TAR

DICTIONARY AND COMPENDIUM

TAROT

DICTIONARY AND COMPENDIUM

JANA RILEY

SAMUEL WEISER, INC.

York Beach, Maine

First published in 1995 by
Samuel Weiser, Inc.
P.O. Box 612
York Beach, ME 03910-0612

Library of Congress Cataloging-in-Publication Data
Riley, Jana
Tarot dictionary & compendium / Jana Riley.
p. cm.
Includes bibliographical references and index.
1. Tarot. I. Title.
BF1879.T2R56 1995
133.3'2424'03—dc20 95-8713
ISBN 0-87728-821-6 CIP
EB

Typeset in 11 point Garamond
Printed in the United States of America

03 02 01 00 99 98 97
10 9 8 7 6 5 4 3 2

The paper used in this publication meets the minimum requirements of the American National Standard for Permanence of Paper Printed Library Materials Z39.48-1984.

TABLE OF CONTENTS

PREFACE

Many years ago, when I first began studying the tarot, I was both delighted and astonished to discover the many tarot books and decks available. Eager to learn, I obtained as many books as I could, and my desk, the coffee table, kitchen and dining tables, and every available—and sometimes not so available—surface was strewn with books, decks of cards, and notes. A friend stopped for coffee one morning and remarked that I had enough material to make a library proud. I felt much like what I imagine an overjoyed flea might feel stumbling on the Westminster Dog Show by accident, so eagerly did I hop from book to book and deck to deck.

It was in this manner that I gradually began to learn the tarot. The tarot sources were plentiful and extremely diverse. What did these sources have in common? If the tarot really works, mustn't it have a methodology that brings all its seemingly diverse and contrary meanings together? And if it doesn't, does this mean that the tarot is nothing more than what many people believe it to be—a collection of classic symbols upon which wishful thinkers and would-be psychics project their own temporal fears and desires? To find the common denominator of the tarot was not an easy task. I would have loved to have had a source, a book, a teacher, to help me get a perspective.

Time and time again I vowed to work with only one or two authors with whom I most identified, to make them my sole mentors, but each time I attempted this, it proved to be an unsatisfactory and short-term course of action. It seemed to me that many writers and artists, each in their own individual way, had something special and unique to contribute. Finally I began to compile my own notebook. This took well over a year, but once it was finished, that notebook became my most valuable source. It enabled me to immediately see the common denominators of the cards and helped me to understand how truly beautiful the holistic symmetry of tarot is.

Well over a decade has passed, and I have come to know many people who share an interest in the tarot—novices, professionals, avid enthusiasts. But from them all—professional, novice, and dabbler alike—I have heard the same remark again and again: "Why doesn't someone write a book that combines some modern interpretations?" If there were many tarot sources ten or twenty years ago, there are even more books and decks available today. There is an old adage: "When all else fails, do it yourself." So I compiled this book. This is a rejuvenated version of my faithful, now dog-eared, tattered notebook.

In compiling this dictionary there have been two major challenges. There are many excellent taroists who have contributed to the wealth of information we have about tarot. Who should I include? At first, foolishly, I thought I was going to have to make this decision, but as anyone who has worked with the tarot knows, these determinations lie far beyond the hands of mere mortals, and who and what to include soon took on a direction of its own. Various contributors, situations, conditions, and coincidences influenced the making of this book. The second challenge I encountered was condensing the monumental works of the remarkable people presented here. What is presented is meant to serve merely as a guideline and does not do justice to the depth and breadth of any individual's work. For readers who wish to pursue the taroists in more scope, the tarot books and decks are listed in the bibliography. Sample cards from the various decks are included here (pp. xix–xxx) so readers can see how varied and individual the decks are. Each deck is truly a work of art and many students will want to collect them all!

This is a tarot dictionary and compendium. It has been written for students, teachers, and practitioners to refer to when learning, teaching, or researching the tarot; when in doubt, when doing a layout, when looking for a different point of view. It can also direct you to the taroists who best provide you with your most familiar symmetries in life. Your personal pattern can be discovered by laying out the cards on a regular basis—perhaps once a week—and consulting the compendium to verify which interpretation ended up being the one most nearly corresponding to the way your week went. This method makes it possible to ascertain the specific taroist, or taroists, who agrees most with your personal point of view. There are always one or two who "hit the nail on the head" time and time again. This accuracy can be downright spooky. From observing the consistent interplay, readings can be focused on the taroists who best fit your personal "angles."

Many good taroists are *not* included here. This is my one regret. This overview is not meant to be the "be-all-end-all"; it merely includes a few of the many outstanding taroists who have dedicated many years to the tarot. It is assumed that the serious reader will not forego exploring other writers, for to do so would be to overlook a vast amount of knowledge and expertise which, because of the limitations of this book, cannot be incorporated here. No one person, or group of persons, holds the key to tarot—its key is universal.

I wish to thank everyone who contributed to *Tarot Dictionary & Compendium*. The taroists and their publishers who helped put it together shared the richness of their knowledge and gave of their spiritual and physical support without question. They have been kind beyond my wildest expectations and have continually made me grateful that I chose to undertake this project. In a world where most of us are too stressed out to figure out how to keep our own pitchers of life halfway full, they have proven that there are some people who have figured out not only how to keep their own pitchers full, but even have enough left over that they are able to pour themselves out for the rest of us.

ACKNOWLEDGMENTS

Many people have contributed to this book. First of all, I want to thank the tarot experts who have allowed me to use portions of their work to help students gain insight into the many ways that we can interpret the cards. They are: Dr. Angeles Arrien, Norma Cowie, Aleister Crowley, Joyce Eakins, Pamela Eakins, Gail Fairfield, Mary Greer, Vicki Noble, Rachel Pollack, Juliet Sharman-Burke, R. J. Stewart, A. E. Waite, Barbara Walker, Dr. James Wanless, and Oswald Wirth.

In addition, I want to thank the publishers who have allowed me to reprint material from the various books published by these esteemed taroists: Arcus Publishing Company (Sonoma, CA) for allowing me to quote from Angeles Arrien's *The Tarot Handbook*; NC Publishing (Blaine, WA) for quotes from Norma Cowie's *Tarot for Successful Living*; Ramp Creek Publishing (Smithville, IN) for Gail Fairfield's *Choice-Centered Tarot*; Newcastle Publishing Company (Van Nuys, CA) for Mary Greer's *Tarot for Your Self; Tarot Constellations* and *The Essence of Magic*; HarperCollins Publishers (New York) for Vicki Noble's *Motherpeace: A Way to the Goddess*; HarperCollins (New York) for Barbara Walker's *The Secrets of the Tarot*; Uitgeverij Schors (Amsterdam) for Rachel Pollack's *The 78 Degrees of Wisdom, Part I*; Richard Curtis Associates (New York) for Rachel Pollack's *The 78 Degrees of Wisdom, Part I and II*; Pan Books, Ltd., an imprint of Macmillan Publisher's Ltd. (London) for Juliet Sharman-Burke's *The Complete Book of the Tarot*; Aquarian Press, an imprint of Thorsons, a division of HarperCollins Publishers, Ltd. (London) for R. J. Stewart's *The Complete Merlin Tarot*; and to Merrill-West Publishing (Carmel, CA) for Dr. James Wanless' *Voyager Tarot: Way of the Great Oracle.*

Because a number of our authors also have created their own tarot decks, I have used various decks to illustrate all the cards in the Major Arcana, and a number of cards in the Minor Arcana. I have not illustrated the cards as they are discussed, for the decks are different, and would confuse readers. However, I wish to extend my sincere thanks to the publishers of the tarot decks that have been used in this book, and I hope that readers will "fall in love" with several decks and use them in their studies. To Aquarian Press, a division of Thorsons, HarperCollins (London) for illustrations from The Dreampower Tarot (R. J. Stewart and Stuart Littlejohn), The Merlin Tarot (R. J. Stewart & Miranda Gray), The Shining Woman Tarot (by Rachel Pollack), and The William Blake Tarot of the Creative Imagination (by Ed Buryn). To Eddison Sadd (London) for illustrations from The Mythic Tarot (created by Juliet Sharman-Burke and Liz Greene, illustrated by Tricia Newell). To Merrill-West (Carmel, CA) for illustrations from The Voyager Tarot (by Dr. James Wanless and Ken Knutson). To U. S. Games Systems, Inc. (Stamford, CT) for illustrations from The Barbara Walker Tarot (by Barbara Walker); for the Motherpeace Round Tarot (by Karen Vogel & Vicki Noble); for the Rider-Waite Tarot (A. E. Waite, artist Pamela Colman); for The Tarot of the Spirit (by Joyce Eakins). To Samuel Weiser for permission to reproduce The Thoth Tarot (by Aleister Crowley and Lady Harris).

Many people gave me special assistance during the making of this book: I want to thank everyone at Samuel Weiser, and Betty Lundsted, Mary Greer, and James Wanless, for their continual insights and encouragement, and for their unerring trust in the universe, which, on occasion, rubs off on me. Thanks to David Schors at Uitgeverij Schors in Amsterdam, and David Daley, former Permissions Controller at HarperCollins in London for their helpfulness.

Thanks to my friends, Jenny Mason and Suzanne Stevens, who, over the years, have offered their unconditional friendship and exceptional words of wisdom and light. I am especially grateful to Dr. E. Otha Wingo, Executive Director of Huna Research, Inc., for lending his expertise in Latin and Greek, and for advice and suggestions for chapter 6 (which I did not always follow, so any errors are mine).

And my deepest thanks to my son, Ryan Bardach, and to my parents, Raymond and Dean Riley, who have continuously given of themselves without expectation, and without any strings attached. It is because they have always seen only the best in me, even when it isn't, that I have eventually gained the faith and fortitude to believe in life as Spirit.

• • •

Quoted material appearing at chapter openings comes from the following sources:

On page 1: *A Course in Miracles* (Glen Ellen, CA: Foundation for Inner Peace, 1985); page 83: Steve Martin—From "A Wild and Crazy Guy" in *The Penguin Dictionary of Modern Humorous Quotations*, compiled by Fred Metcalf (London: Penguin Books, 1987), p. 119; page 163: African Proverb—From *Quotations of Wit and Wisdom*, selected by John W. Gardner and Francesca Reese (New York: W. W. Norton, 1975), p. 115; page 199: J. E. Cirlot, *A Dictionary of Symbols* (New York: Philosophical Library, 1971), p. liv; page 265: Steve Martin—From "A Wild and Crazy Guy," record, 1978, quoted in *The Penguin Dictionary of Modern Humorous Quotations*, compiled by Fred Metcalf (London: Penguin Books, 1987), p. 31.

LIST OF ILLUSTRATIONS

THE MAJOR ARCANA

(All cards in the Major Arcana are illustrated)

THE MINOR ARCANA

(Not all cards in the Minor Arcana are illustrated)

THE MAJOR ARCANA

The Major Arcana are numbered 0-XXI. Some taroists start with 0 (The Fool), and run through XXI (The World). Others start with I (The Magician) and lay (The Fool) after XXI. The illustrations here begin with The Fool. Cards from twelve different decks illustrate the varied presentation of Major Arcana symbolism.

THE HIGH PRIESTESS

III
l'Impératrice

IIII
l'Empereur

V
THE HIEROPHANT

VI Knowledge

VII Experience

8
La Justice
La Giustizia
Justice
Die Gerechtigkeit
La Justicia

IX
Hermit

X
T
WHEEL of FORTUNE.

XVIII STRENGTH

The HANGED WOMAN
12

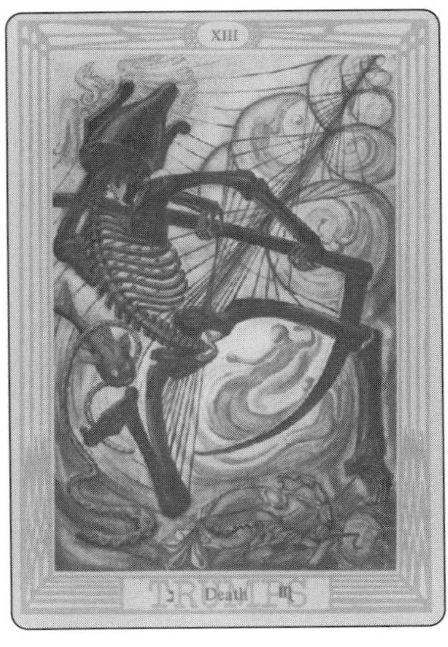
XIII
TRUMPS
Death

TEMPERANCE

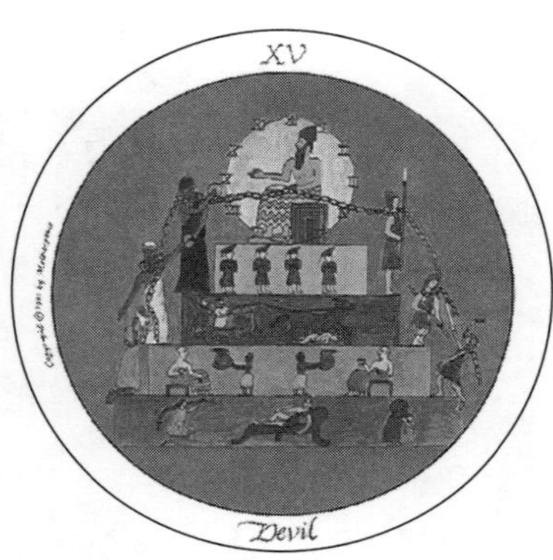
XV
Devil

16
La Maison de Dieu
La Casa di Dio
The House of God
Das Haus Gottes
La Casa de Dios

XVII
Star

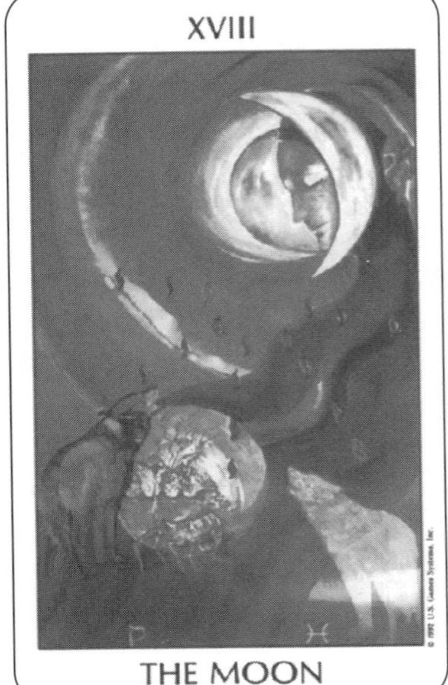
XVIII
THE MOON
© 1992 U.S. Games Systems, Inc.

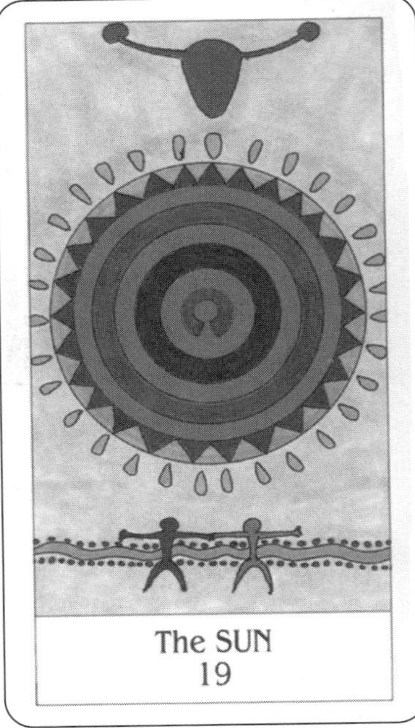
The SUN
19

XX
Time-Space

XXI
The Universe

THE MINOR ARCANA

There are four suits that total fifty-six cards in the Minor Arcana. The four suits illustrated here are called various names by the twelve tarot-card designers included in the following pages. Only a few cards from each suit have been illustrated to show readers the differences in the many decks available today.

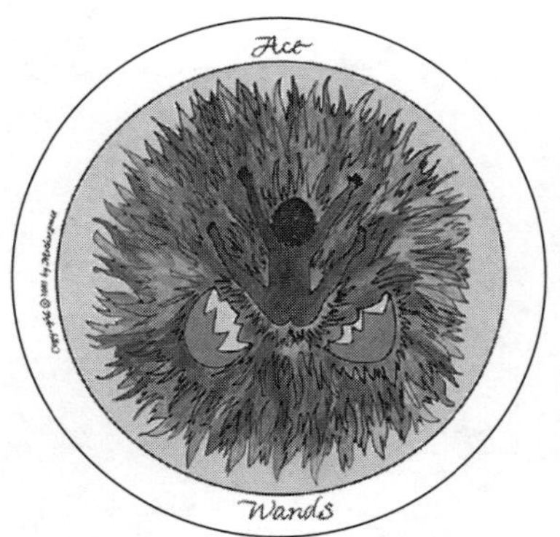

6 of TREES

Swiftness
Time is the mercy of Eternity: without Time's swiftness Which is the swiftest of all things: all were eternal torment
8 of Poetry

Father
FIRE

Ace of Cups

III

FIVE OF CUPS

Passion
Ten of Cups

I
1

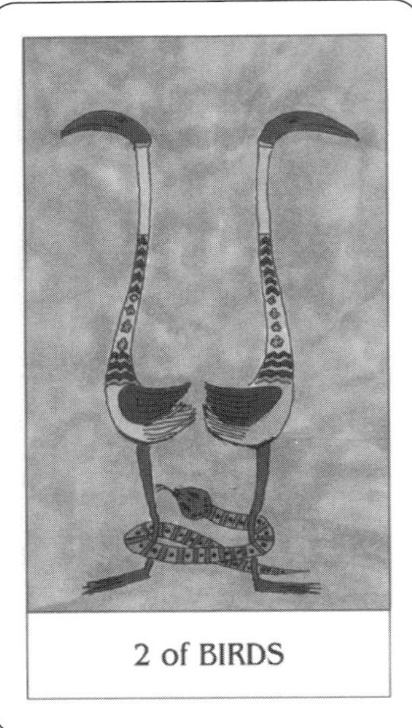
2 of BIRDS

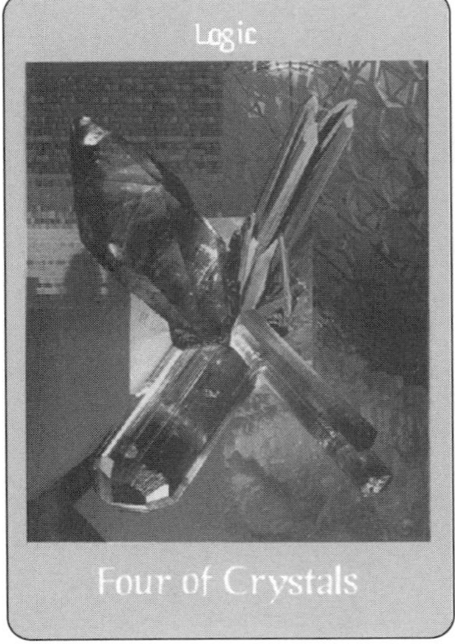
Logic
Four of Crystals

Passage
Tragitto
Passage
Überfahrt
Pasaje
Six des Epées
Sei di Spade
Six of Swords
Sechs-Schwerter
Seis de Espadas

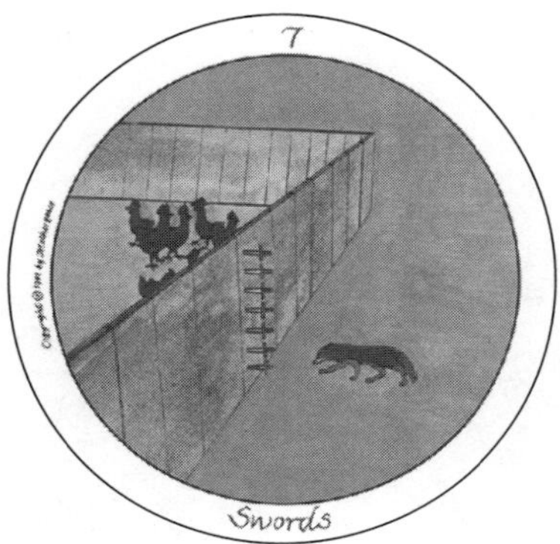
7
Swords

Cavalier d'Epée

One of Earth
FORM

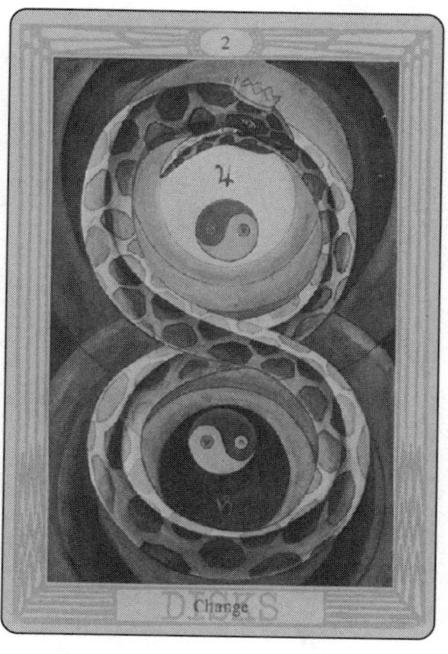
2
Change

Practice
3 of Painting

IX

Merlin

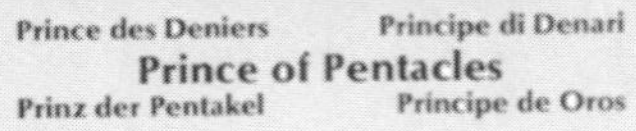
Prince des Deniers
Principe di Denari
Prince of Pentacles
Prinz der Pentakel
Principe de Oros

BEASTS

TAROT

DICTIONARY AND COMPENDIUM

Chapter 1: THE TAROT

> You cannot be aware without interpretation
> for what you perceive is your interpretation.
>
> —A Course in Miracles

The tarot is a collection of 78 pictures presented in the form of a deck of cards. It is divided into three sections: the *Major Arcana*, the *Minor Arcana*, and the *Court Cards*.

For a long time, most people weren't sure what the pictures represented. There were plenty of theories, and opinions abounded, but as far as there being any tangible evidence or any sort of general consensus, the meaning of the tarot, except to a scholarly few, remained elusive. What *was* clear, however, even from the beginning, is that in some way the tarot was a picture compilation of universal imagery and symbology. It contains the symbols found in every civilization—ancient and modern—in the form of paintings, sculptures, drawings, icons, legends, myths, religions, and to make a very long story short, in every physical, mental, emotional, and spiritual form people have ever been able to mold, dream, imagine, express, or squeeze them into. The tarot is cosmogonal. It is a collection of symbols that crosses all boundaries of culture, time, and space; a compilation of inexorable imagery which has existed for eons, and continues to reside in the collective unconscious of all human beings. No one knows exactly how old the tarot is, nor do we know for sure who created it. It is possible that it originated in Egypt or China. It has been associated with the gypsies—descendants of the *Egyptians* who eons ago migrated to Europe, thus the derivation of the name, *gypsies.* There is also evidence it may be associated with the ancient *Taoist* philosophy of China. *Tao* means "the way" or "the path" which is what *tarot* also means, and there are parallels between the ancient writings, meditational practices, and teachings of the Tao and tarot.[1] However, we do not know for sure where, why, or how the tarot originated, and the only thing we can say positively is that it is, without doubt, extremely old. Officially, the first tarot deck goes back to the 14th century, and unofficially, to pre-dynasty Egypt.

In addition to its two factors of universal symbology and enduring antiquity, another significant factor noticed about the tarot is that the Minor Arcana and Court Cards are basically the same as a modern deck of regular playing cards. No one knows how or where playing cards originated either, nor why they are depicted and arranged the specific way they are. Even though at one time, whoever created the tarot and playing cards obviously knew what they were doing, it hasn't been until the 20th century that a prevalent consensus has been reached on what the pictures actually represent. It is now generally accepted that both the tarot and playing cards, each in their own fashion, are representations of the *archetypes.* The archetypes, as they are found in the tarot, and in religion, are divided into a trinity.

MAJOR ARCANA

The Major ***Arc***ana consists of 22 cards depicting the 22 major ***arc***hetypes; hence, their etymological root with the words ***arc***ana and ***arc***hangels. They are called *Major* because they are the archetypes which are contained within the collective unconscious of humanity and all of life, and thus they are universal in content rather than individual.

[1]See *The Secret of the Golden Flower: A Chinese Book of Life.* Translated by Richard Wilhelm (Orlando, FL: Harcourt Brace Jovanovich, 1962).

MINOR ARCANA

The Minor Arcana is a total of 40 cards which show the various ways the 22 archetypes of the Major Arcana are experienced in day-to-day living. C. G. Jung, the father of humanistic psychology, believed that archetypes tend toward manifestation.[2] This being the case, it may be said that the Minor Arcana is the Major manifesting itself on the physical plane, or that universal consciousness is displaying itself in individual consciousness.

COURT CARDS

The Court Cards are pictures of the sixteen different personality types. You may ask why sixteen types, rather than 10 or 20, or any other number? Why specifically sixteen? It seems that, once again, whoever the creators of the tarot were knew *exactly* what they were doing. Between 1913 and 1917 C. G. Jung wrote his now famous book, *Psychological Types*, first published in 1923. In his book Jung describes eight different personality types. Later, Katharine Briggs and Isabel Myers expanded Jung's original theory of eight psychological types into sixteen. Briggs and Myers devised a test, or type indicator, now called the Myers-Briggs Type Indicator (MBTI), which is so uncannily precise that today it is considered by many to be the most accurate tool available to ascertain personality type, and is used in companies, universities, and counseling centers around the world. The MBTI is based on sixteen personality types according to the four Jungian functions of *sensation, emotion, thinking,* and *intuition,* and it is these sixteen archetypal personality types which the Court Cards represent. Although, as far as we know, Jung and Myers-Briggs were in

---

[2]Keith Thompson, *Angels and Aliens: UFO's and the Mythic Imagination* (New York: Addison-Wesley, 1991), p. 46.

no way connected with the Hermetic Order of the Golden Dawn, which in the early 20th century also described the sixteen court cards, the Golden Dawn's descriptions correspond with eerie precision to the personalities established by the MBTI.

The Major Arcana are universal invisible archetypes, sometimes called Archangels, Angels, Spirits, High Selves, Inner Guides, or the superconscious. The Minor cards show how the Major Arcana are displayed in individual archetypal events, situations, or in issues that take place on Earth. And the Court Cards indicate archetypal behavior and personality.

Realizing that the tarot is 78 depictions of archetypes does not, however, enlighten us as to what an archetype precisely *is*. Psychologists, esotericists, and theologians talk about archetypes without providing us with clear definitions. Archetypes form the backbone of modern psychology. They are the images from whence derive the angels and devils of all religions. The heroes and villains of fairy tales, myths, modern novels, and movies, the good guy in the white hat and the bad guy in the black hat, the good guy's trusty steed, and the hapless heroine waiting to be rescued are all archetypal. Archetypes are painted on cathedral walls and holy temples, and corporations unwittingly structure their hierarchy in their image. They appear in the works of Leonardo DaVinci, Michelangelo, Salvador Dali, and all artists and musicians everywhere. Archetypes form the basis of every book ever written, every movie ever made, and every song ever sung. Archetypes are found around us in every form and motion.

To discover what archetypes are in actuality, it is perhaps useful to look at a few of the various ways different scholars over the ages have attempted to define them. Starting far back with the sages of ancient lore, Hermes Thoth Trismegistus, the renowned scholar-magician-savant of Egypt, defined archetypes in much the same manner the Bible's first book of Genesis does. Of archetypes, Hermes wrote:

> Before the visible universe was formed its mold was cast. This mold was called the *Archetype*, and this Archetype was in the Supreme Mind long before the process of creation began. Beholding the Archetypes, the Supreme Mind became enamored with Its own thought; so, taking the Word as a mighty hammer, It gouged out caverns in primordial space and cast the form of the spheres in the Archetypal mold, at the same time sowing in the newly fashioned bodies the seeds of living things. The darkness below, receiving the hammer of the Word, was fashioned into an orderly universe. The elements separated into strata and each brought forth living creatures. The Supreme Being—the Mind—male and female, brought forth the Word—In this manner it was accomplished, O Hermes: The Word moving like a breath through space called forth the Fire by the friction of its motion . . .[3]

As beautifully poetic as this description is, when it comes to explaining what an archetype actually is, it may still leave some of us feeling like our dipsticks are about two quarts low. So let's take a look at a more contemporary definition, one that is perhaps more attuned to our modern way of thinking.

C. G. Jung is the man of our era responsible for once again bringing archetypes to public attention. His entire life was dedicated to their exploration, and he wrote volumes about them. Of archetypes Jung wrote:

> The contents of the collective unconscious are known as archetypes . . . this part of the unconscious is not individual but universal; in contrast to the personal psyche, it has contents and modes of

[3]Manly P. Hall, *The Secret Teachings of All Ages* (Los Angeles, CA: Philosophical Research Society, 1977), p. xxxix. Quoted from "The Vision," believed by some scholars to have been written by Hermes.

> behavior that are more or less the same everywhere and in all individuals. . . . The archetype is essentially an unconscious content that is altered by becoming conscious and by being perceived, and it takes its colour from the individual consciousness in which it happens to appear.[4]

Jung's definition is apropos to tarot for many reasons, not the least because it describes how the Major Arcana ties in with the Minor, how archetypes are first and foremost universal in content (the Major) and then become personal by being perceived through the individual (the Minor). It is also, as the more holistic person may immediately notice, a quasi-clinical way of saying we all create our own realities by that (archetype) of which we are most aware.

However, Jung's definition, as accurate as it is, may still tend to leave some of us a little fuzzy around the mental edges. Even if we do understand Hermes' and Jung's definition of archetypes, they do not tell us how to apply archetypes on a daily basis in our own lives. So let us move on to *Webster's Ninth New Collegiate Dictionary,* where we find archetype defined as: "the original pattern or model of which all things of the same type are representations or copies . . ."[5]

Now, if we think about these three different definitions of archetypes for a little while, it might be possible to arrive at a consolidated definition that goes something like this:

> The original Archetype was a thought in the Mind of God—male and female. The Supreme Mind became enamored with this thought and created life in Its image by the friction of Its Word—or by the motion of Its sound. This caused the Universe to divide into ordered strata, and because creation is

---

[4]C. G. Jung, *The Archetypes & the Collective Unconscious* (Princeton, NJ: Princeton University Press, 1968), pp. 3, 5.

[5]*Webster's Ninth New Collegiate Dictionary,* s.v. "archetype." © (1991 by Merriam-Webster Inc., publisher of the Merriam-Webster ® dictionaries)

> *within* the Mind of God, everything is a model or a copy of the original pattern, which is God.

Or perhaps something to this effect. If there appears to be some confusion as to whether creation is patterned after God Itself or after God's thought, that is probably due to the fact that esoteric scholars have always claimed that thought *is*, God *is*—that thought and God and Mind and Creation are synonymous. We are what we think. And what we think, we are. Likewise, we are also what we speak.

This same concept—of life being patterned after the original Archetype—has been said in many other ways. "As above, so below." "What goes around, comes around." "We reap what we sow." "Like attracts like." "What you do unto others shall be done unto you." "An eye for an eye, a tooth for a tooth." "For every action there is an equal and opposite reaction."

Hunbatz Men, in his book, *Secrets of Mayan Science/Religion,* points out that the bible maintains that God created us in the divine image and likeness, and suggests this is analogous to the idea that God is energy, and that we are a reflection of that intelligent cosmic energy, of cosmic consciousness. In Mayan, the body is called *wuinclil,* which means "to be vibration."[6] This perhaps clarifies again the nature of God's image created by and in the likeness of the word, or sound: for sound is motion, or moving particle-waves of light. In derivation, *wuinclil* sounds suspiciously close to *wunjo,* the runestone of joy and light; to *unihipili,* the low self in the science/religion of Huna which means vitality, energy, body, emotion, and motion; and to the *World,* the 21st Arcanum in the tarot, which means sound, joy, light, life, and dancing, all of which are akin to vibration, energy, light, and sound.

---

[6]Hunbatz Men, *Secrets of Mayan Science/Religion* (Santa Fe, NM: Bear & Company, 1990), p. 81.

From Hermes, Jung, Webster, and Men, we begin to realize that archetypes are difficult to define because archetypes are *everything*—with the additional catch that "everything," or "anything," is always defined through the eyes of the individual. Maybe that's why the word itself, *archetype*, if taken etymologically, also turns out to mean everything as perceived through the eyes of the beholder, for the definition of *arch* is "something that angles," and the definition of *type* is "a kind," so an *archetype* is "a kind of angle." Hermes described everyone having his own personal angle on everything by saying the Archetype separates down through the strata, and Jung described it by saying the archetype is both collective and individual. It would seem that angles, or archetypes, are everything, but at the same time, it is the way we individually see anything that defines its personal reality to us, or the angle in which we are personally perceiving it. That is why Jung says: "the archetype. . .is altered by becoming conscious and by being perceived, and it takes its colour from the individual consciousness in which it happens to appear." The tarot is a magic picturebook presenting 78 angles by which people perceive the One Great Undivided Whole. The power of the tarot lies in its broad application to this universal principle.

The tarot interpretations, correspondences, and layouts which follow are, so to speak, many *angles* on the one God, or on the one life of All That Is. And, as Jung said, we find collectively, if not personally, that these angles "are more or less the same everywhere. . . ." We will see the similarities and the differences in many of the archetypal interpretations. Where interpretations do appear to be at odds, it is because each author approaches the *angel* at a slightly different *angle*.

• • •

By working with the various interpretations, we will eventually understand the many layers of meaning that reside within the archetypal symbolism, but first it is probably appropriate to have a basic consensus of terminology because tarot has a language of its own.

TAROT TERMS & DEFINITIONS

The qualities attributed to the four suits are those usually accepted by most authorities. A difference in the understanding of the meaning of words is sometimes the reason for some seeming discrepancies found in tarot interpretations; for instance, note the distinction between the meaning of *work* (attributed to discs) and *career* (attributed to wands), and between *instincts* (attributed to cups) and *intuition* (attributed to wands). Working with the cards for a prolonged length of time usually makes evident the meaning and the reason for the attribution of certain words to a particular suit. Following are some of the commonly used terms found in tarot.

arcana (plural)—(arcanum-singular): Hidden knowledge, a mystery. The tarot is divided into the Major *Arcana* and the Minor *Arcana* (the Minor plus the court cards), or the greater and lesser secret knowledge.

archetype: A type of arch, or angle, on the Angel(s). Scientifically, any symmetry perceived to be of like-motion or form.

cartomancer: A person who reads a deck of playing cards or a tarot deck.

cartomancy: The art or skill of reading playing cards or a tarot deck.

Celtic Cross Spread (pronounced "Keltic"): One of the oldest and most popular layouts of the cards, with six cards forming the shape of a Celtic Cross and four cards laid in a vertical line to its right. (See chapter on layouts.)

centering: The process of bringing the conscious mind into the center of yourself in order to become more aware. The practice of meditation, or of centering your concentration, usually on the question being asked while shuffling the cards.

client: The person for whom the cartomancer is doing the reading. Also called the querent.

court cards: The sixteen cards of a tarot deck consisting of the King, Queen, Prince, and Princess of each of the four suits. Also called King, Queen, Knight, and Page; or Knight, Queen, Prince, and Princess, respectively. Known by other titles as well, depending on the creator of the deck. In a deck of playing cards, the court cards are the King, Queen, and Jack, it usually being inferred that the Prince and Princess are combined as one within the Jack.

cups: One of the four suits of the Minor Arcana. Also called hearts, chalices, goblets, rivers, cauldrons, bowls, grails, vessels, fish, blossoms, and other titles, depending on the deck. Typically associated with water, feeling, emotions, the heart, dreams, memories, fear, pleasure, instincts, and the subconscious.

discs: One of the four suits of the Minor Arcana. Also called diamonds, coins, pentacles, worlds, circles, nuggets, stones, shields, beasts, and other titles, depending on the deck. Associated with earth, the physical, material, sensation, the five senses, money, work, and all physical bodies.

divination: The practice of perceiving the past, present, and future, or discovering hidden knowledge through esoteric means. In tarot, this is normally done through a "reading" or "laying out the cards."

divine: To discern the past, present, and future, or to discover hidden knowledge through esoteric means.

fortune-telling: Slang for divination.

layout: The placing of cards in a particular arrangement, such as in the Celtic Cross or astrological layout, in order to read the cards. Each position in a layout has a specific meaning. Also called a spread.

Major Arcana: The 22 cards of a tarot deck which depict 22 universal archetypes most closely associated with humanity, the world, and all of life.

Minor Arcana: The 40 cards of a tarot deck consisting of four suits (wands, cups, swords, and discs), each numbered 1 through 10; most authorities also consider the court cards to be part of the Minor, making the total number of the Minor 56.

querent: The person who is asking questions of the reader, cartomancer, or taroist. The person for whom the cards are being read. (See client.)

query: The question being asked.

playing cards: A deck of 52 cards. Four suits of 10 cards each, normally illustrated with pips; and 12 court cards, consisting of three cards in each of the four suits. Normally used for gaming purposes, but can also be read by a cartomancer. The 52 cards of a playing deck are the same as the Minor Arcana and the court cards of the tarot except the tarot has one extra court card in each suit.

significator: A court card, or sometimes another card, chosen prior to the beginning of a reading to represent the querent or query.

spread: Another name for a layout. The cards are spread or laid out in a specific arrangement, each position in the arrangement having a certain meaning. (See layout.)

suit: The four parts of the Minor Arcana of tarot, classically called wands, cups, swords, and discs. In playing cards they are called clubs, hearts, spades, and diamonds, respectively.

swords: One of the four suits of the Minor Arcana. Also sometimes called spades, crystals, trees, birds, wind, epees, blades, lightning, lasers, and other titles, depending on the deck. Associated with air, thinking, judgments, opinions, the intellect, change, and the conscious mind.

tarot: A set of 78 picture cards consisting of 22 Major Arcana and 56 Minor Arcana. Each card in a tarot deck is a unique combination of symbol, number, color, arrangement, and imagery which is specific for that card.

Taroist: (Also tarotist) A person who reads a tarot deck.

trump: A name for each of the 22 cards of the Major Arcana.

wands: One of the four suits of the Minor Arcana. Also called clubs, batons, staffs, staves, scepters, arrows, pipes, spears, rods, serpents, and other titles, depending on the deck. Typically associated with fire, intuition, spirit, inspiration, career, creativity, passion, and the superconscious.

Chapter

2

THE MAJOR ARCANA

The Fool
How dieth the wise man? As the fool.

—Ecclesiastes 2:16

The Major Arcana consists of 22 cards representing the major archetypes. Twenty-two is probably not any more a definitive number for archetypes than any other number, as ancient cultures and religions, along with the more modern, tend to encompass literally hundreds of archetypes, as does Hinduism with its voluminous legion of greater and lesser gods, and Catholicism with its celestial hierarchy of many hundreds of Seraphim, Cherubim, Thrones, Dominions, Virtues, Powers, Principalities, Archangels, and Angels. However, in tarot the Major Arcana are assumed to be those archetypes most imminently connected with the collective unconscious of humanity, and as such, have universal application regardless of one's race, religion, or creed. Taken from the other end of the numerical spectrum, the Major can also be said to consist of only two archetypes—these two being the earth-heaven polarity of yin and yang, positive and negative, or male and female—being expressed in 22 of their complimentary aspects or stages. As a result, most of the Major cards picture either a man or a woman alone, or a man and woman together. But if we are disposed to go even a step further, these two archetypes can also be reduced to only one, which as we have said, is the One, the undivided single Whole, perceived by us as yin and yang on the Earth plane. The One is represented by the Fool. It is for this reason that the Fool is numbered 0, and can be placed either at the beginning or at the end of the Major Arcana.

Tarot, because it does represent cosmology, is a springboard to the infinite and to the eternal. There is no end to it, and that is why taroists have spoken and written volumes of material on it in general and on each archetype specifically. When doing a reading, interpretation depends on who is being read for, the meaning of a specific card, its relation to other cards, the position of each card in the layout, the goal being sought, and for many readers, whether the card is upright or reversed. Add to this the generic possibilities contained within the macrocosm of tarot itself and each card individually, and you've got enough material to last you not one lifetime, but innumerable lifetimes. For this reason, in the interpretations that follow, instead of mentioning the multitudinous possibilities naturally inherent within an archetype, one or two attributes are mentioned. I have tried to avoid covering too much territory. Instead I have chosen brief definitions, although they are incomplete, so readers can get a basic idea from each author.

The Major Arcana is numbered 0 through 21. No one is absolutely certain that the order in which they are numbered today is their correct or original sequence, but except for Arcanum VIII—*Justice*, and Arcanum XI—*Strength*, a general consensus has been reached on the order of their present numbering as established by the Golden Dawn during the early part of the 20th century. Some authorities believe, with not ineffective evidence to support them, that Strength and Justice should be interchanged, making Strength Number VIII and Justice Number XI. Because the order of these two cards has not yet been satisfactorily determined, current tarot decks vary.

The 22 cards of the Major Arcana are defined by Angeles Arrien, Norma Cowie, Aleister Crowley, Pamela Eakins, Gail Fairfield, Mary Greer, Vicki Noble, Rachel Pollack, Juliet Sharman-Burke, R. J. Stewart, A. E. Waite, Barbara Walker,

James Wanless, Oswald Wirth, and myself. I have tried to use prominent material from each taroist's definitions of the cards. Sometimes they use a phrase, or a principle or law which describes the essence of an archetype. When a taroist intentionally stresses an important aspect of an archetype's nature by word or phrase, it is presented first in italic. At the end of each section readers will find space to add their own favorite taroists and personal ideas if they wish. There is also space left after each card in chapter 6 for the same reason.

0—THE FOOL

Arrien—*The Principle of Courage.* State of No Fear. Ecstasy and Peak Experience. One Who Walks without Fear. The ability to give birth to new forms from a place of courage, wonder, and anticipation.

Cowie—*Completes All Motion by Faith.* Walking to your own drumbeat because you believe in what you are doing. Walking with the force of love and laws of the universe.

Crowley—Air. Aleph.

> Know naught!
> All ways are lawful to innocence.
> Pure folly is the key to initiation.
> Silence breaks into rapture.
> Be neither man nor woman, but both in one.
> Be silent, Babe in the egg of blue, that thou
> Mayest grow to bear the Lance and Graal!
> Wander alone, and sing! In the King's palace
> His daughter awaits thee.[1]

Eakins—All is movement, all is change. In the deepest blindness is the deepest sight. The true unraveling of the mystery of eternal life is contingent upon understanding that the knowledge of the many is contained in the one and the knowledge of the one is contained in the many.

Fairfield—Experiencing absolute faith and trust in the universe. No sense of worry or fear and no awareness that worry or fear could even exist. A feeling of protection and a sense that everything will work out; being open to whatever the future brings.

---

[1]Crowley also gives divinatory interpretations, but some of his poetry is included here because it captures the essence of the archetype in the unique way only poetry sometimes can.

Greer—*Realization of Eternal Power.* Spiritual Force. Regeneration. Paradoxical nature of wisdom and foolishness. Leaping off into some new phase of life. Carefree vagabond. Divine nonchalance. Expect the unexpected with this card.

Noble—*Trusting One's Elf.* The void which contains all possibilities. Pure spontaneity: the carefree, irrational impulse; the irrepressible surge of energy that propels.

Pollack—In one aspect, the image of a spirit totally free. In readings, courage and optimism, urging faith in yourself and in life. Beginning, courageously leaping off into some new phase of life. Or a failure to follow your instincts.

Sharman-Burke—An unexpected influence that will soon come into play. There may be a sudden unlooked for opportunity, or the possibility of an adventure or escape. Represents the need to abandon the old ways and start something new and untested. Anything could happen, so hold your nose and jump!

Stewart—Inspiration, spiritual impulse. May indicate naivete or foolish idealism. Often indicates moments of decision or great change and opportunity hidden within apparently difficult situations. The mysterious liberating factor that cuts across form.

Waite—The spirit in search of experience. The Sun which shines behind him knows whence he came, whither he is going, and how he will return by another path after many days. Folly, mania, extravagance, negligence.

Walker—The only Major Arcanum allowed to remain in a standard deck, as the Joker. Suggests the unenlightened person at the start of his journey toward enlightenment.

Wanless—(The Child) Represents the Child within us. The closest and most natural expression of the universe. The beginningless beginning, sourceless source, endless ending, all things, and no-things. Like a fool, dependent and with limited understanding of your purpose, having faith that the universe will take care of you.

Wirth—The person who lacks intellectual and moral existence. Insentient and irresponsible, he drags himself through life as a passive being who does not know where he is going and is led by irrational impulses. The bottomless Abyss. The Absolute. The inaccessible—whatever is beyond our understanding. Everything is made out of nothing and returns to nothing.

Riley—*Trusting Silence.* Receiving protection through your faith and innocence. With this card anything, or nothing, can happen. The Fool is the sum total of all the other cards. God is all things unto all things.

I—THE MAGICIAN

Arrien—*The Principle of Communication and Timing.* The Communicator. Indicates the Magician is supporting and enhancing communications for you now which will transform difficult situations.

Cowie—*All Things are Possible.* As above, so below. The ability to create what one wants.

Crowley—Mercury. Beth.

> The True Self is the meaning of the True Will;
> know Thyself through Thy Way.
> Calculate well the Formula of the Way.
> Create freely; absorb joyously; divide intently.
> consolidate completely.
> Work thou, Omnipotent, Omniscient, Omnipresent,
> in and for Eternity.

Eakins—The magic of universal force traveling through the vehicle of the physical body. Being in tune with the most creative and powerful aspects of your Self, the part of you that directs the flow of creative energy through *focused action,* receives the force and creates reality, changing the structure of the living situation.

Fairfield—Being aware that several different perceptions of reality exist. Able to understand and describe the various points of view. Discriminating between reality and fantasy—among two or more fantasies, or among two or more realities.

Greer—*Principle of Will and Focused Consciousness.* Unity of self. Outer conscious sense of self as a unique, creative individual. Skillfulness. Communication, consciousness, self-expression, initiative, at-one-ment, originality.

Noble—*Dancing the Fire.* Activating power which changes one thing into another. The gift of energy; the motivation to do, to act, to go forth. A time for beginning projects, taking a stand, affirming some idea. A sense of purpose and self-motivation.

Pollack—An awareness of power in your life, of spirit or simple excitement possessing you, or someone else's power affecting you. The actual first steps of beginnings. Inspiration and will-power. The will unified and directed toward goals and having great strength because all your energy is channeled in a specific direction. Or power abused, lack of will, and confusion of purpose.

Sharman-Burke—An important beginning. A time for action. Creative initiative, skill and potential in abundance. The equipment needed is available but steps may not yet have been taken toward achievement of the goal. New opportunities for intellectual or creative pursuits are presented, and the possibilities for new ventures seem assured. A great reserve of power and energy.

Stewart—Usually indicates matters of mental energy, life forces, and creative use of the mind and imagination. Often shows, according to position, those aspects of the situation which would benefit from imaginative effort.

Waite—The descent of grace, virtue, and light drawn from things above and derived to things below. Possession and communication of the Powers and Gifts of the Spirit. Signifies the divine motive in man, reflecting God, the will in the liberation of its union with that which is above. It is also the unity of individual being on all planes, and in a very high sense it is thought, in the fixation thereof.

Walker—Manipulator of the elements. The Conductor of Souls, god of spiritual journeys, and guide to the mysteries of the afterlife. Associated with Hermes Trismegistus, the Egyptian god Thoth, Mercury, and Jesus.

Wanless—*Law of Talent.* The ability to create by transforming and materializing, to conceptualize through *logos* or word, and to externalize this through some medium of communication. To be able, to have power, the ability to make it happen. Making hopes and dreams come true.

Wirth—The great suggestive power of all that is accomplished in the Cosmos; in man, the seat of individual initiative, the center of perception, of conscience, and willpower. Personification of the thinking unity which suggests the idea before its conception. The eternal generator of the Word which takes form. Beginning, unity-principle.

Riley—*Doing It Anyway.* Receiving energy, signs, and answers on the physical plane in the form of synchronicities, coincidences, magic, and miracles. The Messenger who delivers the messages of the gods. "Ask and ye shall receive."

II—THE HIGH PRIESTESS

Arrien—*The Principle of Intuition, Self-Trust, and Self-Resourcefulness.* The Independent Self-Knower. Receiving this card indicates a state of harmony and independence within you that is working easily and effortlessly.

Cowie—*Choice.* Having to make a choice. A time to make a decision to go inward and encounter your feelings.

Crowley—The Moon. Gimel.

> Purity is to live only to the Highest; and the
> Highest is All; be thou as Artemis to Pan.
> Read thou in the Book of the Law, and break
> through the veil of the Virgin.

Eakins—Listening and hearing the message of your own inner teacher guiding you; attuning to faith; accessing hidden or secret knowledge. Remembering—*retaining memory*—the gift of knowing the collective past, present, and future.

Fairfield—Awareness of the greater self—the self that spans realities, exists in many planes, and is part of the stuff of the Universe. A need to ignore the distractions and limitations of the physical world in order to tune into and commune with the expanded self. You may appear to be aloof and removed from the world and from others.

Greer—*Principle of Balanced Judgment Through Intuitive Awareness.* Personal knowledge. Inner truth. Inner, all-knowing self. Intuition, self-sufficiency, self-trust, independence. The power of mystery and inner feminine wisdom. Influence of dreams, cycles, and lunar tides.

Noble—*Paying Attention.* The archetypal feminine receptive mode of consciousness—the inner knowing of the heart. A time when intuition is functioning more strongly than the intellect and thus a time to pay close attention to the body and its natural rhythms, to relax and listen to intuition.

Pollack—A sense of mystery and darkness. The feeling of intuitively understanding the answer to a problem, though perhaps not consciously. Visions, occult, and psychic powers. Or ill-timed passiveness, weakness, and fear of life.

Sharman-Burke—The Spiritual or Celestial Mother. Potential as yet unfulfilled; wisdom; secrets to be revealed; occult and esoteric studies; and development of feminine powers of intuition and natural insight.

Stewart—Relationship between emotions and foundational or sexual energies. Mental and emotional health, matters of sexual attraction, reproduction, and creative work that employ the feelings. Or insights into the inner mysteries of life.

Waite—Represents the Second Marriage of the Prince who is no longer of this world; the spiritual Bride of the just man. When he reads the Law she gives the Divine meaning. Secrets, mystery, the future as yet unrevealed. In some respects this card is the highest and holiest of the Greater Arcana.

Walker—(Papess) Associated with St. Mary Magdalene; Pope Joan (Joannes, A.D. 854); the Great *Shakti* (*Kali*); Greek *Sophia*, the original Great Mother of the Holy Trinity; and the third figure on the Tantric Wheel of Life called *Vijnana*, the stage of development of conscious experience through teaching.

Wanless—*Law of Inherent Wisdom.* Intuiting the truth which comes from within the depths of the universal collective unconscious and from your own personal genetic inheritance. Dreams and meditations bringing to the surface the hidden subconscious, past, and future.

Wirth—The priestess of mystery who unites strict logic and sweet impressionability for the discernment of reality which hides behind the veil of what is apparent to our senses. Wisdom, creative thought, the second person in the Trinity, the wife of God and mother of all things.

Riley—*Listening to Your Inner Self.* Wisdom. Receiving a teaching or message through your feelings, hunches, instincts, or intuition. A time to listen up and to be aware of your subconscious signals and nightly dreams.

III—THE EMPRESS

Arrien—*The Principle of Love with Wisdom.* The Earth Mother. The Nurturer, Comforter, Beautifier. Your capacity to extend and receive love. The power of owning your own maternal and loving nature within.

Cowie—*Abundance.* Experiencing good results with life. The happy, positive life of love.

Crowley—Venus. Daleth.

> This is the Harmony of the Universe, that Love unites the Will to create with the Understanding of that Creation: understand thou thine own Will. Love and let love. Rejoice in every shape of love, and get thy rapture and thy nourishment thereof.

Eakins—Imagination is everything. Opening to all sensuality, reveling in the delights of the senses. A great beauty revealed; all is perfection, receptive, welcoming. Moving with the flow, finding comfort among nature, creatures, and people, and having no need to control.

Fairfield—Giving deep, total love and nurturing. Something or someone needs to be loved, protected, and healed. Being sensitive to the physical and emotional needs of yourself and others and in a position to meet those needs and heal wounds. Highly dedicated to the nurturing, caretaking process.

Greer—*Principle of Love and Creative Imagination.* Personal love. Giving birth to body. Fertile creative Mother. Nurturance, fertility. The archetypal Earth Mother who seeks to connect all opposites, to banish disharmony. Love, beauty, luxury, and sensuality.

Noble—*Giving Forth.* The Great Mother who promises abundance, birth, growth, harmony, community, and relationship. Getting in touch with one's ancient sensual nature. She is fundamentally "in relation" to others, that part of a person which engages a partner or mothers a child.

Pollack—A time of passion when we approach life through our feelings rather than thought. Usually, satisfaction and understanding gained through the emotions. Or expressing emotional aspects in a negative way.

Sharman-Burke—The Earthly Mother. Represents happy, stable relationships, growth, and fertility. Potential fulfilled; a card of love, marriage, or motherhood.

Stewart—Indicates a positive, giving state or condition. May relate to personal emotions or partners, or a fruitful, creative, or beneficial situation. Tends to indicate situations in which nurturing or cultivation are required to truly realise inherent potential.

Waite—The inferior Garden of Eden, the Earthly Paradise, all that is symbolized by the visible house of man. She is above all things in the outer sense of the Word, as there is no direct message which has been given to man like that which is borne by woman; but she does not herself carry its interpretation. Universal fecundity, fruitfulness, activity, initiation.

Walker—The Great All-Mother Goddess known under many names, such as Demeter (St. Demetra), Isis, Hathor, Ishtar, Esther, Stella Maris, Aphrodite, Hera, Cybele, and Lilith. Associated with love, abundance, fertility, giving, and nurturing.

Wanless—*Law of Preservation.* The guardian of life representing your charge to protect the Earth and all that lives. Being nurturing, supportive, loving, and compassionate—

one with all, the Earth and all of its animals, minerals, vegetables, and human beings, everyone and everything.

Wirth—Creative Intelligence, the mother of form, pictures, and ideas. Abstract conception which generates ideas and shapes the Supreme Ideal. Discernment, reflection, comprehension, and the sphere of recognizable and understandable objects.

Riley—*Experiencing Love.* Indication that a warming, gratifying experience will soon occur in your life that brings the peace of love to you.

IV—THE EMPEROR

Arrien—*The Principle of Personal Power and Leadership.* The Pioneer, Builder, Doer, Visionary. The power of owning and demonstrating your own paternal gifts, leadership, and ability to take care of yourself.

Cowie—*Experience.* Using knowledge gained from previous experience.

Crowley—Aries. Tzaddi.

Pour water on thyself: thus shalt thou be
a Fountain to the Universe
Find thou thyself in every Star.
Achieve thou every possibility.

Eakins—Building a firm base of clear knowledge while remaining open and lucid. Power from insight, possessing a global sense of things, and serving those around you.

Fairfield—Identification with a force that has a great deal of power in the world. In fact, you may have chosen to give up some of your individuality or differentness in order to identify with this power. Having made a commitment to rising or falling according to the success of that power, it is to your advantage to energize and support it.

Greer—*Principle of Life Force and Realization of Power.* Archetype of father, boss, and authority figures. Makes rules, sets boundaries, defines, and analyzes. Where we own our authority (or invest it in another). Assertive, forceful, innovative.

Noble—*Separating Off.* A symbol of Patriarchy in its active form. Always an authority figure seeking to establish control and dominance. Being up against an angry, patriarchal structure of some kind, probably rigidity, or even nastiness. A confrontation with authority or some part of oneself which is feeling rigid or afraid.

Pollack—The laws of society, both good and bad, and the power that enforces them. On a deeper level, the structures and laws of existence. The stability of a just society that allows its members to pursue personal needs or the power of unjust laws in a society where stability takes precedence over morality. Or, compassion and mercy.

Sharman-Burke—The Earthly Father. In a spread, points to material success and stability. Authority, ambition, and worldly gain or achievement.

Stewart—Illimitable creative power. A period of opportunity of great benefit. Or opportunities for relationship between inner and outer life and consciousness. May indicate fatherhood or involvement in situations where a fatherly role is undertaken successfully.

Waite—Executive and realization, the power of this world. The lordship of thought rather than of the animal world, but not consciously the wisdom which draws from a higher world. The virile power—will in its embodied form—to which the Empress responds. Stability, power, protection, realization.

Walker—The scepter in a ruler's right hand was based on Shiva's lightning-phallus, giving rise to the Tarot wand. Originally a trident, it was also borne by western phallic gods like Jupiter, Neptune, Hades, Poseidon, Pluto, and Lucifer. Also associated with Osiris and the Guardian of the Holy Grail.

Wanless—*Law of Construction.* Constructing in the material world. Having a goal, making a plan, deciding, and carrying it out.

Wirth—The Worldly Prince who reigns over concrete and corporal things. The substance of the soul darkened through its incarnation and held captive in the very centre of matter at which it must work in order to regain its freedom. Power which gives and spreads life, creative kindness which brings into existence the animating principle, creative light shared out among creatures, and condensed in the centre of each individuality.

Riley—*Making It Happen.* Indicates that energy is being ordered, formed, and realized on the physical plane, your intentions are being manifested, and the job is getting done.

V—THE HIEROPHANT

Arrien—*The Principle of Learning and Teaching.* The Teacher, Counselor, Consultant. Indicates a desire for self-teaching and learning and for making things tangible and practical.

Cowie—*Seeking Guidance.* Consulting with someone who has knowledge and authority.

Crowley—Taurus. Vau.

> Offer thyself Virgin to the Knowledge and Conversation of thine Holy Guardian Angel. All else is a snare.
> Be thou athlete with the eight limbs of Yoga: for without these thou are not disciplined for any fight.

Eakins—Connecting with the higher self and listening for messages surfacing from within. The revelation of the inner voice, or the flash of insight that comes when least expected. Becoming both student and teacher and seeking your inner guides who are waiting to serve you.

Fairfield—Choosing to align yourself with a particular philosophy, religion, or set of beliefs to which you feel a great deal of loyalty. Willing to take on responsibility in order to support the philosophy, to be accountable to it, and to judge yourself by it. You are free to disentangle yourself at any time, but you choose to be involved.

Greer—*Principle of Teaching and Learning.* Learning from authority. Freedom of choice. Social/cultural education. Teacher, Bearer of the "Word." Problem-solving. Practical applications of spiritual truths. Espousing of moral, ethical, and spiritual values.

Noble—*Repressing Others.* The paternal religious authority who transmits orthodoxy. Dealing in some way with conventional morality and patriarchal law. Someone acting as judge and moral preceptor or trying to tell the querent how things are supposed to be. Or the querent acting in a conventional or programmed way—from conditioning rather than from the heart.

Pollack—Our inner sense of obedience. Churches, doctrines, and education in general. Orthodoxy, conformity to society's ideas and codes of behavior, a surrender of responsibility. Or unorthodoxy, gullibility.

Sharman-Burke—The Spiritual or Celestial Father. Assistance from a wise or helpful person, as well as guidance on spiritual matters and the need to find spiritual meaning in life.

Stewart—Shows a spiritual originative power at work within any given situation or query. A defined situation or pattern enlivened by wisdom and truth. Often symbolizes powerful new beginnings in a life cycle or situation.

Waite—The ruling power of external religion. The *summa totius theologiae* when it has passed into the utmost rigidity of expression; but he symbolizes also all things that are righteous and sacred on the manifest side.

Walker—(Pope) Not originally a Christian pope; possibly originated from Bacchus' ruined altar; the Grand Master or Gypsy Prince associated with magic; Pope Leo III or Honorius III, popes known as practitioners of black magic; or perhaps from the Roman legend of a Peter, Petra, or Pater acting as keeper of the keys.

Wanless—*Law of Life-mastery.* Passing the steps or tests of life through a Buddha-like meditative awareness and philosophy that views every experience as a lesson-learning opportunity for growth. Life is the teacher.

Wirth—He who adapts religious knowledge to the needs of humble believers and formulates religious teaching which is addressed to two categories: the credulous and the incredulous. A director of conscience, the doctor of the soul, moral advice.

Riley—*Continuing the Process.* Giving or receiving conscious earth teachings. This most often takes the form of another person, but it can also mean conscious teachings in any physical form, i.e., reading, writing, television. The higher octave of the Hierophant is faith, its lower octave is hope. Because faith is trust without reservation, whereas hope is desire with doubt, faith's foundation is love, and hope's foundation is fear.

VI—THE LOVERS

Arrien—*The Principle of Art and Craft of Relationship.* The Journey of the Twins. Synthesizer of Dualities, Polarities, and Oppositions. A period of making choices about important relationships in your life.

Cowie—*Indecision*: Being confused or uncertain.

Crowley—Gemini. Zain.

> The Oracle of the Gods is the Child-Voice of Love
> in Thine own Soul; hear thou it.
> Heed not the Siren-Voice of Sense, or the Phantom-
> Voice of Reason: rest in Simplicity, and listen to
> the Silence.

Eakins—Recognizing that you are lonely. Being attracted to that with which you wish to merge. The magical image of the power of surrender in which one form is given up in order to gain another. Understanding a sense of sorrow and separation even as you recognize your oneness with all things. In all cases, the experience of the agony of separation and the bliss of union.

Fairfield—Being involved in the process of cooperation. Two or more people or forces joining together and combining forces for a general or specific purpose. The forces will probably never become one unit, they may not work together in all ways, but they do combine energies for a common goal.

Greer—*Principle of Relatedness and Choice.* Urge to unite. Choice to love. Ourselves in relation to others. Attraction and division. Synergy and separation. Exchange. The need to totally reveal and be accepted for who we are without hiding anything. Focus on communication.

Noble—*Joining Together.* Duality and choice; the natural attraction of the yin and yang universal forces for each other. Either working on a present partnership or preparing to begin a new one. The power of sexual surrender to the Goddess within.

Pollack—The importance of love in a person's life. A specific lover, very often marriage or a long relationship. Implies that the particular relationship has been or will prove to be very valuable to the person, leading him or her to a new understanding of life. Or romantic immaturity and prolonged adolescence.

Sharman-Burke—Indicates a relationship or love affair with some sort of trial or choice involved. Marriage may follow such a choice, or it may be what the old books described as "the choice between sacred and profane love."

Stewart—Love and relationships. Usually means positive, harmonious connections with other people. May mean a spiritual or transcendent power within the individual. Balance between male and female which may be outward- or inward-moving.

Waite—The card of human love, here exhibited as part of the way, the truth, and the life. The woman suggests that attraction toward the sensitive life which carries within it the idea of the Fall of Man. But this is the working of a Secret Law of Providence because it is through her imputed lapse that man shall arise ultimately, and only by her can he complete himself. Attraction, love, beauty, trials overcome.

Walker—The message of Tantric philosophy: only through physical union with a female can either a man or a god achieve true reality and the power to deal with it. Shamans, priests, and other holy men required a spiritual/sexual union with the female before they could gain full possession of their powers.

Wanless—*Law of Union.* Oneness through the marriage of opposites, communion with others, and the integration of inner self-polarities. An outer and inner union which creates an androgynous or whole being. Finding your inner lover, your inner "soul mate" which results in finding your "earth mate." The irresistible attraction to another, the wholeness of love, and nonjudgmental acceptance and embracing of the dualities while maintaining the center.

Wirth—The sign of supreme magical power acquired by the individual who with complete self-abnegation puts himself in the service of the "whole" to love to the point of existing only for others. Brings us back to unity through love, for Man becomes divine by loving as God does. The bond uniting all beings. Aspirations and desires on which the beauty of the soul depends.

Riley—*Coming Together.* If you haven't chosen yet, indicates a time of having to choose. If you've already chosen, a time of love and coming together. The life force of masculine and feminine, yin and yang energies bonding together.

VII—THE CHARIOT

Arrien—*Principle of Change.* Movement. Combination of Stillness-Activity. The Generator, Motivator, Traveler. Represents an inherent need to combine quietude with activity. In the next seven weeks or seven months, you will make changes concerned with the job or home, or travel.

Cowie—*Drive.* Having control, therefore having the drive to proceed after goals. Knowing where you are going and being determined to get there.

Crowley—Cancer. Cheth.

The Issue of the Vulture, Two-in-One, conveyed;
this is the Chariot of Power.
TRINC: the last oracle.

Eakins—A new force dissolving old forms. A time of clearing out, moving beyond the past, beginning with new energy, and taking responsibility for your present condition.

Fairfield—Being totally in tune with a fast-moving process or event. Awareness of the tolerances and limitations of the situation, and instinctively knowing how to act and react in order to direct or affect the movement from within. Not standing outside the situation because it can't be controlled from outside. By immersing yourself in it, you become part of it and are therefore able to direct its course.

Greer—*Principle of Mastery Through Change.* Self-mastery, controlled and directed energy, and thus victory. Hero. Warrior for a cause. Confidence in your own abilities. Having a sense of direction, a plan. Movement toward a goal.

Noble—*Winning One's Own Way.* Groundedness and the ability to accomplish tasks on the physical plane. A victory of self-discipline which involves bringing unconscious contents to consciousness for the purpose of accomplishment.

Pollack—The power of focused will. Signifies that the person is successfully controlling some situation through the force of his or her personality. Basically success and victory. Or a situation that has gotten out of control.

Sharman-Burke—Represents the quality of energy needed to fight for a desired goal. A struggle or conflict of interests when a fight for self-assertion may be necessary. However, if well placed in the spread, a successful outcome is assured as it is triumph over difficulties and obstacles.

Stewart—Higher knowledge, scientific inspiration and research, spiritual sciences, esoteric or Hermetic arts. Enlivened energy within the psyche of the inquirer or situation leading to a reasoned resolution inspired by insight.

Waite—Conquest on all planes—in the mind, in science, in progress, in certain trails of initiation. The charioteer is concerned with conquests which are manifest, external, rational, and physical, and not within himself, thus he offers no answers to the world of Grace. Succour, providence, war, triumph, and presumption.

Walker—Carl Jung pointed out that in dreams horses usually represent our uncontrollable emotional drives. On most decks, the charioteer does not hold the reins, and the beasts are heading in opposite directions, the message perhaps implying man is not in control of his Fate, even when he thinks he is.

Wanless—*Law of Motion.* The vehicle or road to self-realization and the highest point of personal attainment by exorcising the inner demon of fear, the greatest obstacle to life and growth. Movement brings change, and change brings new experience, learning, and growth—leading to the achievement of your evolutionary destiny.

Wirth—An ethereal substance playing the role of mediator between the measurable and the imponderable, between the incorporeal and the tangible. Directing intelligence which reconciles basic opposing factors. Triumph, steadfastness, control, direction, legitimate outcome.

Riley—*Riding the Wave.* Usually signifies things are going your way and will work out as you wish—more or less. Each and every single thing works toward the benefit of everything else if allowed to be its own nature and to follow its own natural course.

VIII—JUSTICE

Arrien—*The Principle of Balance.* Justice/Realignment. The Mediator, Adjuster, Arbitrator. Bringing something that is out of balance back into balance, a need to keep things simple and clear.

Cowie—*What You Put Out You Will Get Back.* Every thought, every word, and every action is returned to you. This law is in operation *all* the time.

Crowley—Libra. Teth.

Balance against each thought its exact opposite.
For the Marriage of these is the Annihilation of Illusion.

Eakins—Experiencing karmic adjustments in life from past thoughts and actions which have led to the present state. The nature of things moving into perfect balance by making adjustments to the forces and forms of the universe. All adjustment is good in that it moves us closer to the center of the target of perfection.

Fairfield—Establishing equilibrium or balance in life. A natural process of action and reaction in which the present situation, whatever it is, will pass and be balanced out by its opposite.

Greer—*Principle of Social Wisdom.* Social/Public Truth. Counterpoise or contraposition. Equilibrium. Adjustment. The need to be true to yourself, for neither justice nor mercy are possible without self-honesty. Balance, agreements, negotiations, decisions, and fairness (seen as XI).

Noble—*Setting Things Right.* The laws of Nature, as well as the relentless workings of Fate. Natural connections to all of nature. Coming to consciousness about your place in the universal scheme of things. In some way karma is working in the querent's life.

Pollack—Things have worked out the way they were "meant" to. Receiving what is deserved. A need for absolute honesty to see the truth of the situation. Or dishonesty and unwillingness to see yourself in the true meaning of the event.

Sharman-Burke—The need to weigh things, to find fair and rational solutions, and for reason and thought to override emotion, although at times Justice might need to be tempered with mercy. In short, the need for a balanced mind.

Stewart—Transpersonal energies of adjustment. Related to changes and interactions on a spiritual level. Essential adjustments that lead toward balance either on an immediate personal level or energies adjusting over long time-cycles.

Waite—The moral principle which deals unto every man according to his works. This is justice according to moral principle, and not the spiritual justice of the High Priestess, the latter involving the idea of election, like the dedication of certain men to the highest things and the gracious gifts of the poet. Equity, rightness, probity, executive; triumph of the deserving side of law.

Walker—The Fate-Goddess under various names such as Dike, Ananke, Venus, Nemesis, the Egyptian Mother Maat, Roman Mother of Libya, or Libera. The karmic law "for every action there is an equal and opposite reaction."

Wanless—(Balance) *Law of Action and Reaction.* For every action there is an equal reaction. Things are infinite only because they are constantly changing. The dance of balance amidst ever-present change.

Wirth—The generator of order and organization. Every action, every thought, every desire has its fatal repercussion for good or for ill. Splendour, glory, divinity manifested by order and harmony of nature, the conserving power of things.

Riley—*Taking the Rap.* The manifestation of harmony and balance in life, although sometimes Justice's idea of harmony and balance is not exactly the same as ours. The only *universal* law there is, is that there is no law. God, or life, is always striving away from laws and toward freedom.

IX—THE HERMIT

Arrien—*The Principle of Completion, Introspection, and Space.* The Meditator, Philosopher, Sage, Wise Man. A deep desire to follow that which is extremely meaningful and heartfelt for you.

Cowie—*Knowledge Needed.* Needing more knowledge and having to listen very closely to your inner self to find the answers needed. Meditation and prayer.

Crowley—Virgo. Yod.

Wander alone; bearing the Light and thy Staff.
And be the Light so bright that no man seeth thee.
Be not moved by aught without or within:
keep Silence in all ways.

Eakins—All that *is*, was, and ever shall be. There is nothing new under the Sun. The deepest marriage which is the divine marriage within.

Fairfield—Temporary withdrawal from others or from the usual environment in order to get some perspective on the situation. Gathering enough data and information so that you have enough personal wisdom to sort things out. A feeling that you want to analyze or understand your role within your relationship, group, job, family, or whatever.

Greer—*Principle of Introspection and Personal Integrity.* Completing karma through service. Self-reflection. The Seeker. Old Wise One. Journey into the Underworld. Perfection, patience, authenticity. The inward search to find personal truth in which not only accomplishments and gains, but also despair and isolation, must be accepted. Solitude.

Noble—*Turning Within.* Initiate, seeker, and hermit, representing a stage of life in which wisdom is sought—a time of introversion and spiritual seeking. Almost certainly a time of solitude. Usually comes as a blessing, but at first may include a sense of loneliness.

Pollack—A deliberate emotional withdrawal to work on self-development. Assistance from a definite inner or outer guide. Or withdrawal due to fear of people, or a Peter Pan attitude of fun and games as a way of avoiding the responsibility of doing something with your life.

Sharman-Burke—A time for soul-searching and meditation, the need for patience, and a time to work things out quietly. A degree of solitude is often needed.

Stewart—Looking within for proper answers. Understanding that is found through meditation or self-examination and assessment. May also be the close of a life cycle or period, and a withdrawal of energies accordingly.

Waite—This is a card of attainment rather than quest. It is the man who has the strength to lose himself to such a degree that he finds God. Intimates that, "Where I am, you may also be," because you cannot help getting what you seek in respect of the things that are Divine: it is the law of supply and demand.

Walker—From the Greek Orphics' "little Hermes" came the *Hermit.* Tantric tradition taught that secular life and worldly affairs should be followed by the compensatory life of seclusion and meditation. The Hermit starts a journey in the opposite direction to that of the Fool, into the world of the unconscious and the mystical.

Wanless—*Law of Wholeness.* To become complete by uniting the highest state of attainment in the material and spiritual realms. Using your work in the world as a spiritual path to achieve your higher destiny. Meditation.

Wirth—The Hermit's mission is not to fix beliefs by formulating dogma, for he is not the Hierophant; he does not address the crowds nor let himself be approached easily, and in this way he prepares formidable events, for being unknown to his contemporaries, he becomes the actual maker of the future. With no self interest, he weaves the subtle web of what is to take place. He is the prototype putting the stamp of the species onto individuals.

Riley—*Being Yourself.* Signifies a time to look to yourself for what you really are and what you really want, rather than what you are supposed to be or want. The Hermit is the knowledge that the value of physical life is provisional and is justified only if it allows you to live your love.

X—THE WHEEL OF FORTUNE

Arrien—*The Principle of Opportunity, Breakthrough, and Prosperity.* Abundance, Prosperity, Fortune. During the next 10 weeks or the next 10 months, there are Jupiterian possibilities of creating new opportunities and fortune in your life.

Cowie—*Action.* Involvement in life. Changes through which knowledge is gained. Life moving and being busy.

Crowley—Jupiter. Kaph.

Follow thy Fortune, careless where it lead thee.
The axle moveth not: attain thou that.

Eakins—Fate changing, rising or falling. The turning of the wheel. The whole of experience is necessary, for through this, all manifestations of light and dark ultimately merge and become one.

Fairfield—Something has been triggered that will roll through a natural course of events to its appropriate resting place. Initiation of some action so that the matter has been set in motion and there is nothing more to do but wait to see how the universal energies respond.

Greer—*Principle of Unity in Diversity.* The individual in society. Change, movement. Expansion of ideas. As the wheel turns, new opportunities appear and old projects reach a new turn of the spiral. A card of luck, generally good. Rewards and recognition for things completed.

Noble—*Going the Great Round.* The ancient sense of life as a moving wheel identified in particular with the zodiac. A time when life is in the hands of the Fates—a big event is taking place. A high point, a wish coming true, the manifestation of something anticipated.

Pollack—Some change in the circumstances of a person's life, not usually caused by the person directly but rather as a result of something else simply because life continues. The Wheel turns. Or a struggle against events.

Sharman-Burke—Signifies a new chapter is starting, a decision of importance is to be made, a new run of luck is commencing. The more you are aware of your own power over your destiny, the clearer things will appear.

Stewart—A change of fortune, either positive or negative. Often indicates, in association with other cards, how the individual's reaction will affect a cycle of events.

Waite—The perpetual motion of a fluidic universe and the flux of human life with Providence implied through all. The Divine intention within and the similar intention without wherein lies the denial of chance and the fatality which is implied therein. Destiny, fortune, success, elevation, luck, felicity.

Walker—Goddesses known as Lat, Fortuna, Vortumna, Mena, Tyche, Artemis, Bona Dea, who ruled Time and Fate. Tarot symbolism based on the Oriental-Gnostic concept of cyclic duality, death followed by birth, all things rising and falling.

Wanless—*Law of Abundance* on all levels of being. Fortune comes from following your passions. Your strongest feeling is where your talent lies. Fortune is the manifestation of your talents so that you are rewarded in return.

Wirth—The image of the double whirl which generates the life of each individual. Individual life which proceeds from a vaster life, which Man only manages to preserve to a limited extent, hence the brevity of the individual existence to which the Wheel of Fortune alludes. The Wheel of the Future or of Destiny.

Riley—*Watching Your Destiny.* An intimation that something is happening or will soon happen as a natural and inevitable result of what you have wanted and chosen in the past. The Principle of Karma—what goes around, comes around.

XI—STRENGTH

Arrien—*The Principle of Strength, Passion, and Lustre.* Passion, Awareness, Aliveness. A symbol that you are presently expressing your full creativity and strength and have a strong faith and trust in your abilities.

Cowie—*Strength to Overcome.* Relying on spiritual powers in order to handle the situation at hand, therefore having the help and control you need to overcome obstacles.

Crowley—Leo. Teth.

Migrate Energy with Love; but let Love devour all things.
Worship the name _________, foursquare, mystic, wonderful, and the name of His House 418.

Eakins—The presence of the inner spiritual force creeping to the surface and materializing in waking consciousness. Following your own deep inner light, doing what your heart of heart says is right, seeking bliss to find bliss, and discovering happiness.

Fairfield—Experiencing the gut-level, instinctive drives that are relied on for your protection or survival. Responding to a force that is not logical, and not even intuitive: it is just a compelling drive. It's a biological, emotional, or spiritual survival mechanism that has been triggered without your conscious awareness.

Greer—*The Principle of Courage and Self-Esteem.* Possessing the courage of your convictions. Acknowledging the power within. Enchantress, Animal Nature/Helper. Self-confidence. Perseverance. The balance and integration of opposites. Guidance from rage, anger, instincts. (Seen as VIII.)

Noble—*Finding Magical Helpers.* Matriarchal consciousness which brings sexuality and language to her people. Experiencing being ready and able to get what is wanted in life. Knowing from the heart what is needed.

Pollack—The ability to face life, particularly some difficult problem or time, with hope and eagerness. A person strong within, experiencing life passionately yet peacefully. Or weakness resulting from the passions becoming the enemy.

Sharman-Burke—The strength and endurance necessary to achieve self-control. Obstacles that are overcome through willpower, resulting in a sense of mastery. Courage, strength, determination, self-awareness, potential integration, and individuality.

Stewart—A positive beneficial source of strength. Power or material benefit within a given situation according to position and other cards. Often creative or constructive possibilities within the query situation.

Waite—Fortitude connected with the Divine Mystery of Union, also with *innocentia inviolata*, and the strength which resides in contemplation. This card has nothing to do with self-confidence in the ordinary sense, but concerns the confidence of those whose strength is God, who have found their refuge in Him. The strength of passions liberated in the higher nature. Power, energy, action, courage, magnanimity.

Walker—The Goddesses of Earth from ancient cultures who tamed, rode, and transformed into lions. One of the strongest of the Aryan Gods was Thor, who was married to the Goddess Thrud, whose name meant Strength. She represented the irresistible strength of the Earth.

Wanless—*Law of Self-Dominion*, which translates into rulership and control. The full and free but controlled expression of mind, heart, body, and spirit in yin and yang forms. Total living. Living in full accord with the undiluted multiplicity of your being.

Wirth—Shows Leo who is conquered, or followed, by Virgo in the Zodiac. The Initiate who scorns nothing inferior and considers to be sacred even the least noble of instincts, for they are the stimulant necessary for every action. Life is based on the association of diverging factors unaware of each other's existence which is required to be reconciled in the interest of higher things.

Riley—*Trusting and Allowing.* The card of animals. Holiness is all that lives, equally, for Love excludes not one living thing nor holds it out as more or less than any other.

XII—THE HANGED MAN

Arrien—*The Principle of Surrender, Breaking Old Patterns.* The Transformer. Within the next 12 weeks or the next 12 months you will see clearly restrictive patterns in yourself that you will act upon and break.

Cowie—*Acceptance of Reversals.* Encountering a situation you would rather not have to deal with.

Crowley—Water. Mem.

> Let not the waters whereon thou journeyest wet
> thee. And, being come to shore, plant thou the
> Vine and rejoice without shame.

Eakins—The suspended mind. Being in a time and place of surrender. Letting go and voluntarily retreating to quietude. In losing your self, you find your Self.

Fairfield—A card of timing and effectiveness. A sense of waiting for the appropriate time, situation, or circumstances. You are aware of what you want to do, and you may even be conscious of the next move or direction, but you are also aware that things are not quite set for action yet. Hanging around, suspended in mid-air, waiting to make the next move.

Greer—*Principle of Unconditional Love.* Giving Birth to Soul. Self-sacrifice and submission of the self to higher ideals. The card of the mystic, the shaman, the dreamer. Can literally represent your "hang ups" and addictions, being stuck in old patterns. Reversal. Feeling powerless. Delays. Surrender and devotion.

Noble—*Accepting Initiation.* The voluntary surrender to a death and resurrection process. Losing yourself through a sense of ecstasy and surrender to love. Being suspended in time when it is important to stop action and allow. Yield, wait, and see what happens.

Pollack—Being who you are, even if others think you have everything backwards. The feeling of being deeply connected to life. Can mean a peace that comes after some difficult trial. Or an inability to get free of social pressure to listen to your inner self.

Sharman-Burke—A time of greater understanding, a turning point when control of the conscious ego is surrendered to the unknown inner world. A sacrifice will have to be made, although it is worth remembering that the sacrifice will be made in order to gain something of greater value.

Stewart—Sacrifice of outer form, habits, or situation for a non-personal or transpersonal end. Situations of paradox, loss, or difficulty when a new level of understanding is gained. On a higher level, initiation into the Mysteries of Light.

Waite—The symbolism of the higher nature in which a great awakening is possible and after the sacred Mystery of Death there is a glorious Mystery of Resurrection. A state of mystical death in the form of a change of consciousness. Wisdom, circumspection, discernment, trials, sacrifice, intuition, divination, prophecy.

Walker—The universal version of the dying-god myth who upon crossing the threshold between life and death could see into both worlds. Odin, God of the hanged; Shiva, the sacrificed God; Osiris; Jesus. Also a medieval custom known as "baffling" where debtors were hanged by one foot, sometimes before their execution.

Wanless—*Law of Reversal.* Doing the opposite of what is ordinarily expected to achieve victory brings victory. Salvation is attained by passive surrender rather than by assertiveness and forceful resistance.

Wirth—Passive or Mystic Initiation. Inactivity and powerlessness where the body is concerned, for the soul is freed in order to envelop the physical organism into a subtle atmosphere in which the purest spiritual rays are refracted. Entering into contact with God. Redeeming sacrifice. Activity of the soul. Remote intervention.

Riley—*Obeying the Spirit.* A time when your logic and intuition, or what you want and what is happening, seem to be going in opposite directions at the same speed. Prudence advises, since you don't know up from down now anyway, to accept, to surrender, and above all else, to listen to the Spirit.

XIII—DEATH

Arrien—*The Principle of Letting Go and Moving On.* Release/Detachment. The Releaser, Eliminator, Expander. Cutting through the very bones, the core, in order to release the new in a rebirth.

Cowie—*Rebirth Out of Old Conditions.* Moving away from conditions which cause pain and hurt.

Crowley—Scorpio. Non.

> The Universe is Change; every Change is the effect of an Act of Love: all Acts of Love contain Pure Joy. Die Daily.
> Death is the apex of one curve of the snake Life: behold all opposites as necessary compliments, and rejoice.

Eakins—Being involved in a major transformation, one of the greatest ever known. You must face this change alone and will be reborn into newness, but first your darkest fears must be faced. The darkest hour just before the dawn.

Fairfield—Experiencing total change, transformation, or metamorphosis. The pressures in the current situation are becoming so strong that you are actually choosing to change things. Destroying the old in order to generate something new, getting to the heart of the matter and totally transforming it. Turning the old situation inside out.

Greer—*Principle of Realization of Life Power.* Vital force. Release of outgrown or outmoded forms. Destruction and renewal, immortality and regeneration—eliminating anything restrictive or no longer of service. Giving up your sense of self to a feeling of merging with another or with the cosmos. Pruning and composting.

Noble—*Letting Go.* Change. Almost never signifies physical death, but rather some experience of dying and rebirth. The change is essential and final, and the rebirth is already taking place.

Pollack—A time of change. Often indicates a fear of change. A cleaning away of old habits and rigidness to allow a new life to emerge. Dealing with the issue of death in your life. Or being afraid of death or being stuck in old habits.

Sharman-Burke—Heralds the inevitable ending of something, but with the promise of a new beginning. The pain that is suffered under the effect of Death is related to the willingness or unwillingness of the seeker to surrender to the inevitability of change.

Stewart—Initially a change for the better. Frequently changes which arise from deep inner or spiritual drives, causing outer form or patterns in the personal life to dissolve, thus may be areas of personal tension and inner conflict that can be resolved only by true change.

Waite—The natural transit of man to the next stage of his being. The ascent of the spirit in the divine spheres. Creation and destruction, perpetual movement, rebirth, destination, renewal.

Walker—Similar to the *danse macabre* of the Grim Reaper. A Teutonic shaman who was allowed to visit the Crone-goddess, Hilde or Hel, in her underworld. First users of the Reaper's scythe may have been the Scythians, a matriarchal Amazonian people. Mother Hel was called Scatha by the Irish and Skadi, or Skathi, by the Vikings.

Wanless—*Law of Impermanence.* The dissolution of obstruction, a freeing-up, the breakup of blockage and constriction which is represented by the Hanged Man. All things must come to an end, but like a snake which sheds its skin, death is a life-giving transformation which means a shedding of the old to be reborn.

Wirth—What "is" changes its aspect but is never destroyed: everything persists by being changed indefinitely by the action of the great transformer to whom individual beings owe their origin. By decomposing forms that have worn out and are no longer capable of fulfilling the job for which they were destined, Death intervenes as a rejuvenator to set free energies to enter into new combinations of life. We owe our transitory existence to what we call Death. It allows us to be born and leads to rebirth.

Riley—*Letting Go.* A time when perception of one thing is lost and another is gained. There is no creation or destruction—only motion, or change. A change of form by which a reliance on human consciousness is reduced and a reliance on spiritual consciousness increased.

XIV—TEMPERANCE

Arrien—*The Principle of Integration, Synthesis, and Synergy.* The Creator, the Alchemist. Indicates that whatever life dream or visions are important to you may be actualized or fall into place within the next 14 weeks or 14 months.

Cowie—*Blending of All Circumstances to Create Balance.* Balancing the different conditions of life. Knowledge to blend different life aspects, thereby creating harmony.

Crowley—Sagittarius. Samech.

> Pour thine all freely from the Vase in thy right
> hand, and lose no drop. Hath not thy left hand a vase?
> Transmute all wholly into the Image of thy Will,
> bringing each to its true token of Perfection.
> Dissolve the Pearl in the Wine-cup; drink, and
> make manifest the Virtue of that Pearl.

Eakins—Trials and temptations which lead toward integration, the "middle way." Through acting in moderation, stretching spiritually, and allowing inner growth, fears are conquered and you arrive at a period of profound realization.

Fairfield—Blending of diverse elements to create something new. Combining the many elements, allowing them to affect and transform each other so that no one element dominates. Together they mesh and blend into a new whole. Awareness that the whole is truly greater than the sum of its parts.

Greer—*Principle of Spiritual Education.* Compassion. Freedom of action. Learning by experience. Assimilating and integrating. Tempering, adjusting, and redistribution. The promise that there is a solution to every problem. The Healing Angel working by correcting imbalances.

Noble—*Grounding Cosmic Energy.* The empowerment of Alchemy, the process of blending the parts of the self until fusion is achieved. An integration of the emotional forces with the physical—a blessed union of opposites within and without. Being in balance. Experiencing a union.

Pollack—Moderation, calm. Right action, doing the correct thing in whatever situation arises, very often nothing. Blending activities and feelings to produce harmony and peace. Or a warning that life has become fragmented and extreme.

Sharman-Burke—Cooperation, successful blending of opposites, and compromise in marriage and partnerships. Denotes balanced emotions.

Stewart—May simply be temperance or balance within the query situation. On a higher level, grace or power from unknown sources. Occasionally a direct spiritual influence at work within the query.

Waite—Changes in the seasons, perpetual movement of life, and the combination of ideas. When the rule of Temperance obtains in our consciousness, it tempers, combines, and harmonizes the psychic and material natures. Under that rule we know in our rational part something of whence we came and whither we are going.

Walker—The transmuting and transforming nature of love which turns all things into its own nature. The mystery of love beyond death, such as the Egyptian savior Osiris who was carried to his love-death in the form of water in a vase.

Wanless—(Art) *Law of Creativity.* Being a creative artist in all aspects of being and in all endeavors of worldly life. Weaving together the opposites so that all elements of inner self are woven together, resulting in creation and becoming naturally whole and healed.

Wirth—Far from suppressing life, death provides for eternal rejuvenation. It decomposes the "container" in order to liberate the "contained." This is envisioned as a vital liquid unceasingly poured from a silver urn into a gold one without one drop being wasted by Temperance who becomes the angel of universal life. The animating fluid which restores spent energy.

Riley—*Sharing With Your Angel.* On a physical level, harmonious balance, or patience and acceptance. On a whole spiritual level, it means no separation, for *unconditional* love does not involve *perceiving* the other, but *being* the other.

XV—THE DEVIL

Arrien—*The Principle of Mirth Combined with Stability.* Humor at What "Bedevils" Us. The Joker, Worker, Stabilizer. Handling life from a place of humor. During the next 15 weeks or 15 months, you may be attracted to creative people, projects, and inspirational events.

Cowie—*Beware of Emotions.* Emotions close to or out of control. Warning that even with the best of intentions, one may be wrong.

Crowley—Capricornus. Ain.

> With they right Eye create all for thyself, and with
> the left accept all that be created otherwise.

Eakins—The world of the dark subconscious. A struggle for truth amid seeming contradictions and haphazard or incomplete information through which there are glimpses of light. Accepting the presence of paradox and realizing your own truth. Celebrating life, laughter, play, and dancing upon the Earth.

Fairfield—Experiencing boundaries and limits. Seeing that options and choices are being narrowed and your life is becoming more structured and somewhat less flexible. Making certain assumptions or establishing baseline conditions, which rules out some of the options.

Greer—*Principle of Urge to Separate.* Choice to fear. Obsessions and limitations. Material form. Projections of what is hidden or repressed. The "shadow" self. Raw, untamed power and creativity which calls for a sense of humor and being able to laugh at yourself and your own self-importance. Social and sexual taboos.

Noble—*Denying the Spirit.* Being in bondage to some power. In some way subscribing to the dominance-submission mentality, and the issue of power is at stake. Maybe abusing power in some way, exercising personal will over others, or letting the ego take the reins. The soul in need of liberation.

Pollack—A narrow materialistic view of life. Any form of misery or depression with illusion that no alternatives are possible. Being the slave of desires or a controlling obsession. A feeling of helplessness or shame. On a deeper level, going into your own darkness. Or, freeing yourself from oppression.

Sharman-Burke—Inhibitions and blocks that hinder growth but which may be removed. Carries the promise that if removed, great growth and progress is possible. "Out of apparent evil, much good can come."

Stewart—Energies of purification, disillusionment, and rebalance. Restriction for positive ends, or thresholds beyond which it is dangerous to cross. Often provides the key to solutions for difficult or negative problems in life.

Waite—The chain and fatality of the material life. Being sustained by the evil that is within and blind to the liberty of service. Signifies the Dweller on the Threshold without the Mystical Garden when those are driven forth therefrom who have eaten the forbidden fruit. Ravage, violence, vehemence, extraordinary efforts, force, fatality: that which is predestined and is not for this reason evil.

Walker—The ancient Lord of the Underworld worshiped under such names as Pluto, Hades, Nergal, Saturn, Zeus Chthonios, Apollyon, and Ahriman. His identification with the Underworld developed the belief that he controlled all the mineral wealth, including buried treasure, hence the Christian notion that he could make a person rich.

Wanless—(Devil's Play) To live fully and joyously, and to work and play to the point where play and work are the same. Celebrating the expression of creative energy.

Wirth—The Prince of the Material World which could not exist without him because he is at the base of all differentiation between one individual and another. The one who differentiates, the enemy of unity. He sets the worlds against the World and having incited people to wish to be like God, then indicates the instinct which relates everything to themselves, as if they were the centre around which everything must gravitate.

Riley—*Butting In.* The hubris, or speciesism, of the human race, people believing they are better than other life. Or mirth. Receiving this card is a reminder to live life just for the fun of it, for what other reason is there? If it isn't close to laughter, it isn't close to God.

XVI—THE TOWER

Arrien—*The Principle of Restoration and Renovation.* The Restorer, Healer, Renovator. During the next 16 weeks or 16 months you will be eliminating from your life that which is false-to-fact, artificial, and no longer useful to you.

Cowie—*Unexpected Events.* Something completely unexpected will happen, and you will need to "let go."

Crowley—Mars. Peh.
Break down the fortress of thine Individual
Self, that thy Truth may spring free from the ruins.

Eakins—A series of insights which propel to a new awareness. Outgrowing the old physical or mental structure in order to make room for new structures which are needed. Disturbing flashes of truth which become the source of liberation.

Fairfield—Deciding to change a basic or core belief in life. Because you have believed certain things, those things have manifested in your life as foundations upon which your life's structure has been built. When you change a core belief, you are seeing a new "truth" about the way things are. A flash of enlightenment that starts off a whole chain reaction.

Greer—*Principle of Breakthrough.* Illuminating energy unleashed. Insight that strikes and shatters whatever is rigid and unyielding. Anger. Eruptions. A major change in life that catapults the individual into a whole new direction.

Noble—*Shattering the Structure.* Ego death. The end of mental control. Brace yourself—you're in for a change. A radical shift, a flash of illumination. At the same time the "high self" can understand and handle what is happening, the personality self may be freaking out.

Pollack—A period of literal or psychological upheaval, the break-up of situations or relationships in anger or violence. Clearing away some situation that has built up intolerable pressure that can lead to new beginnings. On a deeper level, revelations.

Sharman-Burke—The necessary breaking down of existing forms to make way for new life and new ways. Rigid or imprisoning structures that need to be torn down and replaced. The defeat of false philosophies and the triumph of true ones.

Stewart—Breakdown and collapse of unhealthy, false, or unnaturally rigid conditions. Destruction of illusions or delusions.

Waite—The materialization of the spiritual word. The ruin of the House of Life when evil has prevailed therein, the rending of a House of Doctrine, a House of Falsehood. Misery, distress, indigence, adversity, calamity, disgrace, deception, ruin; a card in particular of unforeseen catastrophe.

Walker—The Holy Roman Empire was sometimes called "the proud tower," and if the card is seen to prophesy the Empire's fall, then the two figures falling from the tower are pope and emperor, the combination of church and state.

Wanless—*Law of Purification.* A revolutionary self-cleansing of mankind's ego and the structures he builds to support his vanity. Moving away from the daily world of habitual living and seeing with a new clarity.

Wirth—The principle which determines all materialization and the tendency towards materialization. Human rapacity, the source of all despotisms, perhaps with regard to the intensive exploitation of the earth and of human energies on which the present age prides itself. The systematic reproach of all moderation that leads toward a terrifying social cataclysm. Pride, presumption, restrictive hoarding.

Riley—*Getting Off the Fence.* When physical illusions are released and spiritual truth descends into materialization, causing a sudden release and manifest direction to previously pent up or distressing conditions. Heaven's answer to "Dial-a-Prayer."

XVII—THE STAR

Arrien—*The Principle of Self-Esteem and Confidence.* Self-sufficiency and Talent Recognized by Others. During the next 17 weeks or 17 months, you increase and maintain your own self-esteem to such a point you may assist others with theirs.

Cowie—*Knowledge Being Given Out.* Help by giving out love and understanding. Balance is maintained by giving out what is received in a controlled, balanced manner.

Crowley—Aquarius. Daleth.

> Use all thine energy to rule thy thought: burn
> up thy thought as the Phoenix.

Eakins—Following your own star, meditating upon the nature at the center of the true self. The *natural intelligence* of the universal mind which is found in the great ocean of the dark subconscious. Hearing your own song through meditation and then moving with love, calm, and peaceful agility.

Fairfield—Experiencing the boundless, free abundance of the Universe. Sensing a flow of pure energy and resources that can be used for many purposes. Knowing that you have these infinite resources at your disposal, and you can channel this energy wherever you want.

Greer—*Principle of Courage to be Ourselves.* Acknowledging the power from Source. Self-esteem. Spiritual regeneration. Hope in a vision of the future. The individual freed from all masks and restrictions and being replenished by the waters of the unconscious. Interdependency of nature.

Noble—*Opening to the Goddess.* The calm after the storm. Passing to a new level. Trusting in the ability of the universe to heal and being ready to begin the process of transformation. Often a peaceful, restful period which connects you to others or to divine spirit in the world.

Pollack—Hope, a sense of healing and wholeness, especially after emotional storms. Inner calm. The unconscious activated in a very benign way. Or weakness, impotence, and fear sometimes masked as arrogance.

Sharman-Burke—A happy message of promise, good fortune, optimism, and joy. Suggests inspiration, a sense of purpose, and the renewal of life's forces and energies.

Stewart—A profound spiritual impulse or transcendent energy at work usually within the individual, but sometimes a collective or cosmic energy pattern involving the inquirer and many other people.

Waite—The mottos of this card are "Waters of Life freely," and "Gifts of the Spirit." The Great Mother in the Kabalistic *Sephira Binah*, which is supernal Understanding who communicates to the *Sephiroth* that are below in the measure that they can receive her influx. Hope, immortality, interior light, Truth unveiled.

Walker—The mystic's "astral body" is literally the star-body, based on the ancient notion that our inner being is a star. The Goddess Artemis governed stars and appeared as Ursa Major, the Great Bear, or what we now call the Big Dipper, greatly venerated by the ancients because of its position at the apex of heaven and because it forever circles the North Star.

Wanless—*Law of Luminosity.* Seeing things as they really are. Inspiration, aspiration, upliftment, and affirmation. Recognition of the star light within you so that you succeed and star on all levels of being. Giving of yourself with compassion in service to others so they may find their star light.

Wirth—The stars and lights above which encourage us and make us feel that we are not abandoned. What the gods originally called "the shining ones" who watch over us and direct us with the aim of fulfilling our destiny, for no one is created without his destiny being traced in its broad outlines, without an aim being assigned to the earthly traveller. Life shared out among creatures.

Riley—*Gaining an Inner View.* Receiving and recognizing the love of your spirit for you. Being the rose and its thorns; a light enveloped by the universe; a verse held within the One Song. Also passion, because passion is soul's recognition of her spirit.

XVIII—THE MOON

Arrien—*The Principle of Choice and Authenticity.* The Chooser, the Romantic. During the next 18 weeks or 18 months you will make choices which require that you drop old illusions, delusions, and self-deceptions in order to reclaim your own authenticity.

Cowie—*Watch Motives.* A time to be careful of decisions and actions and to check motives to make sure they are honest and you are not deceiving yourself.

Crowley—Pisces. Koph.

> Let the Illusion of the World pass over thee, unheeded, as thou goest from the Midnight to the Morning.

Eakins—Unable to see the future clearly. Trusting intuition and staying on the Path of *corporal intelligence* that connects the emotions and psychic upwelling with the physical body, leading to physical manifestation and spiritual unfoldment.

Fairfield—Being guided by your greater, or Universal, self. Some doors are opening for you and others are closing. Guidance appearing in an intuitive or symbolic form, showing you the path you need to follow. Trusting something other than your logical mind to be your guide.

Greer—*Principle of Completing Karma Through Evolution.* Journeying within. The Source. Spiritual Evolution. Journey into the unknown. Intuition. Functioning in the realm of the unconscious where you become aware that reality is a dream, that time and space and physical bodies are merely conceptions, and therefore deep cellular change is possible.

Noble—*Experiencing the Mystery.* The shamanic call to enter into the darkness. Unconscious desires and fears that accompany the sense of losing control or falling into the unconscious. Nothing to do but yield to the feelings. Flowing with the darkness and the unknown. A good time for dreaming.

Pollack—An excitement of the unconscious. The imagination enriching life through strange emotions, dreams, fears, or even hallucinations. Or a struggle against this experience leading to fear and disturbed emotions.

Sharman-Burke—Usually a phase of fluctuation and change. Often indicates uncertainty and even illusion. It can also suggest that solutions to problems can be found through dreams and intuitions rather than through logic and reason.

Stewart—Unconscious forces or unseen influences from within materializing into outer life. Matters relating to birth and death, dreams, and desires. Sometimes the early stages of inner transformation or initiation.

Waite—Represents life of the imagination apart from life of the spirit. The intellectual light is a reflection, and beyond it is the unknown mystery which it cannot shew forth. The message is: "Peace, be still; and it may be there shall come a calm upon the animal nature, while the abyss beneath shall cease from giving up a form." Hidden enemies, danger, calumny, darkness, terror, deception, occult forces, error.

Walker—The moon has always been associated with the Great Goddess in all of her three forms—maiden, mother, and crone. The Moon card was sometimes called Hecate, or the Dogs of Hecate, who guarded Death's gate, as souls were said to go to the Moon upon death where the Moon Mother conceived them to be born again onto Earth.

Wanless—*Law of Cycles and Phases.* Inner changes brought through contemplation that will in time quietly usher in a new phase. It is not a disruptive revolutionary force, but is instead a conservative change, a preservation through "continuity transformation" that ensures the flow of gentle evolutionary completions and beginnings.

Wirth—The theatre where human existence is played out. Illusions of materiality. Maya. The path of earthly life with its trials, falls, and bruises which leads us to recognize error, lose our illusions, and make our way toward the dawn of full light. Outward appearance. What comes within our senses.

Riley—*Giving Up*. An issue hidden from the conscious for the present, and there is no ability to reach it. It is out of your hands; things are happening on the inner planes, and there's nothing to do but to go about your business, or better yet, go back to bed.

XIX—THE SUN

Arrien—*The Principle of Collaboration, Teamwork, and Partnership.* Co-operation. The Originator, Co-creator, Co-operator. The child-like innocence and curiosity within your own creative nature that wants to be expressed in all aspects of your life.

Cowie—*Growth, Reward, Truth, and Progress.* Beginning a new cycle of life. Ready to achieve on the inner plane what the Sun accomplishes in giving life and warmth to the Earth.

Crowley—Sun. Resh.

Give forth thy light to all without doubt;
the clouds and shadows are no matter for thee.
Make Speech and Silence, Energy and Stillness,
twin forms of thy play.

Eakins—The truest love. The coming of a divine marriage which is physical, mental, or spiritual. Everything now makes sense, is as good as it could possibly be. Liberation from the limitations of physical matter and circumstances through conscious self-identification with the One Life.

Fairfield—Experiencing a time of rekindled enthusiasm. Revitalizing something that has previously existed in your life. You have learned a great deal from past experiences and are now ready to make refinements and adjustments so that you can re-do something you've done before in a new and more effective manner.

Greer—*Principle of Unity in Spirit.* All as one. Wholeness, achievement, and revelation. Affirming life. Enlightenment, comprehension, clarity, wisdom. Things previously unclear have come into the light of day. Joyous, radiant sense of well-being. Optimism.

Noble—*Raising Consciousness.* Rebirth. Consciousness and the active, awakened understanding of, and appreciation for, life. Full mental understanding bursts into consciousness, and you see what is. A good day, week, or year. Probably experiencing a great deal of expansiveness and pleasure.

Pollack—Joy, happiness, and a great sense of the beauty of life. Clarity. In its deepest sense, it means looking at the world in a wholly new way, seeing all life united in joy and light. Above all it is a card of optimism, energy, and wonder. Or a time when life is still giving simple happiness, but it cannot be seen so clearly, as if the sun has become clouded over.

Sharman-Burke—Energy and a source of strength. Success, prosperity, happiness, and true friends. It seems to brighten all the cards surrounding it, adding a sense of optimism and good cheer.

Stewart—Powerful harmonising, centralising influence or energy upon life patterns. Emergence of new meaning, knowledge, and higher levels of awareness.

Waite—Signifies the transit from the manifest light of this world to the light of the world to come. Consciousness in the spirit—the direct light as the antithesis of the reflected light. When the self-knowing spirit has dawned in the consciousness above the natural mind. Material happiness, fortunate marriage, contentment.

Walker—Represents emergence from the dark night of gestation between lives. The children on the card were seen as the young lunar-solar twins of a new creation.

Wanless—*Law of Radiance.* The emitter of light and heat which awakens and gives life. Brings consciousness.

Wirth—Reveals the reality of things and shows them as they really are without the veil of illusion. The primordial light which puts order into chaos. The Word which enlightens all men that come into this world. Superhuman Reason which inspires all minds.

Riley—*Seeing the Light.* The rise of previously unconscious material to the conscious mind. Becoming aware of something you didn't know. The pieces of a puzzle, or something, coming together for you. Or just having a good time.

XX—JUDGEMENT

Arrien—*The Principle of Good Judgment.* Discernment. The Analyst, Evaluator, Seer. During the next 20 weeks or five months, you are determined to change judgmental attitudes you might hold in order to look at all situations you are currently facing with more objectivity.

Cowie—*Accepting Results of Your Decision.* Experiencing the results of a previous choice.

Crowley—Fire. Shin.

> Be every Act an Act of Love and Worship.
> Be every Act the Fiat of a God.
> Be every Act a Source of radiant Glory.

Eakins—Dissolving of personal perceptions and consciousness to be replaced by the deepest understanding possible. The final stage of knowledge as it has been known, resurrection into a completely new stage. Freedom from judgment. Spiritual rebirth of the recognition of the One Life, the unity of all things.

Fairfield—Experiencing the natural process of growth and maturation. The old phase in life is ending because of maturation through the passage of time. Reaching a phase because you're growing up; celebrating your "coming of age" through a rite of passage or ritual. A sense of passing from one phase of life into another.

Greer—*Principle of Cosmic Understanding.* Spiritual Truth. Change and transformation. Recognizing a purpose behind the events. Family and/or social consciousness. Resurrection or awakening in all its various forms. Criticism and conscience.

Noble—*Healing the Earth.* The cycle of return, the time of healing and planetary regeneration. An important decision has been made by the "high Self" which alters your reality for good, even though you may not be consciously aware of what has happened.

Pollack—A push, a call from within to make some important change. In effect, the person, old self, or situation has already changed, and it is simply a matter of recognizing it. Or trying to deny the call, usually from a fear of the unknown.

Sharman-Burke—The final settlement of a matter, a "clean slate"—paying off old debts and a preparedness for the resurrection of a new beginning. Indicates that things which have lain fallow will come to life, and reward for past effort will finally be forthcoming. A time for rejoicing and renewal.

Stewart—Outwardly a matter of judgement in a situation or a judgement to be made, often with profound or far-reaching effects. Also collective or ancestral matters, such as national situations and seemingly unavoidable influences.

Waite—Signifies the accomplishment of the great work of transformation in answer to the summons of the Supernal whose summons is heard and answered from within. The resurrection of the triad of human life—father, mother, child—the generative forces of life. A card of eternal life. Change of position, renewal, outcome.

Walker—The regenerated Self in the sense of a new being discovered within the present physical body. The original ancient belief that there is constant destruction and renewal, which the Christians made linear and static.

Wanless—(Time-Space) *Law of Karma.* The new life which comes after the judgment of death to old karmic patterns that are self-destructive. Called "Time-Space" because it implies the ability to see into past patterns that create present realities, which in turn predict future patterns. A total overview of where you have been, are, and are going.

Wirth—Intervention for the purpose of distinguishing the spiritual from the material, the deep significance from the expressive form, the living word from the dead letter. Everything is a symbol, for everything proceeds from a generating idea which is related to transcendent conception. Penetration into the depths of things. The Holy Ghost. Inspiration. Communication with divine spirit.

Riley—*Beginning Again.* Astral transformation which will soon result in physical manifestation, or vice-versa. When we finally become totally aware spiritually, we need never leave that which we have loved, for all that we truly become aware of, we become, so that always it is with us.

XXI—THE UNIVERSE

Arrien—*The Principle of Totality, Individuation, and Wholeness.* The Completion, the Initiator. In the next 21 weeks you are building new worlds internally and externally, and actualizing them in your life.

Cowie—*Attainment.* Attainment of goals and overcoming of difficulties. The positive and negative are balanced, the material and spiritual have blended. Protection, happiness, and contentment.

Crowley—Saturn. Earth. Tau.

> Treat time and all conditions of Event as Servants of thy Will, appointed to present the Universe to thee in the form of thy Plan.
>
> And: blessing and worship to the prophet of the lovely Star.

Eakins—The individual's whole world is in balance. Endeavors have been successful, every undertaking has paid off. The end of a long journey whose purpose was the discovery of the inner self, and the closing of the circle by discovering that you are the source of your own love.

Fairfield—Having everything available to you and being at center stage in your life, aware that you can simply reach out and choose one of many options. You know that the choices are complex, and you are aware of the multiple factors that you need to take into consideration to make your choice.

Greer—*Principle of Universal Love.* Giving Birth to Spirit. Strong connections to the Earth. Finding freedom within structure. Free to maximize your own potential. The self-actualization of the joy of being alive and the rapture of being. Learning to dance on your limitations.

Noble—*Casting the Circle.* The Divine Androgyny, integrating male and female energies. The liberation of consciousness that is not *of* bliss, but *is* bliss. Mastering in some way the three planes of mind, body, and emotions. Reaching completion on some work, the end of one phase, and the very expansive beginning of another.

Pollack—Success, achievement, satisfaction. To greater or lesser degree, a unification of the inner sense of being with outer activities. Or stagnation.

Sharman-Burke—The completion of one phase or stage of life; promises success, harmony, and triumphant achievement. The realization of a sought-after prize or goal.

Stewart—May simply mean worldly or material concerns. Balance of elements or energies within the individual. Also a direct indicator of where the greatest power may be found in any situation, according to the position of the card.

Waite—Refers to that day in the past when all was declared to be good, when the morning stars sang together, and all the Sons of God shouted for joy. The perfection and end of the Cosmos, the secret which is within it, the rapture of the universe when it understands itself in God. The state of the soul in the consciousness of Divine Vision, reflected from the self-knowing spirit.

Walker—The unveiled Goddess dancing in the wreath of the world womb, representing the basic, primary symbol of creation and re-creation of reincarnation. The Lady Soul of a "thousand names" who was cosmic energy, the power source of every deity and every living thing.

Wanless—(Universe) *Law of Universality.* At one in consciousness with all phenomena. Each of us is a microcosm of the macrocosm, carrying within our genes the gifts and qualities of the universe, thus possessing a literal universe of possibilities.

Wirth—The world which swirls in a perpetual dance where nothing stops. Everything turns ceaselessly in it, for movement is the generator of things. From this movement, flows life. Cosmos. The ordered universe. Reign of God. Totality. Re-integration. Complete success. Reward.

Riley—*Understanding the Reason for Your Being.* Discovering and/or living your purpose in life. Living life to the fullness of your being. The selves rejoicing with the Self.

NOTES

THE MINOR ARCANA

Judgment (Day)
What! You been keeping records on me? I wasn't so bad! How many times did I take the Lord's name in vain? One million and six? Jesus Ch. . . . !

—Steve Martin

The Minor Arcana consists of 40 cards—10 cards numbered 1 through 10 in each of the four suits. The four suits are wands, cups, swords, and discs. (The Minor Arcana is usually also thought to include the court cards. These are covered in the next chapter.) The four suits are representative of the four elements and are extremely important because they show the only four ways that we are able to perceive anything. All human awareness is filtered either through our 1) intuition or spirit (wands); 2) emotions (cups); 3) thoughts (swords); or 4) the five physical senses (discs). If a stimulus is not being received through one or more of these four perceptive mechanisms, then we remain unaware of its presence.

In psychology, these four functions are called *intuition, feeling, thinking,* and *sensation,* respectively. Also psychologically speaking, wands (intuition) correspond to the superconscious, cups (emotions) to the subconscious, swords (thinking) to the conscious, and discs (sensation) to the physical. The four suits are fundamental to our existence on Earth, and their correlations are found in countless ways, such as in the King, Queen, Prince, and Princess of the court cards; the four seasons of Spring, Summer, Fall, and Winter; and the four directions of South, East, West, and North. In astrology and alchemy they are called the four elements of Fire, Water, Air, and Earth, and in numerology they are the numbers 1 through 4.

The four suits have different names and titles, depending in which context they are being used and what subject is being discussed, but regardless, each suit bears the same attributes, i.e., the suit of wands maintains the same characteristics as Fire, the number 1, intuition, Spring, and the space called South.

Following are some more properties commonly attributed to the suits. Different taroists vary somewhat on these correspondences, but in general, they remain fairly consistent. These may be further explored by the interpretations offered in this book and in each taroist's published works.

WANDS

The Spiritual World of Creativity. The time of Spring and the space of South. Enterprise, career, wisdom, imagination, inspiration, creativity, freedom, intuition, energy, power, passion, spirit, light, and the superconscious. Wands' colors are those of light, lightning, fire, flame, the aurora borealis, rainbows, and the Sun, because, although all things are composed of light, these are closest to purest light or refractions of light in the physical.

CUPS

The Emotional World of Feeling. The time of Summer and the space of East. Receptivity, emotions, feelings, security, survival, instincts, memory, psychism, yearnings, fears, dreams, fantasies, and the subconscious. Cups' colors are those of water, lakes, ponds, rivers, rain, the sea, and blood. Blood is actually deep blue until it is exposed to air which is why our veins look blue beneath our skin.

SWORDS

The Mental World of Thinking. The time of Fall and the space of West. Change, new ventures and ideas, the intellect, the mind, reasoning, analysis, planning, communication, logic, thought processes, opinions, judgments, and the conscious. Swords' colors are those of air, clouds, smoke, and the sky. The air and the sky are both pale blue. The physicist K. C. Cole says: "Air is blue for the same reason that the sky (which is made of air) is blue—namely that clusters of air molecules scatter blue light more than all the other colors in sunlight . . . (You might say that air is very, very, very, very light blue)."[1]

Air, clouds, and the sky may not at first seem very colorful to us, but perhaps there is nothing more beautiful—or colorful—in their own ways than the sky, clouds, and air during a violent thunderstorm; the wavering, silently massive flush of the atmosphere over desert; or the breathtaking intensity of the painted sky during sunrise and sunset.

DISCS

The Material World of Visible Physical Objects. The time of Winter and the space of North. The material, objects, matter, structure, form, money, finances, earthly rewards for effort, business, work, material success, possessions, and all physical bodies. Discs' colors are those both of the Earthbody herself, and those of her physical children—creatures, people, trees, plants, and all vegetation.

[1]K.C. Cole, *Sympathetic Vibrations: Reflections on Physics as a Way of Life* (New York: William Morrow, 1985), p. 24.

NUMBERS AND SUITS

Preceding the interpretation of the Minor Arcana in this chapter is a chart of each taroist's suggestion on the numbers of the suits (see pages 87–89). It may be kept in mind that these are greatly abbreviated, thus do not fully explain the entire nature of the number. For example, an Ace is often called a "beginning," but the word "beginning" does not explain that an Ace is often unseen, invisible in the physical world, because of the fact that it *is* a beginning. Like an embryo still in the womb, it has been conceived but not yet born. Nor do the words "beginning" or "conception" for an Ace tell us that because the Ace is a beginning that also means it is a completion, because there can never be a beginning of anything without the ending of whatever it was that caused its birth to begin with. Thus it sometimes appears key words differ, when in reality they don't.

Each number applies only to its own suit. Using the 9 as an example, if the card is the 9 of Cups, it means the completion of something emotional, whereas if it is the 9 of Discs, it is the completion of something physical.

Taroist's Suggestions on the Numbers of the Suit.

Number	Arrien	Cowie	Crowley	Eakins
Ace	Creativity, clarity & communication.	Beginning. Initiation.	The root or seed of the element.	Gate of Potential: Begins to open up.
2	Initiation & intention.	Balance. Choice.	The first manifestation.	Gate of Force: Becomes polarized.
3	Love & healing.	Expression of creation.	Understanding.	Gate of Form: Becomes dimensional.
4	Personal power & leadership.	Experience. Steadfastness.	Solidification. Materialization.	Gate of Will: Becomes stable.
5	Challenge & wisdom.	Scattering of energy.	Motion coming to the aid of matter.	Gate of Severity: Begins to move.
6	Relationship & relating.	Service. Movement.	Harmony & balance in form.	Gate of Truth: Restabilizes.
7	Movement & change.	Stationary. Reconciliation.	Degeneration & weakness.	Gate of Vision: Becomes highly complex.
8	Alignment & balance.	Power. Achievement.	Alleviation.	Gate of the Lightening Path: Grows.
9	Introspection & completion.	Completion. Togetherness.	Full impact of the elemental force.	Gate of the Portal: Comes into highest point.
10	Abundance, prosperity & expansion.	Ending, with new beginning.	The end or total of the element.	Gate of Communion: Fulfills itself.

Taroist's Suggestions on the Numbers of the Suit.

Number	Fairfield	Greer	Noble	Pollack
Ace	A point. Beginning.	Types of consciousness.	Gifts.	Gifts & essence of suit.
2	A line. Affirming.	Gifts & tests of judgment. Choice.	Balance.	Union. Balance.
3	A plane. Planning.	Gifts & tests of creative imagination and love.	Synthesis.	Understanding. Development.
4	A solid. Manifesting.	Gifts & tests of personal power. Stabilization.	Stability.	Statis. Solidity.
5	Time. Adjusting.	Gifts & tests of fears. Struggle.	Struggle.	Loss. Conflict.
6	Cycle. Cycling.	Gifts & tests of relatedness (or reciprocity).	Exuberance.	Sharing. Giving & receiving.
7	Imagination. Imagining.	Gifts & tests of proving yourself. Challenges.	Inner work.	Struggle. Problems.
8	Order. Organizing.	Gifts & tests of transforming hope into reality. Re-evaluation.	Change.	Movement.
9	Integration. Integrating.	Gifts & tests of completion. Solitude.	Completion.	Compromise.
10	Transition. Hesitating.	Results & rewards of completion.	Transformation.	Being filled with the suit's quality.

Taroist's Suggestions on the Numbers of the Suit.

Number	Sharman-Burke	Stewart	Wanless	Wirth	Riley
Ace	Beginning.	First movement or seed emerging.	Success.	Crown.	Conceiving.
2	Opposites in conflict or balance.	Wisdom & definition.	Reflection.	Wisdom.	Unfolding.
3	Growth & expansion.	Understanding & depth.	Nurturing.	Intelligence.	Developing.
4	Reality, logic & reason.	Mercy & giving.	Commencement.	Kindness.	Manifesting.
5	Uncertainty.	Taking & severity.	Setback.	Fear.	Moving.
6	Equilibrium, harmony & balance.	Harmony & beauty.	Synergy.	Beauty.	Flowing.
7	Wisdom. Completion of a cycle.	Victory & triumph.	Breakthrough.	Steadfastness.	Resting.
8	Regeneration & balance.	Communication & honor.	Change.	Splendour.	Resolving.
9	Summation & foundation.	Foundation.	Harvest.	Basis.	Completing.
10	Perfection through completion.	Manifestation.	Reward.	Kingdom.	Fulfilling.

ACE OF WANDS

Arrien—*The Torch of Fire.* A deep spiritual desire and opportunity for self-discovery and self-realization that the individual has to draw upon for a year's time.

Cowie—*New Idea.* Having a new thought.

Crowley—*The Root of the Powers of Fire.* The essence of the element of Fire in its inception. The primordial Energy of the Divine manifesting in Matter at so early a stage that it is not yet definitely formulated as Will.

Eakins—*Force.* Transformative high energy. Great energy of new beginnings. A newly discovered source of power. Excitement. Exhilaration.

Fairfield—*A New Identity.* Planting the seeds for a new, public identity. Beginning to create a new name for yourself or taking on a new role in life.

Greer—Inspired Consciousness. Consciousness Raising. Desire for self-growth. New idea. Burst of energy. The first impulse and the passionate will to begin.

Noble—The beginning of fire—spirit, intuition, energy. A rebirth of the spirit. The passions are aroused and creativity is assured. Expansive activity and willpower for whatever your goals dictate.

Pollack—A gift of strength, power, great sexual energy, and of the love of living. Or chaos and things falling apart.

Sharman-Burke—Positive new beginnings and ideas in the element of fire. Creativity, energy, and initiative. Can symbolize a new business venture, a new undertaking, new foundation, and creative power with plenty of potential and ambition to progress and succeed.

Stewart—*Fire/Light.* In one sense the burning flame, while in a higher octave universal light, the energy of being. A balancing, affirmed power, an energy increasing in potency. The god of light in harmony and balance with the dragon power.

Waite—Creation, invention, enterprise, the powers which result in these; principle, beginning, source; birth, family, origin, and in a sense the virility which is behind them. The starting point of enterprises; money, fortune, inheritance.

Walker—*Power.* Power and the masculine element of fire with its connotations of heat, vigor, aspiration, contest, enlightenment, and avidity to consume.

Wanless—*Illumination.* Purity, clarity, and honesty. State of enlightenment. Understanding. Having the courage to change and expand. Knowing what gives you energy and vitality.

Riley—*Evokes the Force.* Unseen self-organizing. The Spirit rising up from within. The dawning of desire, passion, enthusiasm, creativity. Indicates some form of *I desire.*

TWO OF WANDS

Arrien—*Spiritual Sovereignty, Power.* A state of integration and optimum balance. Moving forward in a new direction from a place of full power, dominion, and balance.

Cowie—*Contemplating Ideas.* New ideas which are being contemplated in relation to older, fixed ideas.

Crowley—*The Lord of Dominion.* Mars in Aries. The energy of fire in its best and highest form. Ideal Will independent of any given object. Pure will, unassuaged of purpose, delivered from the lust of result, is in every way perfect.

Eakins—*Convergence.* Unfocused energy becoming clear and polarized. A strong direction. Moving with the burning energy of the male force toward that which is most receptive and tempering, maintaining the internal balance of male and female at all times.

Fairfield—*Claiming and Validating the Self.* Affirming or claiming a new self-concept.

Greer—Personal power through synthesis of abilities. Ability to make choices and stand by them. Control over the situation.

Noble—Harnessing of your personal power—learning how to use the fire that was born in the Ace. The intuition is awakening.

Pollack—A card of accomplishment with a feeling of no real satisfaction. Or surprise, wonder, enchantment, trouble, or fear.

Sharman-Burke—Indicates a well-balanced nature, but the essence of the card remains potential as yet unfulfilled. High ideals and aims, a desire for travel and a new outlook from present environment. A change in the air and a feeling of restlessness. Promises success through strength and vision.

Stewart—*Choice.* Wisdom of Fire: Choose well between right and left. Represents the two pillars of any choice, any balancing or polarizing situation that defines and enables the other.

Waite—On one hand, riches, fortune, magnificence; on the other, physical suffering, disease, chagrin, sadness, mortification. Suggests the malady, the mortification, the sadness of Alexander [the Great] amidst the grandeur of this world's wealth.

Walker—*Alliance.* A partnership of two powers having different individual capacities, each one reflecting the other.

Wanless—*Purity.* Seeing yourself purely or honestly as you truly are as opposed to who you are supposed to be or were taught to be. Honest self-observation and clear awareness of self. Living authentically, uncontaminated by conditioning inappropriate to you.

Riley—*Self-confidence.* Affirming and approving yourself. Feeling good or not feeling good about yourself.

THREE OF WANDS

Arrien—*Spiritual Integrity, Honesty.* The three aspects of self—body, mind, and spirit—conjoined. Looking at your self and external situations from a place of maximum integrity, honesty, and with no compromise from the three aspects of self.

Cowie—*Putting Thoughts into Action.* Your ideas are firm, and you are now ready to put them to the test in life.

Crowley—*The Lord of Virtue.* Sun in Aries. Establishment of the primeval energy of fire. The Will has been transmitted to the Mother, who now conceives, prepares, and gives birth to its manifestation. Comparable to the beginning of Spring, its meaning is harmonious.

Eakins—*Birth of Light.* Staying on the path; keeping on with present activities; everything is coming to fruition. The holy balance of the Three.

Fairfield—*Defining and Clarifying the Identity.* Understanding and seeing yourself more clearly.

Greer—Ability to envision the possibilities, often long before they become actuality. Established strength. Synthesis of your ideas through foresight and planning.

Noble—Communication and the joy of self-expression.

Pollack—Combinations and achievements. A solid basis while continuing to open new areas and interests. Or failure of some exploration, being disturbed by memories.

Sharman-Burke—Making a decision and proceeding further. Efforts are rewarded, and an initial completion of some work or goal is achieved. Satisfaction and challenge at the same time, for although one thing is achieved, there is much more yet to do.

Stewart—*Intention.* Understanding of Fire. Will and increasing energy. Inner Fire and light, the spiritual power inherent within our bodies.

Waite—Established strength, enterprise, effort, trade, commerce, discovery; co-operation in business. Collaboration will favour enterprise. A very good card.

Walker—*Fate.* In conjunction with other cards, implies that it is impossible to change what the other cards indicate.

Wanless—*Compassion.* Acceptance, understanding, and tolerance of others.

Riley—*Expressing Yourself.* Enhanced development of your will, desires, or goals. Fate. One of the most powerful cards in the Minor Arcana in that it represents the Trinity of the Spirit. As with all the threes, it is a timing card and indicates a wand event will occur in three to four months.

FOUR OF WANDS

Arrien—*Spiritual and Holistic Completion.* The ability to look at your self and external situations holistically. Something is being completed, and there is a desire to begin something new.

Cowie—*Ideas Firmly Established.* Ideas have been tested and have flourished. Now it is time to celebrate the reward they have brought.

Crowley—*The Lord of Completion.* Venus in Aries. The Lord of all manifested active Power. The original Will of the Two has been transmitted through the Three and is now built up into a solid system—Order, Law, Government. Completion and limitation of the original work where there is no intention to increase the scope but bears in itself the seeds of disorder.

Eakins—*Flame of Spirit.* A phase of development is complete, solidified, and successful, and a new beginning will soon occur.

Fairfield—*Manifesting a New Identity.* Acting on a sense of direction. Doing something definite and taking action based on who you are.

Greer—Sense of completion that comes when opposing energies harmonize. Celebration and thanksgiving after labor. Arrival. Optimism. Completion of an enterprise. Rites of passage.

Noble—A rite of passage. Joyful celebration.

Pollack—Freedom. Opening up a situation. A domestic environment filled with Fire optimism, eagerness, and celebration. Or a happy environment that is not so obvious.

Sharman-Burke—Celebration and reward after labor, a pause in activities and a tranquil time of rest. There may be holidays due, or a time of relaxation.

Stewart—*Generosity.* Fire of Compassion and Merciful Dragon. A card of giving without cost. The potential of giving that comes from a total selflessness, an established energy attuned to the universal power of Mercy that flows through us and out of us.

Waite—Country life, haven of refuge, a species of domestic harvest-home, repose, concord, harmony, prosperity, peace, and the perfected work of these. Unexpected good fortune.

Walker—*Success.* The reward of effort, the first establishment of a secure position in the world.

Wanless—*Aspiration.* Aspiring to fulfill all the potentials of your being, the heights of personal attainment. Acting with inspired idealism.

Riley—*Inactivity.* Perfected Work. Achievement. Status-quo. Reaching a stage of satisfaction, enjoying it, and feeling good about your situation.

FIVE OF WANDS

Arrien—*Spiritual Frustration, Conflict.* A deep sense of frustration, conflict, and anxiety is being experienced in relation to creative expression, or there is a feeling of being restricted in creative expression by a Leo person.

Cowie—*Confusion of Ideas.* The mind has many ideas running around in it, and they have become confused.

Crowley—*The Lord of Strife.* Saturn in Leo. A purely active force. There is no limit to the scope of this volcanic energy whose authority is derived from the superiors. It is purgation through fire and the resurrection of the energy from its ashes.

Eakins—*The Struggle.* A sense of conflict. A feeling of striving and being immobilized at the same time. Relinquishing that which has grown obsolete.

Fairfield—*Adjusting the Identity.* Being challenged to adapt and change. Perhaps self-doubt.

Greer—Ideas tested through conflict and disagreements. Exchange of ideas. Energetic and competitive games. Parts of self with differing needs and desires.

Noble—Struggle and strife without pain. An agreement that this struggle be fair, resulting in an effort to win.

Pollack—Conflict and competition for the joy of action. Or conflict with a more serious tone.

Sharman-Burke—A struggle in life and love. Petty obstacles and annoyances, short-term difficulties in communication which, once overcome, can change things for the better. In the short run, seems as if nothing works out quite right in work and play.

Stewart—*Retribution.* Purifying Fire and the Flaming Pentagram. Retribution is tribute assigned back or paid back, balancing return for either good or evil. The active power of rebalance.

Waite—Imitation as in a sham fight or mimic warfare, but also the strenuous competition, struggle, and search after riches and fortune. In this sense it connects with the battle of life. Success in financial speculation.

Walker—*Impasse.* Powerlessness. Earlier security collapses into acute insecurity. A time of trial and difficulty which may serve a higher goal not immediately present.

Wanless—*Oppression.* Self-created oppression through one's own ignorance, through lack of self-awareness.

Riley—*Activity.* Being busy. Too much activity or sometimes just the right amount.

SIX OF WANDS

Arrien—*Spiritual Revitalization and Expansion.* An indication that some major breakthrough has happened in relation to creativity, insight, or perception.

Cowie—*Victory is Assured.* The person's ideas will be victorious. Putting ideas into practice.

Crowley—*The Lord of Victory.* Jupiter in Leo. The Energy of fire in completely balanced manifestation. The Five has broken up the closed forces of the Four. and a marriage has taken place between them, resulting in self-supporting stabilization, reception, and reflection.

Eakins—*Glory.* The fruit of the battle. A state of harmony and beauty; experiencing a maturation of understanding. The realization that deep within you there is a harmonious internal flame which cannot be quelled.

Fairfield—*A Predictable Personality.* Being secure with your identity and possessing a sense of purpose or direction.

Greer—The gift of victory that comes from working with others to achieve a goal. Self-confidence in your leadership abilities. Setting a direction.

Noble—A joyful card, expansive and warm, an emblem of personal creative power. Victory, self-confidence, balance, leadership, and glory.

Pollack—Unification with Fire. Optimism producing the very success it desires and expects. The Fire belief in life that wands give to the people around them. Or covering doubts with bluster or illusion, leading to fear and weakness. A self-fulfilling prophecy, either for success or defeat.

Sharman-Burke—Achievement, fulfillment of hopes and wishes, and great satisfaction in career. Acclaim received from others, and due recognition awarded for success. Promotion after good work, or reward for effort expended in a good cause.

Stewart—*Balance.* Illuminating Beauty and Perfected Fire. Energies in a condition of balanced power and poise that are not resting or static, but energizing and active like the sun which emits the positive and negative poles from its still centre.

Waite—The victor triumphing. Great news, such as might be carried in state by the King's courier. Expectation crowned with its own desire, the crown of hope.

Walker—*Glory.* A period of short-lived glory, a sense of victory with all blockages overcome.

Wanless—*Trust.* Confidence and belief in yourself and in the universe. Trusting your own instincts and intuitions.

Riley—*Stability.* Victory. Trusting and flowing with your Higher Self. Depth of prayer or any form of concentration.

SEVEN OF WANDS

Arrien—*Spiritual Courage, Bravery.* A rising of spiritual courage, the willingness to take risks for spiritual growth, the stirring of spiritual energy, all desiring a creative outlet.

Cowie—*Unsure of Ideas.* Needing more confidence in yourself and in your ideas.

Crowley—*The Lord of Valour.* Mars in Leo. A departure from the balance so low that there is a loss of confidence. The initial energy has degenerated, and there is a departure from equilibrium and balance. If victory is to be won, it is by dint of individual valour.

Eakins— *Courage.* Intensifying of conditions. Developing strengths and a sense of self-confidence that will continue to grow if you have the courage of your convictions.

Fairfield—*Experimenting with Different Roles.* Exploring new aspects of yourself.

Greer—The need to test your mettle, to prove yourself against competition. Facing up to a situation and asserting your point. Holding your own in the face of opposition.

Noble—Responsibility. Standing completely on your own and trusting yourself to know how to handle the most difficult of situations.

Pollack—Exhilarating conflict. Or anxiety, indecision, embarrassment.

Sharman-Burke—Deep purpose and valour. A successful change in profession, but strength and determination are necessary to achieve success. A card of knowledge that incorporates skills in teaching, lecturing, or writing.

Stewart—*Ability.* Victorious Fire and Triumph of Illumination. Increasing manipulation or organizing power of will. Fusing of intent and feelings.

Waite—Valour. On the intellectual plane, signifies discussion and wordy strife. In business, negotiations, war of trade, barter, competition. A card of success with the combatant on top where his enemies may be unable to reach him.

Walker—*Challenge.* Holding victory against challenges, a dynamic equilibrium preserved only by constant effort, skill, and courage.

Wanless—*Courage.* The courage to face and study your fears. Wherever there is fear, there is courage. Fear is the ally, the tool to realize your highest destiny through encouraging yourself, being a warrior, and trusting.

Riley—*Slowdown.* Outer inaction while essential inner action is taking place. Results are not yet seen from the efforts you have expended.

EIGHT OF WANDS

Arrien—*Spiritual Velocity, Haste, Acceleration.* A spiritual bridge to wholeness using intuition and spiritual vision. Processing a high intensity of spiritual energy very rapidly.

Cowie—*Ideas Will Very Soon be in Physical Existence.* The ideas in your mind are soon going to become reality.

Crowley—*The Lord of Swiftness.* Mercury in Sagittarius. The subtilizing of the fire Energy bringing down from Chokmah the message of the original Will. Light has been turned into electrical rays, sustaining, or even constituting Matter by their vibrating energy. Interplay, correlation, the card of the energy of high velocity.

Eakins—*The Lightning Path.* A high energy period for initiating change. A sense of fast movement and rapid growth. The card of transmuting spirit, energy flowing from the primal universal force, sometimes called "the descent of power."

Fairfield—*Re-examining the Identity.* Figuring out what you like and don't like about yourself.

Greer—Moving to express energies creatively. Activities and energy speeding up. Rapid growth and development. Fast thinking and communication. Being swept off your feet. Falling in love.

Noble—Energy. Taking a risk, trying something new, letting passions fly. A phone call, visitors, or any expression of life force and high energy.

Pollack—Swiftness and movement. Action taken in a love affair, seduction, proposals made and accepted. Or continuance with no conclusion in sight. Jealousy.

Sharman-Burke—The need to be "up and doing" activities and new beginnings. Marks the end of a period of delay or stagnation, and a time for initiative and action to begin. A busy exciting time ahead, suggesting travel and moves.

Stewart—*Expediency.* Creating Possibilities, Glory of Wands, Wisdom of Serpents. Constant interchange of energies moving with great rapidity that takes whatever action is necessary to rebalance and enable the intent of the mind.

Waite—Activity in undertakings, the path of such activity—swiftness—as that of an express messenger. Great haste and great hope; speed towards an end which promises assured felicity; generally that which is on the move; also the arrows of love.

Walker—*Fall.* An important journey, motion, and progress which could all be ruined by overeagerness, overconfidence, or excessive activity. Pride that goeth before a fall.

Wanless—*Harmony.* The perfection and order in life. The unifying spirit which sees how everything fits together, blending all seeming opposites into a harmonious whole.

Riley—*Swiftness.* Going forward. The end of delay and being almost there. A time when activities and energy are being released and you're expanding your horizons.

NINE OF WANDS

Arrien—*Spiritual Power, Potency, Force.* Internal strength; strength in communications, insight, intuition, and vision. There is conscious awareness and trust of your own inner and outer strengths.

Cowie—*Defending Ideas.* Believing in your ideas and having the strength of your convictions but sometimes having to defend them.

Crowley—*The Lord of Strength.* Moon in Sagittarius. Energy brought back into balance. This is the fullest development of the Force in its relation with the Forces above it. The Nine may be considered as the best that can be obtained from the type involved, regarded from a practical and material standpoint. It is a double influence, hence the aphorism, "Change is stability."

Eakins—*Eye of Fire.* Arriving at a peak experience. Reaching the right wavelength, the right current, attuning to the right frequency. Seeing things clearly and accurately which leads to solid creations which will endure over time.

Fairfield—*The Integrated Self.* Acting naturally and in accordance with your true being.

Greer—The opportunity to face your greatest fears with the gift of strength of purpose. Wisdom and discipline from experience. Independence. Dedication.

Noble—An accumulation of energy—knowledge of energy retention which leads to its wise storage and competent use.

Pollack—Strength, physical power, and mental alertness dealing with problems. Or defense and tenseness.

Sharman-Burke—Strength and determination. Even when you feel as though you have come to the end of your fighting powers, there is strength in reserve. Being in a very strong position that suggests victory through courage and endurance.

Stewart—*Endurance.* Enduring Fire or Immutable Foundation. The endurance of will in which we hold ourselves together through all misfortunes. The will creating images in the inner light, the imaginative pool out of which dreams are made substantial and expressed as outer patterns. Fusion of will and imagination.

Waite—Strength in opposition. If attacked, the person will meet an onslaught boldly, and his build shews that he may prove a formidable antagonist. With this main significance, there are all its possible adjuncts—delay, suspension, adjournment. Generally speaking, a bad card.

Walker—*Defense.* A barrier that either keeps things in or keeps things out, depending on any given situation.

Wanless—*Integrity.* Unbending self-determination. The vision, aspiration, and strength of character to express the truth.

Riley—*Great Strength.* Persistence. Obtaining trust and know-how in your own perceptions and being comfortable with them. Good health. Expectation of change.

TEN OF WANDS

Arrien—*Spiritual Restraint, Repression*—Self-oppression, or withholding communications for fear of how they will be received.

Cowie—*Too Many Ideas.* The mind is so busy thinking about many things it has become its own worst enemy. It cannot see the forest for the trees.

Crowley—*The Lord of Oppression.* Saturn in Sagittarius. The Force detached from its spiritual sources. Fire in its most destructive aspect; a blind force which suggests oppression and repression. It is what happens when one uses force, force, and nothing else but force all the time.

Eakins—*The Cage.* Feeling trapped or oppressed. Or a tremendous opportunity to become a co-creator with the primal force on the physical plane. Applying the peak experience of the 9 of fire to daily life.

Fairfield—*An Identity Question.* Feeling comfortable with yourself but aware that this is a choice point. For now, sitting on the fence.

Greer—Creativity blocked by too many responsibilities, or the importance of developing a sense of responsibility. Perseverance in meeting a goal. Burdens.

Noble—A release of all energies that have built up over time that now and then overwhelm the personality.

Pollack—Burden and oppression by life, especially by responsibility. Too many burdens or throwing off the burdens.

Sharman-Burke—A burden is soon to be lifted or a problem solved. The burden can be physical, mental, or emotional, and is often self-imposed, but something can be done to lighten the weight now.

Stewart—*Responsibility.* Express Intent, Manifest Power, Action and Reaction. The bundle of a manifest will. If intent is aligned with the will of Light, a potent force of balance and control. If separated from the Light within, a burden or the seeming effect of energies and forces upon us rather than through us.

Waite—The chief meaning is oppression simply, but it is also fortune, gain, any kind of success, and then the oppression of these things. A card of false-seeming, disguise, and perfidy.

Walker—*Oppression.* Triumph of tyranny, misuse of power, selfish authority, excessive pressure, punishment of ambition.

Wanless—*Growth.* Accelerated growth through conscious effort. Aspiring higher, stretching to limits, and extending yourself. Reaching higher consciousness through manifesting your dreams and passions.

Riley—*Energy in Extreme.* Reaching the full glory of fire—passion, intuition, spirit, and *joie de vivre*; or reaching the opposite extreme of fire—burnout.

ACE OF CUPS

Arrien—*Emotional Balance.* Not over-extending or under-extending the emotions; reflecting and expressing accurately what is going on within your nature. The gift of emotional balance is available to be used and drawn upon for the next year's time.

Cowie—*New Attitude Brings Rewards.* Applying a new attitude to life which brings rewards when in tune with the laws of the universe.

Crowley—*The Root of the Powers of Water.* The element of Water in its most secret and original form. The feminine complement of the Ace of Wands, derived from the Yoni and the Moon exactly as the Ace of Wands is from the Lingam and the Sun. As it is the virtue of this card to conceive and to produce the second form of its Nature, the liquid is shown as water, transforming either into Wine or Blood as may be required.

Eakins—*The Open Channel.* Experiencing a burst of feeling, sentiment, empathy, sympathy, or enthusiasm. A time for connecting, staying open, and becoming vulnerable in order to receive.

Fairfield—*A New Emotion or Insight.* Feeling something new, maybe something not felt before, such as a new emotion, a new relationship, or a new awareness about an existing relationship.

Greer—Love Consciousness. Heart Opening. The beginning of love, pleasure. The opening of psychic, spiritual, or unconscious channels. Receptivity.

Noble—The gift of love—a dive into your deepest feelings. A surrender to emotions and beauty, an influx of pleasure, inspiration, imagination.

Pollack—Love underpinning life. A time of happiness, a gift of joy. Or disruption. Not recognizing what life offers us. Love, and ultimately life, cannot be seized but only accepted.

Sharman-Burke—The purest aspect of emotional energy. The beginning of a new relationship, the renewal of strong emotions, love, marriage, motherhood, and great joy or reward gained from a loving union.

Stewart—*Water/Love.* Reveals Love, either in a personal context or in a deeper spiritual sense, depending upon other cards present. Associated with perfection and ideal spiritual vision, the Blessed Realm, physical birth and death, and the vessel or gate between worlds. The Mystery of spiritual redemption and regeneration. Human fertility and situations involving fruitful interaction.

Waite—House of the true heart, joy, content, abode, nourishment, abundance, fertility; Holy Table, felicity hereof.

Walker—*Love.* Birth, beginning, fruitfulness, pleasure, happiness, home, nourishment, satisfaction, and caring. An enhancement of other good influences, or a mitigating power over bad ones.

Wanless—*Ecstasy.* An intensity of feeling that comes with a love for life in its entirety, accepting and revering all. The courage to completely live out the full range of your emotions, feeling everything, expressing all feelings.

Riley—*Channels the Force.* Absorption and assimilation. Emotions or love rising up from within. The beginning of new emotions or feelings. Indicates some mode of *I feel.*

TWO OF CUPS

Arrien—*Deep Love Relationship*—A deep, very significant love in a person's life, either a relationship with another or toward some form of creativity. There is a desire to fully experience and to be open to this love at this point in time.

Cowie—*Communication.* Opening up to listen and respond to others.

Crowley—*The Lord of Love.* Venus in Cancer. The Two always represents the Word and the Will. It is the first manifestation. As such, this card refers to Love which recovers unity from dividuality by mutual annihilation. It is Love under Will, the harmony of the male and the female interpreted in the largest sense; perfect and placid harmony, radiating an intensity of joy and ecstasy.

Eakins—*Sacred Cord.* The joyful merger of opposites. A great sense of connection and bliss. Receiving just as you have been received.

Fairfield—*Validating a Feeling.* Choosing a feeling or relationship, or validating a psychic or intuitive experience.

Greer—Compassionate and caring response. A loving and healing union of opposites. The conscious and unconscious working together so that seeming oppositions are reconciled.

Noble—The pull of the attraction force on the unconscious level of the emotions. Union resulting from the merging of unconscious desires with conscious love of the heart.

Pollack—The pledging of friendship, the beginning of a love affair. The linking of action and spirit. Or the breakdown of a love affair or friendship, a split between action and emotion.

Sharman-Burke—The beginning of a romance or well-balanced friendship. Ideas generated between two partners with harmony and co-operation. An engagement, or commitment to romance or friendship. Reconciliation of opposites or the resolution of quarrels and disputes.

Stewart—*Freedom.* The Wisdom of Love. An easeful threshold. A sense of release, of freedom. Love frees the soul toward its spiritual origins.

Waite—Love, passion, friendship, affinity, union, concord, sympathy, the inter-relation of the sexes, and—as a suggestion apart from all offices of divination—that desire which is not in Nature, but by which Nature is sanctified. Favorable in things of pleasure and business, as well as love; also wealth and honour.

Walker—*Romance.* Trust, sympathy, consummation of desires, vows, promises, engagements, marriage, and intimate friendship. All permutations of active partnership.

Wanless—*Equilibrium.* Emotional stability and self-sufficiency. The even flow of emotional vitality.

Riley—*Love.* Inner peace. Being wounded by the knowledge of your own love. Healing union of opposites, the merging of lover and beloved.

THREE OF CUPS

Arrien—*Emotional Abundance.* An outpouring of love and positive feeling toward three very significant people in your life and your desire to communicate this to them.

Cowie—*Happiness.* A happy and full life.

Crowley—*The Lord of Abundance.* Mercury in Cancer. Here is the fulfillment of the Will of Love in abounding joy. The idea of love has come to fruition. This card requires great subtlety of interpretation, and the lesson seems to be that the good things of life, although enjoyed, should be distrusted.

Eakins—*Stream of Love.* A sublime state of harmonious pleasure; a grace period. A sense of wondrous creation and feeling very loved by all that is.

Fairfield—*Emotional or Intuitive Clarification.* Becoming clearer about what your feelings and intuition are saying.

Greer—The gifts of friendship and hospitality. Support and enjoyment of others. Celebration and joy. Shared ideals.

Noble—An expression of happiness and joyful time shared. Sharing pleasure together, having fun with others. Letting the spirit come through your feelings and emotions.

Pollack—Joy, celebration, and sharing the wonder of life. A sharing of experience. Or a loss of some happiness, perhaps excess in physical enjoyment and the pleasures of the senses.

Sharman-Burke—A celebration or joyful occasion. A marriage or birth, emotional growth, and a feeling of happiness and achievement. Can also indicate the conclusion of a happy matter or a healing of wounds. As with all the threes, there is a sense that it's important to enjoy the moment of rejoicing for there is still hard work ahead.

Stewart—*Affection.* Understanding of Water. The steady and constant timeless affection that is more powerful than personal emotion or romantic love that seeks gratification. That deep affection which is an unconditional state of love.

Waite—The conclusion of any matter in plenty, perfection and merriment. Happy issue, victory, fulfillment, solace, healing.

Walker—*Grace.* The classic image of the three female Graces dancing together. The epitome of all forms of love, based on mother-love, the root of them all, exemplified by the Goddess. Kindly gracious fate as gifts of bestowed love.

Wanless—*Love.* Receiving and giving love. Following the heart. The life essence that holds all things together and moves everything forward. Reverences for all that lives, unconditionally.

Riley—*Experiencing Feelings.* The Dance of Love. Augmentation of your emotions, feelings, needs, or of a relationship. Sometimes called *Grace* and *Love* because it can be a temporary state of *being,* rather than feeling. In timing, indicates something of an emotional nature will occur within the week.

FOUR OF CUPS

Arrien—*Emotional Luxury*—The capacity for being able to make people feel emotionally secure, happy, satisfied, and comfortable. A time when things are working, running smoothly, and you consciously know why you are feeling good.

Cowie—*Being More Aware of What is Occurring.* Viewing your life and feeling you have everything that you need. Not open to other suggestions.

Crowley—*The Lord of Luxury.* Moon in Cancer. The energy, although ordered, balanced, and stabilized, has lost the original purity of the conception. Implies a certain weakness, an abandonment to desire. Because it is not quite strong enough to control itself properly, the solidification of the four is a little unstable.

Eakins—*The Flood.* Outgrowing a period of contentment. Things that were once good now seem stale, and things have grown old. The edge of a completion, and a new vision of love beginning to formulate.

Fairfield—*Acting on What You Feel.* Acting on your psychic, intuitional, or emotional perceptions.

Greer—Both gift and challenge of a fallow period. The ability to let things take their course, trusting the cycle of change. Or lethargy, boredom, apathy, and discontent. Awaiting inspiration.

Noble—A time for getting clear, refining things down to simple truth. Feelings are hurt. Things don't feel quite right. A time of uncertainty.

Pollack—Apathy resulting from a dull, unstimulating environment. Opportunities overlooked. Nothing worth getting up for, worth doing. Or enthusiasm and the seizing of opportunities.

Sharman-Burke—"Divine discontent." Caught between the worlds of thought and action. Discontentment in which the emotions are turned inward.

Stewart— *Promise.* Promise of Mercy or Creative Compassion. Healing, empathy, transpersonal love, forgiveness and taking away, washing, or dissolution of soul-burdens. Promise of expansion, material increase, and procreation.

The flow of sexual energies in humans in which personal focus is washed away and compassionate powers are established beyond our usual experience of such energies.

Waite—Discontent with one's environment. Weariness, disgust, aversion, imaginary vexations. Also blended pleasure.

Walker—*Decline.* Stage in any relationship known as the end of the honeymoon with hints of new insights to come.

Wanless—*Anger.* Frustration from fear, insecurity, or not reaching goals. Using anger to breakout and get going.

Riley—*Contentment.* Comfort, enjoyment, and ease.

FIVE OF CUPS[2]

Arrien—*Emotional Disappointment.* An indication that there is some disappointment either currently being experienced or that has been experienced in the past that still has a charge and is being felt deeply.

Cowie—*Crying Over Past Events.* Grieving over what has been lost.

[2]If given the opportunity, which they are not given here, these taroists would point out that every card is experienced according to the perception, or consciousness, of the individual involved. No card is good or bad—people create their own reality. The 5 of Cups is held as the number of change, motion, and movement from the placid 4, and thus it is often experienced as disruption. John Anthony West points out in his book, *Serpent in the Sky,* that in Pythagorean numerology the number 5 also means *love* because it is the union of the masculine 3 and the feminine 2. Thus it is also creativity, the number of magic, humanity, and the possibility of wholeness.

Crowley—*The Lord of Disappointment.* Mars in Scorpio. The idea of disturbance, when least expected, in a time of ease. Frustration of the anticipated pleasure. Whereas Fire delights in superabundant energy, the water of Pleasure is naturally placid, so any disturbance of ease can only be regarded as misfortune.

Eakins—*Spilling.* A feeling that relationships are transient, impermanent, and painful. Relying too much on others for love. Discovering your own source of internal love.

Fairfield—*Emotional or Intuitive Adjustments.* Feelings in flux. Emotional or intuitive uncertainty, or adaptation.

Greer—Being shaken from complacency. Loss and disappointment. Progress hindered. Loss of harmony but love is still there. Learning from mistakes and experience. Sometimes grieving.

Noble—Disappointment in love, being on the verge of despair.

Pollack—Sorrow but also acceptance. Regret, loss, and separation. Or, beginning a process of recovery.

Sharman-Burke—Possible regret over past actions. A situation where something is lost but something remains, and there are new alternatives to be explored within the loss.

Stewart—*Sorrow.* Flowing Away or Ebb-Tide. Longing, sorrow, and that mysterious grief for our lost paradise or primal world. May represent personal sorrow in a direct situation, but more frequently defines the deep sorrow of the soul.

Waite—A card of loss, but something remains over. Inheritance, patrimony, transmission, but not corresponding to expectations.

Walker—*Regret.* A sense of turning away from old ties and looking forward to new interests, needs, and meanings. Something comes to an end with a sense of regret but there exists the possibility of new interests.

Wanless—*Disappointment.* Sadness as a result of emotional attachment to an expectation that is unfulfilled. Or setting goals but living 'in the moment' without attachment to the outcome, so as not to be disappointed.

Riley—*Emotional Activity.* Emotions in motion.

SIX OF CUPS

Arrien—*Emotional Pleasure.* The experiencing of receiving pleasure and the giving of pleasure to others. Your emotional nature is being renewed and regenerated, and you are going through a healing process, which is giving way to a feeling of enjoyment.

Cowie—*Happy Memories of the Past.* Reliving happy memories.

Crowley—*The Lord of Pleasure.* Sun in Scorpio. One of the best cards in the pack, it is well-being, harmony of natural forces without effort or strain, ease, satisfaction. Foreign to the idea of the card is the gratification of natural or artificial desires, for it is pleasure understood in its highest sense.

Eakins—*Faith.* A surrender to faith. Innocence and taking great pleasure in your childlike qualities. Experiencing the world as if seeing it for the first time. Being taken care of in all ways.

Fairfield—*A Regular Emotional Cycle.* A level of understanding in feelings, relationships, or psychic processes that is reliable or predictable.

Greer—The exchange of love and pleasure that two people can bring to each other. Memory or renewal of something from the past. Gifts. Friendship. Ecstasy. Being overwhelmed.

Noble—An orgasmic rush of feelings, a wave of ecstasy. Even if your feelings are sad, the active expression of them provides a release that feels good.

Pollack—Sweet memories. Giving and receiving. Sometimes, over-idealizing the past. Or a move toward the future rather than the past.

Sharman-Burke—You may be reconsidering something with roots in the past. Past efforts which may bring present or future rewards. Can bring a meeting with an old friend, acquaintance, or lover, or mean that you are living too much in the past or are being too nostalgic.

Stewart—*Joy.* Singing Harmony and Sea of Beauty. Flowing, giving, receiving. A selfless joy often found as the ecstasy of spiritual enlightenment. The joy of union that comes with sexual and mystical ecstasy. The joy of creation, of souls mingling.

Waite—Pleasant memories. Looking back on the past and memories—on childhood. Happiness and enjoyment coming from the past, from things that have vanished. Or new relations, new knowledge, new environment.

Walker—*Childhood.* A psychic return to early experiences of love and faded memories of the deep past.

Wanless—*Sorrow.* Emotional state of expressing sadness or grief. Release.

Riley—*Harmony.* Sense of well-being. Pleasure, peace. Subtlety of feelings and understanding of surrounding conditions that come from the natural flow of psychic energy.

SEVEN OF CUPS

Arrien—*Emotional Over-extension*—Experiencing depression and attempting to ease the pain by overindulgence through habits or patterns which deplete the energies.

Cowie—*Imagination at Work.* The imagination running away with itself. The need to become more realistic and accept life as it is.

Crowley—*The Lord of Debauch.* Venus in Scorpio. The invariable weakness arising from lack of balance and loss of direct touch with Kether, the Highest. The sinking into the mire of false pleasure, it represents almost the "evil and averse" image of the Six.

Eakins—*Insight.* Filling the empty space of the soul and moving into deeper spiritual realms. The pursuit of love, the longing for reconciliation with the One and for movement back to wholeness again.

Fairfield—*Emotional Variety and Exploration.* Experiencing variety and activity in emotions, relationships, dreams, or psychic work.

Greer—The ability to conjure up visions, fantasies, and dreams. Experiencing an altered state of consciousness. Test of appropriate choice. Not knowing what to do.

Noble—Spaciness, imagination, and dreaminess, watery visions, fantasy. Difficulty in deciding among an abundance of choices.

Pollack—Dreams, visions, emotions, or imagination that do not connect to anything in real life. Or a determination to make something from dreams.

Sharman-Burke—A choice has to be made, and much care and consideration need to be devoted to it. A time when the imagination works overtime and choices seem innumerable. Accompanying the confusion over the choice is also an abundance of creative and artistic talent and energy.

Stewart—*Humour.* Star of Laughter or Triumph of Feeling. That sense of humour which is spontaneous and deep, bringing clear laughter, free of personality or pose. Sometimes a sense of self-delusion, but the humourous heart will always clarify delusions so as not to take itself too seriously.

Waite—Fairy favours, images of reflection, sentiment, imagination, things seen in the glass of contemplation; some attainment in these degrees, but nothing permanent or substantial is suggested.

Walker—*Dream.* On one hand true vision, talent, and insight: on the other, fantasy, illusion, and unrealistic attitudes. Interpretation decided by the context.

Wanless—*Fear.* Diving into your fears, or worry and anxiety. Feeling fear and using its energy in order to move through it. Stopping to understand and reflect in order to be prudent and not act impulsively and to go forward with courage.

Riley—*Insight.* Meditation. Or a waiting "to see" that is not wanted now but necessary. Sometimes called "the card of choice" because a choice is being made or will have to be made.

EIGHT OF CUPS

Arrien—*Emotional Stagnation*—Being overly tired, drained, depleted, and exhausted. There is a need for some structure or discipline to set some limits on over-extension.

Cowie—*Leaving What is Known and Going into the Unknown.* Leaving past ways of thinking, values, or residency and going into the unknown.

Crowley—*The Lord of Indolence.* Saturn in Pisces. Time and sorrow have descended upon pleasure, and there is no strength to react against it. The very apex of unpleasantness. Nothing good. The German Measles of Christian Mysticism.

Eakins—*Still Waters.* A state of withdrawal which is necessary and good at this time in order to become clear. Charging your self and renewing resources within a space of protection.

Fairfield—*Evaluating Feelings.* Reflecting on relationships and what is liked and not liked about them.

Greer—The ability to go deep within to regenerate energies. Withdrawal of activities into self. Retreat or time out. Energy drain. Self-pity. Sense of aimlessness.

Noble—An unconscious kind of change taking place—one happening on the very deep feeling level.

Pollack—Leaving a stable situation. Time to move on. Or a refusal to leave some situation even though you know you have taken all you can from it. Or, the importance of staying in a situation.

Sharman-Burke—The end of something and the beginning of something new. Leaving the past behind and abandoning a situation through disappointment or disillusionment. The seeker has no choice but to abandon it in search of what is right.

Stewart—*Excitement.* Forming Glory, Cascade of Energy, The Swimming Shoal. The power of fluid motion. The infinite flow of potentials. Reproduction, artistic creation, the excitement of forming a work. Cooperation of many potentials flowing together.

Waite—Usually shews the decline of a matter, or that a matter which has been thought to be important is really of slight consequence—either for good or evil.

Walker—*Loss.* Unavoidable regret at leaving something valuable during a passage into a new phase of life.

Wanless—*Stagnation.* Emotional state when things have reached a point of stasis or stillness. Rest and regeneration.

Riley—*Emotional Progression.* Leaving behind the known for the unknown and progressing to feelings which are new, different, and somehow changed.

NINE OF CUPS

Arrien—*Emotional Fulfillment and Happiness.* A time of emotional expansion evolving from a feeling of fulfillment and completion. An ability to go into emotional depths to integrate and balance feelings.

Cowie—*Contentment and Satisfaction.* A fully happy life that should continue.

Crowley—*The Lord of Happiness.* Jupiter in Pisces. The restoration of stability that was lost in the Eight. The culmination and perfection of the original force; a benediction; water in its most complete, most beneficent, and highest material manifestation. Happiness, complete satiety, but as with the Nine of Wands, there is nothing permanent in this; there is no rest from the Universe. "Change guarantees stability. Stability guarantees change."

Eakins—*Rainbow Mirror.* A strong sense of internal integrity and inner security. Enjoying self-esteem and inner joy. Acceptance of self that brings a new sense of wisdom and harmony.

Fairfield—*Flowing Feelings.* Experiencing a flow of emotions with purpose and direction. Perhaps flashes of intuition and inspiration.

Greer—The opportunity to create your own reality with the gift of creative imagination. Visualizing. Satisfaction. Wishes fulfilled. Sensual pleasures. Self-indulgence.

Noble—Physical and mental enjoyment and well-being. A visionary card. A card of optimism and trust in the future, a time of wishing for what you want and trusting to receive it.

Pollack—Avoiding worry and problems by concentrating on ordinary pleasures. Physical contentment and a simple good time. Or victory and liberation by clinging to "truth, loyalty, liberty."

Sharman-Burke—The "wish" card signifying the fulfillment of a desire of paramount importance. Emotional stability as well as physical and material happiness. Sensual pleasure is also satisfied.

Stewart—*Fulfillment.* Fountain of Full Moon, The Giving Mother, Waters of Life and Love. A card of great blessing. The fusion of will and imagination becoming fluid and flowing out into expression; thus, it is the realization, or making real in manifest terms, of that which has been imagined. Fecundity, production, reproduction.

Waite—Concord, contentment, physical *bien-être;* also victory, success, advantage. Satisfaction for the Querent or person being read for.

Walker—*Happiness.* Amalgamating sexuality and sensuality with kindness, goodwill, contentment, fruitfulness, physical health, and emotional stability.

Wanless—*Fulfillment.* State of emotional satisfaction upon the completion of a task. Pleasure from doing your purpose.

Riley—*Happiness.* Doing what you love. Flowing feelings. The card of wishes fulfilled.

TEN OF CUPS

Arrien—*Emotional Contentment.* A great deal of emotional passion and vitality being experienced internally and radiating out to others. Feeling peaceful and content.

Cowie—*Happiness and Contentment for Everyone.* Receiving rewards, and happy because of it. Accomplishing goals by your own endeavors and by the energy of the universe.

Crowley—*The Lord of Satiety.* Mars in Pisces. The work proper to water is complete, and disturbance is due. A conflicting element due to the gross, violent, and disruptive force of Mars in peaceful and spiritualized Pisces. The pursuit of pleasure has been crowned with perfect success, and having got everything one wanted, it is constantly discovered one did not want it after all.

Eakins—*Fountain of Love.* When motivated by love, the unfolding of highest wisdom. Feeling showered by a fountain of love; a time of rarefied and spiritual joy, exquisite beauty, and deep sharing.

Fairfield—*An Emotional or Intuitive Crossroads.* Experiencing an emotion, relationship, or psychic work that is stable and satisfying with awareness that it will soon be time to move on.

Greer—The gift of bringing light and good cheer to others. Being "at home" with yourself and others. Wholeness and completion. Affirming joy in your life. Unrealistic dreams. The family.

Noble—Communication with Source. Gratitude, contentment, and happiness.

Pollack—Domestic happiness. Any situation that brings a surge of joy. Recognition of valuable qualities in a situation. Or some emotional situation has gone wrong. Not recognizing the happiness life offers.

Sharman-Burke—The ultimate of what the Cups can bring in the way of love and happiness. A happy family life, inspired from above, with lasting contentment. A lot of love is available both to give and to receive.

Stewart—*Friendship.* Great Sharing, Collective Creation, Children of Earth. A power of collective Love. The inherently friendly nature of humanity's collective existence, sharing, interacting, creating, and living together. Caring and respect for the Earth and all living creatures on it.

Waite—Contentment, repose of the entire heart; the perfection of that state; also perfection of human love and friendship.

Walker—*Salvation.* Attainment of any long-sought goal as well as salvation through love.

Wanless—*Passion.* Fortune is where your passion is. Listening to your passions, following the beat of your heart, abandoning reservations, and doing it! Living fully, richly, and courageously by following your desires and dreams.

Riley—*Being Full of Emotion.* Feeling grateful. Reaching the peak of your emotions, whether for happy or sad. If emotions were stars, you'd be the Milky Way right now.

ACE OF SWORDS

Arrien—*Mental Clarity, Inventiveness, and Originality.* The gifts of inspired intellect, decisiveness, and mental clarity are available to be utilized and manifested for the next 12 months.

Cowie—*Problems being Overcome.* A problem that can be risen above and brought to a resolution.

Crowley—*The Root of the Powers of Air.* The primordial Energy of Air which has no self-generated impulse of its own. It is the Wind "which bloweth whithersoever it listeth," but once set in motion by its Father of Fire and Mother of Water, its power is manifestly terrific. All-embracing, all-wandering, all-penetrating, all-consuming.

Eakins—*Dawn.* The beginning of the intellectual process. An important new idea is taking hold in the mind. Paying attention to new thought. Clear, original, creative thinking.

Fairfield—*A New Idea.* The potential for a brand new lifestyle direction, schedule, or routine. Recognizing that you could begin to communicate in a different way.

Greer—Reasoning (focused) Consciousness. Mind Expanding. Analysis of what needs to be done. Acting with logic and discrimination.

Noble—Force, particularly on the mental plane. The gift of intellect. A choice is made to do something specific.

Pollack—Intellect, truth, emotional force in extreme form. Or illusion, confused ideas and feelings, overpowering emotions.

Sharman-Burke—Strength in adversity. Often indicates that out of evil something good will come. A situation that looks bleak can surprisingly turn out to be extremely promising. A sense of inevitable change, "the old order changeth." A card of great power, force, and strength.

Stewart—*Air/Life.* Powerful and disturbing new openings, beginnings, changes. Can bring benefit or difficulty, life or death, depending upon other cards present in a pattern. A card of great but unrealized potential, of originative energy.

Waite—Triumph, the excessive degree in everything, conquest, triumph of force. A card of great force, in love as well as in hatred. Great prosperity or great misery.

Walker—*Doom.* The card of Morgan the Fate, Fata Morgana, who carried dead heroes to her Fortunate Isles. Finality, tragedy, and ultimate fate, but also at times a release, freedom from restraint, a new lightness, or a kind of salvation.

Wanless— (Crystals) *Brilliance.* The quality of insight. Seeing and understanding insightfully with a driving curiosity. Concentration, organization, and imagination which brings the ability to be creative.

Riley—*Changes the Force.* Expansion and celebration. Change rising up from within. The beginning of an idea or information. Indicates some form of *I think.*

TWO OF SWORDS

Arrien—*Peace of Mind.* Two issues, situations, choices, or relationships have been integrated at a subconscious level, and the mind is now at peace. You will soon experience outward signs and evidence of this mental integration.

Cowie—*Not Accepting Realities.* Not accepting what is in front of you. The need to be more tolerant towards other's ideas and suggestions and to not embrace your own so strongly.

Crowley—*The Lord of Peace.* Moon in Libra. As with all the Twos, this card manifests the very best idea possible to the suit. But Swords, governing all intellectual manifestations, are always complicated, disordered, and subject to change as is no other suit. Thus this card is comparative calm abiding above the onslaught of disruption.

Eakins—*The Crossing.* A temporary balance. A sense of release from captivity. Maintaining gentle balance and peace. Using wisdom and understanding to assess the situation.

Fairfield—*Affirming a Philosophy or Lifestyle.* Identifying and affirming a new belief, opinion, lifestyle, schedule, or communication.

Greer—Making peace. Suspending judgment. Blocked emotions. Uncertainty or stalemate. Procrastination. Compromise. Waiting for the tide to turn.

Noble—An attempt to gain mental balance and peace. The mind wants to be still. A respite before change.

Pollack—Handling a problem or situation by not facing it. A precarious balance held by denial of emotions. Or the balance is lost.

Sharman-Burke—Stalemate: balanced forces immobilizing each other. Conflict at an impasse. The person feels by not confronting the issues at hand they might go away. However, with courage, a change can be made, and often good comes out of what appears to be a bad situation.

Stewart—*Doubt.* Wisdom of Air: All life is uncertain; all is relative. The doubt that comes at the very brink of daybreak, at the point of stepping over. A pattern in which the outcome seems impossible to predetermine.

Waite—Conformity and the equipoise which it suggests; courage, friendship, concord in a state of arms.

Walker—*Balance.* A balance of opposing forces leading to a stalemate, a temporary truce in the midst of strife, or a new equilibrium after difficult adjustments.

Wanless—*Equanimity.* A heightened state of balanced awareness. Objectivity and mental stability achieved through dispassionate analysis. A state of detachment and noninvolvement where you can see with nonjudgemental awareness according to the higher laws and values of the universe.

Riley—*Peace.* Acceptance and agreement. The intellect is agreeing with the heart. Your heart and mind are going together.

THREE OF SWORDS

Arrien—*Thoughts of Sorrow.* Patterns or events that have not been released from the past that are currently producing sorrow. Also triangular relationships.

Cowie—*Disappointment and Heartbreak.* Suffering from heartbreak and emotional upset due to disappointments in life.

Crowley—*The Lord of Sorrow.* Saturn in Libra. This is not vulgar sorrow dependent upon any individual disappointment or discontent, but universal sorrow; it is the quality of melancholy. There is an intense lurking passion to create, but its children are monsters. Secrecy and perversion.

Eakins—*Recognition.* Giving up to gain. Surrendering in order to achieve. Feeling frustrated which is a normal part of the creative process. Bouts of anxiety intermingling with bouts of joy.

Fairfield—*Planning a Philosophy or Lifestyle.* Clarifying and articulating your lifestyle, schedule, communications, or beliefs.

Greer—The gift of sorrow. Ability to experience emotions fully so that you don't become blocked. Creative heartbreak. Separation. Jealousy. Feeling hurt.

Noble—The merging of mental energies through struggle. A dance of power in which difficulty precedes harmony.

Pollack—Sorrow, pain, and heartbreak, either with acceptance or non-acceptance.

Sharman-Burke—Stormy weather for the emotions. Maybe quarrels or separations; maybe tears over a faithless lover. A sense of clearing the ground for something new, amid sorrow, for the "darkest hour is before the dawn." Signifies a flash of understanding or insight into a situation as it really is.

Stewart—*Suffering.* The Understanding of Air, the Suffering of the Mother. The inner suffering that leads to understanding, to realization in the sense of "being-made-real."

Waite—Removal, absence, delay, division, rupture, dispersion.

Walker—*Sorrow.* Sorrow for any cause, any disappointment, any reason for self-pity. A sense of isolation and endurance of inner pain.

Wanless—*Creativity.* The creative mind. New ideas and creativity born out of love for what you have to offer to the world.

Riley—*Indecision.* Or further development, advancement, and achievement of an idea, change, or plan. In timing, indicates either a mental decision or mental snafu is already occurring or will occur within the next few hours or days.

FOUR OF SWORDS

Arrien—*Mental Expansion, Resolution.* Mental understanding of an issue, relationship, or of something that has now come to full resolution on all four levels of awareness—the mental, emotional, spiritual, and physical.

Cowie—*The Answer Lies Within.* Problems that should not be ignored. If you will listen to your inner you will know the answer.

Crowley—*The Lord of Truce.* Jupiter in Libra. The idea of authority in the intellectual world, hence the establishment of dogma and law concerning it. It represents a refuge from mental chaos, chosen in an arbitrary manner. It argues for convention, appeasement, and compromise bringing social harmony.

Eakins—*Mastery.* A holding pattern after mastering a difficult task. Enjoying rewards and success from having understood the task. Authority in the intellectual world.

Fairfield—*Acting on What You Think.* Speaking up. Writing. Acting on ideas or manifesting a personal philosophy.

Greer—Stress as a health factor. Need for healing. Illness. A problem or dilemma being worked on in the mind or in dreams. Retreat. Rest and recovery. Taking time out. Need to ask for professional or spiritual advice.

Noble—Creation of a protected mental space. The personality needs time to withdraw, be alone, and think about things in order to heal and renew.

Pollack—Rest, retreat, or withdrawal, either to hide or to heal. Or a return to the world.

Sharman-Burke—A time of rest or retreat after a struggle: a quiet period for thinking things through, a slackening of tension and a relaxation of anxiety. Convalescence or recuperation.

Stewart—*Truce.* Merciful Air and Spirit of Compassion. A giving-pause during which the turbulent, irresistible force of the Ace of Swords is balanced. Awareness of potentials.

Waite—Vigilance, retreat, solitude, hermit's repose, exile, tomb and coffin. A bad card, but if reversed a qualified success may be expected by wise administration of affairs.

Walker—*Seclusion.* A card of insight generated by seclusion, like the insight of Delphi's fatidic priestess. Sometimes prophetic powers invoked in secret, seclusion of exile, imprisonment, convalescence, voluntary isolation, or rest and recuperation in the midst of adversity.

Wanless—*Logic.* Discriminate intelligence, structure, integrity, thinking, and planning. Putting things into a workable whole, creating a practical system, and building a solid foundation by seeing how every piece is related to the whole. Recognizing that all phenomena in the universe have an order.

Riley—*Rest.* R&R. Time out. Sometimes illness in order to recuperate. The intellect relinquishing its control.

FIVE OF SWORDS

Arrien—*Fear of Defeat, Memory of Defeat.* Some fear of defeat is weighing on the mind, making the individual afraid to try again now in a new relationship or with some new idea. There is a desire and possibility of breaking through this fear in the next five weeks to five months.

Cowie—*Conflict.* Involvement in a conflict that appears to have been won but leaves the individual with problems.

Crowley—*The Lord of Defeat.* Venus in Aquarius. Five, as always, brings disruption, but here it is weakness rather than an excess of strength which seems the cause. Defeat is due to pacifism. The intellect has been enfeebled by sentiment.

Eakins—*Fear.* A sense of weakness. Fear of a painful, frightening, or unknown situation. Being trapped in a self-designed prison of negative energy from the past.

Fairfield—*Philosophical Adjustments.* Challenge or change of lifestyle. Adapting your beliefs or your communication.

Greer—Difficulty in communicating your ideas to others. Thinking may be fragmented and decisions difficult, bringing confusion and doubt. An empty victory using unfair means. Personal or political strife. No win situation. Divisiveness.

Noble—A powerful negative experience, such as a defeat on the mental level.

Pollack—Defeat with a sense of humiliation and weakness.

Sharman-Burke—A need to give up fighting a situation. Advises swallowing pride, acknowledging and accepting limitations, and proceeding in a new direction.

Stewart—*Loss.* The Taking Wind and The Birds of Loss. Often loss or abandonment in early phases of a situation. Separation and breaking up of established patterns.

Waite—Degradation, destruction, revocation, infamy, dishonour, loss, with the variant and analogues of these. An attack on the fortune of the Querent.

Walker—*Defeat.* A defeat decreed by the Fates, to be accepted without protest and by patient endurance and passive courage.

Wanless—*Negativity.* Doubt and pessimism, defeatist thinking based on the mind's interpretation.

Riley—*Mental Activity.* A time of mental exercise and energy, either mind expansion or a temporary mental maze.

SIX OF SWORDS

Arrien—*Objective, Logical, Rational Thinking.* Strong analytical ability, logical scientific thinking that is felt internally and externally. Communication about something which is completely new in such a logical, objective way that it is easily understood and well received by others.

Cowie—*Problems which Will Soon be Ended.* Feeling laden down with responsibilities but doing the correct things to solve them.

Crowley—*The Lord of Science.* Mercury in Aquarius. The fullest interpretation of this card is the perfect balance of all mental and moral faculties, hardly won, and almost impossible to hold in an ever-changing world. The full establishment and balance of intelligence with humanity.

Eakins—*Clarity.* Sudden clarity. A keen ability to analyze. Mental and moral faculties in true balance which causes jubilation and a beautiful sense of reverence.

Fairfield—*A Reliable Philosophy or Communication Pattern.* A rhythmic and cyclical lifestyle. Acceptance and reiteration of beliefs and attitudes.

Greer—The gift of support in adversity. Moving away from danger. Journey in consciousness or mental travel. Solving problems. Getting distance to see things in perspective—objectivity.

Noble—The most spiritual of the Swords, after the Ace. The ability to see things as a whole. Perspective, getting distance, and taking care of the hurt parts of yourself.

Pollack—A quiet passage through a difficult time. A time of easy transition. Functioning in some difficult situation without addressing the fundamental problems. Sometimes keeping silent about pain or anger, especially in family history. Or balance is disturbed. Breaking silence.

Sharman-Burke—The moving away from difficulties toward more peaceful times. Can mean a literal journey, a move to a more pleasing environment, but the journey could also be on an inner level. A release of tension and anxiety after a period of strain, and a sense of prevailing harmony.

Stewart—*Transition.* Beautiful Flight or Harmony of Birds. Movement from one state to another in a balanced transition. A sense of movement towards sanctuary, safety, or settlement.

Waite—Journey by water, route, way, envoy, comissionary, expedient. The journey will be pleasant.

Walker—*Passage.* A difficult anxious time, a journey toward a dark, unknowable future which sometimes presages success.

Wanless—*Confusion.* Extreme mental activity and agitation, mental conflict, ambiguity, and indecision. Out of this conflict can come resolution and synthesis and great ideas can be born.

Riley—*Overview.* The mind watching itself. The power of safe passage from one world to another. You may not always be aware of it at this time, but Michael *is* rowing your boat ashore.

SEVEN OF SWORDS

Arrien—*Thoughts of Futility.* Wanting something and believing you can't have it. A sense of resignation, giving up. There is the desire and possibility of breaking through this feeling of futility within the next seven weeks or seven months.

Cowie—*Creating Problems for Yourself.* Creating problems by taking on guilt feelings or resentments.

Crowley—*The Lord of Futility.* Moon in Aquarius. There is vacillation, a wish to compromise, a certain toleration. This card suggests the policy of appeasement, a contest between the many feeble and the one strong, a striving in vain.

Eakins—*Many Tongues.* A sense of futility. Too many ways to go, as if hearing or speaking several languages at once and there is no sense to be made of anything.

Fairfield—*Mental Flexibility.* Experimenting with schedule, lifestyle, daily routine, beliefs, or communication.

Greer—Wit and cunning with ability to create plans and stratagems. Research: collecting the knowledge and ideas of others. Preparation. Lying and sneaking around. Avoiding confrontation.

Noble—Mental strategy. The mind creates a plan to get what it wants.

Pollack—Schemes and actions that do not solve anything, perhaps a sense of isolation. Craftiness combined with hiding your true intentions. Or acting to find help or advice from others.

Sharman-Burke—The necessity for prudence and evasion in order to gain an objective—a time for brain, not brawn. If the card is badly placed, a flight from a dishonourable act might be indicated.

Stewart—*Dishonesty.* Original Victory and Dawn of Feeling. Often self-deceit in which the mind talks itself out of truth and the emotions are disrupted. In broader terms, a card of complex movement, an essential inspirational and disruptive force that originates the tension of power to be used creatively.

Waite—Design, attempt, wish, hope, confidence; also quarreling, a plan that may fail, annoyance. A good card; it promises a country life after a competence has been secured.

Walker—*Opposition.* Being "at sword's points." Quarrels, difficulties, and hampering of movement.

Wanless—*Dullness.* A stable state of mind amidst great movement. Rest or boredom of the mind. Giving the mind the opportunity to regroup and renew.

Riley—*Avoiding Confrontation.* Evasive tactics and moving under cover. New plans and preparations are being laid in the mind, but it is not yet clearly seen how to arrive at their completion.

EIGHT OF SWORDS

Arrien—*Mental Interference.* The desire for expansion concerning any duality. Indication of over-analyzation, doubt, or confusion about a choice needing to be made. There is a desire and possibility for resolution with the next eight weeks to eight months.

Cowie—*Temporary Problems.* The feeling that nothing will work—that the fight for dreams has been lost.

Crowley—*The Lord of Interference.* Jupiter in Gemini. Signifies a lack of persistence in matters of the intellect and of contest. Due to the influence of Jupiter in Gemini, good fortune attends even these weakened efforts, yet the Will is constantly thwarted by accidental interference.

Eakins—*Power Shield.* Indecision which leads to a sense of imprisonment. Energy wasted, external obstacles, disillusionment. By surrendering to love, the way becomes clear, and you will become internally empowered.

Fairfield—*Organizing Thoughts and Communication.* Organizing and re-working your lifestyle, schedule, or attitudes to more closely align them with values.

Greer—Bound by mental obstructions. Waiting to be rescued. Too many ideas with no direction. Lack of persistence. Fenced in by own beliefs. Restrictions. Ignoring the opinions of others.

Noble—The activity of fighting your way out of a box created by the mind—a stuck place, an obstacle holding you back from success.

Pollack—Confusion, oppressive ideas, isolation. Feeling trapped, ashamed. Or the first step in liberation from some oppressive situation.

Sharman-Burke—Afraid of moving out of a situation which is binding and restricting. Positively, a sign will come to show the way.

Stewart—*Danger.* Encircling Wind, Ceaseless Change, Restless Motion. Uncertainty. Potential destructive or disruptive energy. The danger that may be passed through and must be addressed, either in potential or in reality, come what may. Uncentered restlessness, mental disturbance, imbalance, and confusion.

Waite—Bad news, violent chagrin, crisis, censure, power in trammels, conflict, calumny; also sickness. Yet it is a card of temporary durance rather than irretrievable bondage.

Walker—*Disillusion.* Loss of faith, inner turmoil, depression, and possibly discovery of formerly honored principles and beliefs proved false.

Wanless—*Synthesis.* Balance and synthesis of the mind's abilities. The full and integrated use of the mental facilities which allows you to create wholeness, heal, and to view it all holistically.

Riley—*Mental Direction.* The mind arrives at pure individual reason, which either results in being out of touch with your emotions and thus confused, or a light dawns and the intellect knows how to proceed.

NINE OF SWORDS

Arrien—*Mental Self-Cruelty.* Negative thinking and mental degradation being felt both dynamically and receptively which bring the individual down. There is a desire and possibility to break this general pattern of negativity within the next nine weeks to nine months.

Cowie—*Feeling Sorry for Yourself.* Being hurt by life and crying about it rather than moving ahead.

Crowley—*The Lord of Cruelty.* Mars in Gemini. Here the original disruption inherent in Swords is raised to its highest power. The suit has been constantly degenerating, thought has gone through every possible stage, and the conclusion is despair. The original pure intellect is now more the automatic stirring of heartless passions. Consciousness has fallen into a realm unenlightened by reason.

Eakins—*The Screen.* Being threatened or appearing threatening to others. Being hurt and having hurt others. Fear of cruelty, judgment, and pain. A sense of anger which leads to seclusion. A need to analyze, think clearly, and to get in touch with your night dreams for direction and understanding.

Fairfield—*Integrated Thoughts.* Smooth and well-integrated lifestyle, communication, and belief system.

Greer—The opportunity to grieve, face the demons, or weather the nightmares through time and patience. Depression. Guilt. Grieving. Going within.

Noble—A ghastly nightmare, the rising up from the unconscious of all the fears and projections the mind has made during its process of thought. Worry or anguish.

Pollack—Deepest sorrow, utmost mental pain, the moment of agony and dissolution. Or oppression, depression, and suspicion rather than tragedy.

Sharman-Burke—A sense of impending doom and disaster which may be unfounded. A difficult decision to be made or situation to face in which the fear is far worse than the outcome.

Stewart—*Misfortune.* Bringer of the Whirlwind, Birth of Sorrow. Associated with pain, with birth pangs and death pangs. The spiritual pain of the Sorrowing Mother of all Being, or physical pain of the birth or death of any life-phase. The power of separation that brings beginnings.

Waite—Utter desolation. Death, failure, miscarriage, delay, deception, disappointment, despair. Generally, a card of bad omen.

Walker—*Cruelty.* Mental or physical suffering, anxiety about the imminent possibility of pain, or callous indifference to the pain of another.

Wanless—*Narrowness.* Focus on priorities. Concentrating on what is most important to complete, keeping to the straight and narrow, and trusting yourself and the course that you have committed to. Or narrow-mindedness.

Riley—*Mental Conclusion.* Much thinking, which either results in mental pain, illness, or insomnia; or finally arriving at a long-sought-for solution to a mental problem, resulting in relief and gratification.

TEN OF SWORDS

Arrien—*Fear of Ruin.* Mental despair, helplessness, and hopelessness about an emotional relationship or about finances. There is the desire to release this fear of ruin and the possibility of doing so within the next ten weeks to ten months.

Cowie—*End of Problems.* A condition definitely coming to an end in a short while.

Crowley—*The Lord of Ruin.* Sun in Gemini. The damping down of the Creative impulse, weakness, corruption, or mirage. Reason divorced from reality. This card teaches the lesson that if one goes on fighting long enough, all ends in destruction. But ruin can never be complete because as soon as things are bad enough, one begins to build up again.

Eakins—*The Way of the Cross.* Death coming to an old way of thinking. Transcending old patterns of thought which have kept you caged in a reality which no longer serves. Resignation to a higher form of thinking: divine reason. The spirit rising on the winds of change.

Fairfield—*A Philosophical Choice Point.* Comfortable and safe communications, lifestyle, beliefs, and values that will soon evolve but for now are not ready to change.

Greer—Feeling pinned down, or stabbed in the back. The end of a problem. Letting go. Acceptance and resignation. Paralysis. Back problems.

Noble—The final letting go of some idea to which the ego has been attached. The struggle has ended. The ego has no choice but to let go.

Pollack—Being filled with pain. Or temporary advantage.

Sharman-Burke—The end of something—of a relationship, particular circumstance, or of a false way of seeing a situation. Truth and clarity of vision which brings about an inevitable death while clearing the ground for something new.

Stewart—*Disaster.* Collapsing Form, Cutting Free, The Bitter Wind. The ultimate cut which manifests right through into substance and brings a complete separation, dividing any form or pattern into its constituent parts. The transition between night and day—the end of dark comforting night and the dawn of a harsh morning.

Waite—Pain, affliction, tears, sadness, desolation, imprisonment, treason. It is not especially a card of violent death.

Walker—*Ruin.* A new birth of hope born out of despair, desolation, and pain.

Wanless—*Delusion.* Delusion is really a delusion in itself, a false title. Every vision is an illusion until it is manifested on the physical level of reality. But even then, everything is an interpretation of the mind, so follow the illusion/vision of your choice—what your heart wants to do, where your passion lays, and be entertained.

Riley—*Mental Ending.* No choice but to let go. A critical point reached that releases astral thought into physical manifestation. Although this can be a great time—a real megamoment if you've got your act together, it can also be the final force in which your act is brought together for you.

ACE OF DISCS

Arrien—*Grounded, Practical, Organized.* Union between the spiritual and physical aspects of your self. Radiating the higher aspect of your self and bringing it into physical manifestation. The gift of being centered, grounded, and productive is available to be used and drawn upon for the next year's time.

Cowie—*New Material Conditions.* Beginning a new pathway in life which will bring satisfaction.

Crowley—*The Root of the Powers of Earth.* As with all the Aces, this is not the element itself but the seed of the element. This card is the affirmation of the New Aeon in which the the Sun and Earth are recognized as living Beings, as one's constant companions in a Universe of Pure Joy.

Eakins—*Form.* Receiving a gift of productivity, something new physically or materially. Engaging in promising new endeavors. Moving toward a state of true external success and internal harmony. The beginning of material gain and physical delight.

Fairfield—*A New Physical Form or Pattern.* Planting seeds for a new home, job, career, or form of security. Perhaps getting some urges to begin a new direction in health or finances.

Greer—Crystallizing Consciousness. Body Sustaining. A business or work possibility. Materialization of ideas. Centering or grounding your energy. Stability and skills to get results.

Noble—A gift of earth energy—the birth of something in material form. Something manifesting. Sometimes a time of meditation, an inward pull of energy.

Pollack—A gift of the Earth: nature, wealth, security, a joyful life. Protection. Or corruption by wealth, end of protection. Leaving security to move into the wider world.

Sharman-Burke—The body, matter, material gain, worldly status and achievement, financial security, or wealth. Good beginnings for financial propositions, business ventures, or enterprises. It can mean the successful founding of a busieness which will bring financial rewards, prosperity and security firmly based. Might also indicate a lump sum of money or gifts, perhaps of gold.

Stewart—*Earth/Law.* Manifest or expressed power often concerned with outer or material circumstances. Law and Wisdom, the Mystery of Night and Winter, thus can indicate a force or restriction that leads to liberation. The Winter that precedes Spring, the wisdom of endings that bring beginnings.

Waite—Perfect contentment, felicity, ecstasy; also speedy intelligence; gold. Shews prosperity and comfortable material conditions. The most favourable of all cards. Even reversed, it is a share in the finding of treasure.

Walker—*Reward.* The reward of practical effort in the worldly sense, such as opportunities, security, stable foundations, and ownership.

Wanless—(Worlds) *Success.* Ability to achieve goals and to succeed in the world. Bringing together internal and external resources and talents, and thus also getting it together in the material world of work, money, relationships, health, and home.

Riley—*Grounds the Force.* Remembering and memory. The rising up of physical manifestation. The beginning of any new physical form. Indicates some form of *I do.*

TWO OF DISCS

Arrien—*Physical Transition, Transformation.* A balance which is achieved through change that takes place externally in order to make things more secure, stable, and solid. The symbol of infinity, ongoingness of change unending.

Cowie—*Trying to Balance the Material Affairs of Life.* Juggling affairs.

Crowley—*The Lord of Change.* Jupiter in Capricorn. Appropriate to two, this is energy in its most fixed form, thus it is change in its most fixed form according to the doctrine that Change is the support of stability. Earth is the throne of spirit, or having gotten to the bottom, one immediately comes out at the top, hence, it represents the harmonious interplay of the Four Elements in constant movement.

Eakins—*Cause and Effect.* The process of discovering that every action entails a reaction. Recognition of infinite process, yin and yang. The sacred space of infinite ambivalence.

Fairfield—*Choosing a Physical Path.* Affirming and nurturing a new form of financial, material, or inner stability.

Greer—Ability to handle two or more situations at once. Expanding your horizons. Adaptability. Mobility. Change. Travel. Play.

Noble—Trying to balance more than one project at a time, or handling both inner growth and outer achievement at once.

Pollack—Juggling life. Having a good time and enjoying life. Or pretending to take everything lightly.

Sharman-Burke—The necessity to keep several propositions going at once. A flow of movement when skilful manipulation achieves success. Change, particularly with regard to financial matters, but also harmony within the change if you can be flexible enough to keep everything moving.

Stewart—*Change.* The Wisdom of Earth: All things change. Change arising out of darkness, night, stillness. From light we move toward darkness, from darkness toward light. The gate toward major transitions and movements of energy in any cycle.

Waite—On one hand it is a card of gaiety, recreation, and its connexions, but it is read also as news and messages in writing, and as obstacles, agitation, trouble, and embroilment. Troubles are more imaginary than real.

Walker—*Change.* A particularly important card implying that opposites are illusion, and all things are ultimately different forms of the same thing.

Wanless—*Reflection.* Time off to take a good look at the situation. Contemplation, evaluation, thinking, or patience before acting.

Riley—*Daily Living.* The physical condition of dualities. Yin and yang. The ability to recognize and integrate polarities.

THREE OF DISCS

Arrien—*Physical Persistence, Tenacity, Endurance.* Strong determination to give any external situation the "works"; full commitment to a situation regardless of difficulties. Operating at a high level of energy.

Cowie—*Aware of Responsibilities.* Being aware of responsibilities and that people are observing.

Crowley—*The Lord of Work.* Mars in Capricorn. The material establishment, the basic form of the idea of the Universe; the Earth, the crystallization of forces. The energy is constructive and Mars is at his best. Something has definitely been done.

Eakins—*Works.* A time of inventing, creating, or engineering. All things material moving into alignment to work for success as long as the sense of heart and spirit is not lost.

Fairfield—*Planning Secure Structures.* Planning for the kinds of physical, financial, or security needs that are really wanted.

Greer—Love of work. Working out practical plans using creative skills and abilities. Practicality. The gift of working together with others. The card of the craftsperson. Displaying work for approval.

Noble—Work done together—a communal act of building. The ability to work together. Craft and dexterity.

Pollack—Hard work and dedication resulting in mastery. Conscious practical work which may serve self-development. Or mediocrity.

Sharman-Burke—A basic form or structure that is finished, sound, and complete, and finishing touches can now be added. Material gain or success through effort. Approval and recognition given by others and a sense of achievement deservedly experienced.

Stewart—*Effort.* The Understanding of Earth: Expressive Comprehension. Right effort towards a graceful or wise end.

Waite—*Metier,* trade, skilled labour; usually, however, regarded as a card of nobility, aristocracy, renown, glory.

Walker—*Work.* Work undertaken, especially with others. Material gain as a result of creative skills.

Wanless—*Nurturing.* Support with patience and tender loving care. Love of your creations.

Riley—*Working.* Increasing and producing on the physical level, usually with a sense of love and/or satisfaction. In timing, indicates something will manifest on the physical plane within the next 3 to 4 week period.

FOUR OF DISCS

Arrien—*Physical Potency, Vitality, Forcefulness.* Owning your own personal energy, power, and vitality. A feeling of self-assuredness. Expressing vitality and creativity in the external world.

Cowie—*Holding on Tightly.* Holding on closely to what you have, material possessions or emotions.

Crowley—*The Lord of Power.* Sun in Capricorn. Generation and establishment in its full material sense. It is the power which dominates and stabilizes everything, but manages its affairs more by negotiation, by pacific methods, than by any assertion of itself. It is the Law, the Constitution, with no aggressive element.

Eakins—*Power.* The unfoldment of power. Perhaps a feeling of closing off the outside world. Power which will be maintained if offered in the service of love.

Fairfield—*Making Something Tangible.* Taking concrete steps toward creating security in the physical world. Taking action to feel grounded and centered.

Greer—Gift of drawing resources that are needed. Awareness of personal value and worth. Power. Giving structure to or establishing order in a situation. Centeredness or selfishness. Possessiveness.

Noble—An inner sanctuary of some kind, perhaps a room or house where a person can be alone and sheltered. A need for silence.

Pollack—Dependence on material comfort and security for stability. Selfishness, greed, or confinement. Giving structure and meaning to the material universe. Self-protection. Or inability to give structure.

Sharman-Burke—Holding on to something and risking nothing, but neither is there gain. "Nothing ventured nothing gained."

Stewart—*Increase.* Merciful Earth. Growth. Gives power in any existing situation and expands it.

Waite—The surety of possessions, cleaving to that which one has. Gift, legacy, inheritance.

Walker—*Avarice.* Blockages of thought and action which naturally follow from excessive devotion to materialistic rewards.

Wanless—*Commencement.* Movement of energy with swiftness. The exercise and expression of your talents and dreams. Ramming ahead, taking the leap.

Riley—*Power.* Enjoyment of a physical situation. Being content and pleased with the way things are, feeling as protected as if you are within the walls of a strong castle, under the dominion of a benevolent power of strength.

FIVE OF DISCS

Arrien—*Physical Concern, Anxiety, Rumination.* Worry about finances, health, external situations, or relationships. A state of *being/consciousness* that goes back to the *past* or forward into the *future,* but never handles the now of the *present.*

Cowie—*Out in the Cold.* Feeling left out because of a lack of money or left out of social activities.

Crowley—*The Lord of Worry.* Mercury in Taurus. This is instability in the very foundation of matter. The soft quiet of the Four has been completely overthrown. Discs being what they are, stolid and obstinate, the general effect is one of intense strain coupled with long-continued inaction. There is no action, at least not in its own ambit, that can affect the issue.

Eakins—*The Nadir.* A sense of worry, darkness, alienation, or feeling alone and on the outside. The stage of the dark night which is passed by tuning into love and the message of the heart.

Fairfield—*Physical Adjustments.* Adapting or changing security, health, or practical matters.

Greer—Challenges of deprivation, insecurity, and exclusion. Uncertainty creating anxiety, worry, and strain. Feeling "out in the cold." Voluntary simplicity and unconventionality. Scarcity consciousness.

Noble—Tension held in the body. Worry. Probably the mind is focused on survival issues of some kind—money, housing, jobs. Inertia.

Pollack—Material troubles, such as poverty or illness. A situation where outside forces cannot help. Or collapse of survival, new possibilities.

Sharman-Burke—Strain or anxiety over money, or a loss of spiritual direction. Signifies the need to pay attention to detail—financial, emotional, or spiritual—for there is a warning that without due care something important or valuable may otherwise be lost.

Stewart—*Conflict.* Earth's Severity or The Breaking Earth. Tension or conflict. Adjustment of pattern, energies, and entities seeking the balance of a new cycle or further pattern.

Waite—A card with many alternatives, concordance, affinities, disorder, but the foretelling of material trouble above all.

Walker—*Hardship.* Hard times, worry, loss or lack of comfort without help from fair-weather friends and institutions.

Wanless—*Setback.* Difficulties and conflict. Strategic review, retreat, regrouping, realignment, and redirection due to a setback.

Riley—*Physical Activity.* A time when calm is disrupted, and you are temporarily disequalized. Letting go of status quo and moving on. Or when your idea of getting around is running in circles.

SIX OF DISCS

Arrien—*Physical Attainment, Accomplishment.* A deep desire to be successful at some external venture. Success, achievement in all aspects of life by being willing to risk, being committed, and trusting your intuition.

Cowie—*Having to Put Out.* Because of the Law of Karma you are now having to put out. You will receive it back at a later date.

Crowley—*The Lord of Success.* Moon in Taurus. The full harmonious establishment of the Energy of Earth. This is a card of settling down, wholly lacking in imagination, and somewhat dreamy. Because the weight of Earth will ultimately drag the current down to a mere eventuation of material things, change is soon coming upon it. Yet, for the time being, there is a balanced system.

Eakins—*Beauty.* The Beauty Way. Experiencing the joy of giving. Healing through the pursuit of beauty. The balanced and harmonious establishment of material energy coming from a higher consciousness.

Fairfield—*A Predictable Physical Cycle.* Income or security is steady and predictable.

Greer—The gift of success in relationships, achieved through sharing of resources. Drawing what is needed. Sensitivity to others' needs. An "energy exchange." Can be codependency. Getting paid.

Noble—Generosity, having more than enough, sharing health and good fortune.

Pollack—Sharing, generosity, charity. A relationship or situation in which one person dominates others. Giving people what they are able to receive. Or lack of receiving and giving.

Sharman-Burke—Suggests that money owing will be paid; you will receive what is rightfully yours. Maybe financial help received from a generous friend or employer, and money affairs put on a stable footing. Also suggests that present prosperity should be shared with others.

Stewart—*Benefit.* Harmony of Earth or Beautiful Land. A healing and redemptive force. A benefit often through shape, pattern, or form which is not rigid structure, but beauty, flow, and living shape in which are found the elemental flow patterns.

Waite—Presents, gifts, gratification. Attention, vigilance. Now is the accepted time. Present prosperity.

Walker—*Charity.* Gifts, help from someone, material gain, with a warning against excessive expenditure of resources through misplaced generosity.

Wanless—*Synergy.* The ability to bring resources together to create an alliance of power and success. Combining your own resources or those of others.

Riley—*Success.* Steadiness in realization. Having enough health, physical energy, or resources in yourself to be able to include others.

SEVEN OF DISCS

Arrien—*Physical Failure, Nonsuccess.* The fear of failure with finances, health, relationships, or any external situation. There is a determination to release fears of failure within the next seven weeks to seven months.

Cowie—*Keep On, Your Project Will be Completed Soon.* Being tired and feeling as if you will never finish the task, but it is nearly completed.

Crowley—*The Lord of Failure.* Saturn in Taurus. Sevens are the degeneration of the element, its utmost weakness. In this card, it is the extreme of passivity. There is no effort, not even dream. Labour itself is abandoned, and everything is sunk in sloth. But in one sense this is the fullest possible establishment of matter—the lowest fallen and therefore the highest exalted.

Eakins—*The Garden.* A pause during growth in which the seeds of new growth and a better and more rewarding path are discovered. Using wisdom and understanding to do what is right.

Fairfield—*Physical Experimentation.* Experimenting with money, material resources, or body. Exploring ways to feel centered, safe, and grounded.

Greer—No matter what a person does, there is a certain point at which they have to wait for the results. Delay. Evaluating the results of your efforts. Observing the cycles and processes. Patience.

Noble—Growth and waiting. The message of the card is, "Be patient—there is nothing to do but wait." There is no way to hurry this birth, no way to see inside for certain.

Pollack—The moment of being able to look back with satisfaction on something accomplished. Or pervasive dissatisfaction that comes from unsatisfying jobs or commitments.

Sharman-Burke—A pause during the development of an enterprise or business. Assessing what has been achieved and what needs to be done.

Stewart—*Attention.* Attending the Earth and Venus Reflecting. Building, structuring, defining in readiness and preparation for a further step. Expanding toward expression or manifestation.

Waite—Extremely contradictory divinatory meanings, but in the main, a card of money, business, and barter.

Walker—*Failure.* Deep-seated blockage, deceived hopes, self-induced anxiety, loss of capacity to inspire.

Wanless—*Breakthrough.* Breaking through blocks that have prevented achievement of goals and aspirations. Free up of talents and resources.

Riley—*Waiting.* Delay. Unable to take physical action. This is a good time to do something while you wait—like do your favorite hobby, reflect, or catch up on things around the house.

EIGHT OF DISCS

Arrien—*Physical Caution, Carefulness, Prudence.* Wisdom operating from a place of balance and integration; making sure all bases are covered. Not overextending or underextending your self externally and operating from near the center.

Cowie—*Working Steadfastly, or Beginning a New Endeavour.* Working steadfastly, beginning a new project, and having others later on.

Crowley—*The Lord of Prudence.* Sun in Virgo. Signifies loving intelligence lovingly applied to material matters. A "retiring"—the secret withdrawing of Energy into the fallow Earth—in a sense, birth. In purely material matters, this is a sort of strength in doing nothing at all. It is sowing the seed, sitting back, and waiting.

Eakins—*The Mountain.* Perseverance, commitment, and discipline. Learning, practicing, growing, and blossoming. A deeper understanding of the position of the Self in the external world and what needs to be created in order to nurture the Inner Self.

Fairfield—*Organizing Physical Things.* Making choices so that the material world more closely conforms with your needs.

Greer—Ability to develop and refine skill or craft. Self-discipline. Preparation. Repetitiveness. Productivity. Getting finances and resources in order.

Noble—Craft—apprenticeship in a skill that will take you through life in a grounded way. A sharing of skills between people.

Pollack—Training that brings both discipline and skill. Thinking about the work itself without the goal of reward. Or impatience, frustration, unfulfilled ambition.

Sharman-Burke—The card of "talent." The possibility of turning a skill or talent into a profession, or money earned through such a skill. Hard work and practical ideas forming the stable basis for building up a new and profitable career both in emotional and financial terms.

Stewart—*Skill.* Glorious Expression or Honourable Mind, Quicksilver. Mind working with substance. Skill to work with energies and forms. The manipulative skill of the fingers working upon substance.

Waite—Work employment, commission, craftsmanship, skill in craft and business, perhaps in the preparatory stage.

Walker—*Learning.* A quest for unstealable rewards of knowledge and the extension of learning into new areas.

Wanless—*Change.* The way of keeping the balance. The only constant in life is change, so adapt to new realities by change of attitudes, feelings, energies, and situations.

Riley—*Learning.* Utilizing and doing what brings you satisfaction. Moving forward, expanding, action, and working toward a desired goal.

NINE OF DISCS

Arrien— *Physical Profit, Benefit, Gain.* Physical gain in external reality from projects, relationships, or situations.

Cowie—*Contentment and Peace of Mind.* Peace and quiet and security from having worked hard.

Crowley—*The Lord of Gain.* Venus in Virgo. The balance of Force in fulfillment. Good luck attending material affairs; favour and popularity; the mingling of good luck and good management. One becomes more and more stolid, and feels that "everything is for the best in the best of all possible worlds."

Eakins—*The Zenith.* A sense of accomplishment, reward, happiness, balance, joy, splendor, unity, love, radiance, beauty, and light. Success in life from learning that the importance of the ego pales next to that of the soul.

Fairfield—*Integrated Security.* Money, resources, health, or security base operating in a coordinated, smooth manner.

Greer—Luxury and material well-being. Reward for efforts. Enjoyment of solitary leisure. Relaxation. Ease. Harvest. Cut off from instincts and freedom.

Noble—The solitary person who is learning through art, dreams, meditation, books, or from spirit guides. The development of strength and courage.

Pollack—Awareness and the ability to distinguish what matters in life. Success and certainty from knowing you have made the right choices, done the right thing, and taken necessary actions. Self-discipline. Or lack of discipline and the failure that comes from it.

Sharman-Burke—Material well-being. Enjoying the good things in life, even though alone. A solitary pleasure in physical comfort and material success because you are at peace within and therefore do not *need* constant companionship to feel content. Material benefits are promised and appreciated.

Stewart—*Means.* Founded within the Earth, The Ninefold Womb, Expressive Moon. Manifesting energy and ideas taking shape. All means toward realization: dreams, seeds, life patterns, sexual fertility, spiritual truth, inner birth, vision, wisdom teachings. The last step before physical life, and the first step after it.

Waite—Suggests plenty in all things, possibly in one's own possessions, and testifies to material well-being. Prudence, safety, success, accomplishment, certitude, and discernment. Prompt fulfillment of what is presaged by neighbouring cards.

Walker—*Accomplishment.* Achievement in the sense of gestation, productivity, careful cultivation, the nurturing and love of beauty and nature.

Wanless—*Harvest.* The fruition of hard work. Reaping what has been sown and nurtured. Harvesting the fruits of labor.

Riley—*Gain.* Solitary creative work. Accomplishment which comes as a result of following your own path. The possibility of realizing what Nietzsche called *Amor fati*, the "love of your fate."

TEN OF DISCS

Arrien—*Physical Prosperity, Abundance.* A state of wealth and prosperity on all levels of consciousness that is now manifesting in the external world.

Cowie—*Material Success.* Dominant happiness and material well-being, especially family well-being.

Crowley—*The Lord of Wealth.* Mercury in Virgo. The accumulation of wealth. The great and final solidification, not only of the suit of Discs, but like XXI, The Universe is to the Trump cards, is the sum total of the other thirty-five small cards. The force completely expended resulting in death and rebirth, shown by the *Conjuntio*, or union, of Mercury in Virgo.

Eakins—*The Great Work*. A sense of order, design, tension, balance, and harmony. Life moving with a wonderful rhythm. Realizing that the true meaning of wealth is following the spiritual path.

Fairfield—*A Physical Crossroads.* Current security is stable and steady but not stimulating. The time for taking security risks is approaching but hasn't yet arrived.

Greer—Using the wealth of resources and talents to build lasting structures in the world. Established or inherited traditions and conventions. Endurance and permanence. Prosperity and wealth. Family and home.

Noble—A circle of support in which manifestation takes place. A sense of being part of some family or group. A symbol of wealth—everything the querent needs for survival and more is contained within the power of the group energy.

Pollack—Established home, good life, security, and comfort. The magic and blessings of nature and the universe. Or taking emotional or financial risks.

Sharman-Burke—Financial stability and firm foundations for home and family life. Suggests property acquired for the founding of new generations, or traditions being passed down in the family with a feeling of continuity and security. A materially settled way of life.

Stewart—*Opportunity.* Sacred Body, Holy Earth, Perfected Kingdom, Earth Mother, Regenerating Substance. The ultimate Earth of Earth, the planetary body, our own body, and all matter-energy. Material and spiritual opportunity in any situation.

Waite—Gain, riches; family matters, archives, extraction, the abode of a family. Represents house or dwelling and derives its value from the other cards.

Walker—*Protection.* A charm of surpassing power implying protection in the material sense, not self-created but provided by the work of someone else.

Wanless—*Reward.* Being successful in the material world. Abundance from flow of income and output. Taking risks, expanding, thinking optimistically and abundantly—not stopping.

Riley—*Satiety.* Reaching fullness and the extreme, whether for good or bad, of something physical—health, the body, work, money, security. Or winning the pie-eating contest and wishing you hadn't.

NOTES

NOTES

THE COURT CARDS

The Devil
Evil is a hill, everyone gets on his own and speaks about someone else's.

—African Proverb

It has often been noted that in all the tarot, the court cards present the most confusing picture. Some authorities interpret the court cards as events, some as people, and some as both people *and* events. Some taroists see the court cards as certain specific individuals who are present in one's life, while others view them as personality traits that manifest in all of us.

Fortunately, this profusion of meaning is not nearly as contradictory as it may at first appear, and there is even good reason for it, the reason being because *people are nearly always involved in events that are like some aspect of themselves.* Because everything is really one, there is no clear separation between what we experience in the outer world and what we are on an inner level. When reading tarot, to try to divide the person from the event that is occurring is perilous at worst and foolish at best. Nevertheless, it is probably because of this that the court cards often remain the least understood part of the tarot. Many people are not aware that everything their lives consist of is what they *are*, or as C. G. Jung once pointed out: "A man's life is characteristic of himself." When it comes to the court cards, interpretations are sometimes misunderstood because of the very common belief that a great deal of the events, situations, and people we encounter in our personal lives are things that happen to us *in spite of* ourselves, rather than events that happen to us *because* of ourselves. Most of the taroists in this book, however, know this, so some have chosen to define the court cards in light of events, others in the nature of personality, while still others swing both ways. Regardless, taroists are describing the same thing—the only difference being that one is psychic and the other physical. Once this is understood, the similarity in seemingly diversified interpretations becomes more evident.

To sum up, court cards can be interpreted as 1) people in general, 2) specific people in your life, 3) yourself, 4) events and situations happening to someone else, or 5) events and situations happening to you. When reading the following interpretations it helps to keep in mind that their meaning may apply in any one or more of these contexts and should be applied according to what the querent is seeking. Or if this is too confusing (which it certainly is for me), a more homogeneous way is to establish, as most taroists have, one or two specific ways that you read the court cards. After becoming familiar with the court cards, you can choose for yourself which manner of meaning you attribute to them. Or still an even older, more traditional way of using them is simply to eliminate the above altogether and to use the court cards *only* as significators. A significator is a court card chosen to represent the person receiving the reading. It is chosen prior to the reading, laid at the center of the layout, and used as the focal point for concentration and to consistently refer back to for clarification during the reading. It enables the reader to ascertain and confirm the querent's actions and reactions, and the nature of the personality which brings the reading's various causes and effects into play.

Some of the taroists in this book have created their own tarot decks and use different titles for the court cards. The name of the deck and its court card titles are footnoted after the taroist's name in the following section: *King of Wands.*

KING OF WANDS

Arrien—*The Spiritual Evolutionary.* Evolution and change taking place at a deep core level; old perceptions are being shed in order for there to be new extended insight and spiritual birth.

Cowie—*Projecting Ideas.* Balanced judgments due to perception and future projections being well thought out.

Crowley[1]—The fiery part of Fire. Rules in the zodiac from 21° Scorpio to 20° Sagittarius. Moral qualities of activity, generosity, fierceness, impetuosity, impulsiveness, and swiftness in unpredictable actions.

Eakins[2]—*The Spirit of Flame.* Experiencing a sense of conviction. Much movement, energy, and the power of leadership. Moving rapidly toward a new way of knowing, a new viewpoint or perspective on matters.

Fairfield—*Releasing an Old Identity.* Letting go of an old identity or self-image that it is time to end. Reaching the end of a phase of personal development.

Greer—Establishment of self. The ability to be yourself. Achievement-oriented, creative, and self-expressive. Entrepreneur. Politician.

Noble[3]—Positive male power. A powerful personality capable of accomplishing long-term goals and handling extremely complex situations.

---

[1]The *Thoth* deck by Aleister Crowley and Lady Harris. Court cards are Knight, Queen, Prince, and Princess.
[2]The *Tarot of the Spirit* deck by Joyce Eakins. Court cards are Father, Mother, Brother, and Sister.
[3]*Motherpeace Round Tarot* deck by Vicki Noble and Karen Vogel. Court cards are Shaman, Priestess, Son, and Daughter.

Pollack[4]—A strong-minded person able to dominate others by his strength of will. The wands energy controlled and turned into useful projects or long-term careers. Naturally honest, positive, and optimistic, but sometimes intolerant.

Sharman-Burke[5]—A master of wit and charm. Warm and generous with a good sense of humour and a strong liking for fun. He can persuade anyone into anything, could even "sell ice to Eskimos" because he is so amusing and optimistic. An abundance of vision and foresight.

Stewart[6]—*Decisive.* A mature male in whom the potential of inner and outer being is well harmonized. Powerful, creative, strong-willed, and ceaseless energy. May be a highly empowered spiritual being, but exercise must be cautioned in this interpretation.

Waite[7]—Dark man, friendly, countryman, generally married, honest and conscientious. Generally favorable and always signifies honesty. May mean news concerning an unexpected heritage before very long or signify a good marriage.

Walker[8]—*Valraven.* A god who gave the secrets of magic to men, and according to the Danes, became Hel's king and a lord of the underworld. A powerful person of a fiery nature: energetic, active, hard to control, attractive, but sometimes dangerous.

---

[4]*Shining Woman Tarot* by Rachel Pollack. Court cards are Place, Knower, Gift, and Speaker.

[5]*The Mythic Tarot* was created by Juliet Sharman-Burke, Liz Greene and Tricia Newell. Court cards are King, Queen, Knight, and Page.

[6]*Merlin Tarot* deck by R. J. Stewart and Miranda Gray. Court cards are King, Queen, Warrior, and Page.

[7]*Rider-Waite Tarot* deck by Arthur Edward Waite and Pamela Colman Smith. Court cards are King, Queen, Knight, and Page.

[8]*Barbara Walker Tarot* deck by Barbara Walker. Court cards are King, Queen, Prince, and Princess.

Wanless[9]—(Man) *The Actor.* Mastery of Aspiration and Oppression. The free spirit capable of being anyone and doing anything.

Riley—*Extraverted Intuition with Thinking* (ENTP).[10] The Fulfiller. Able to delegate responsibilities to others to obtain his own aim. A natural leader because he is perceptive of the views of others and has the ability to manifest self-confidence in his actions.

QUEEN OF WANDS

Arrien—*The Spiritual Self-Explorer/Discoverer.* A person in the process of self-discovery who deeply desires more self-knowledge and understanding.

Cowie—*Tendency to be Side-Tracked from Goals because of Emotions.* This person knows where she wants her ideas to take her, but there is a tendency to allow emotions to rule.

Crowley—Water of Fire. Rules in the zodiac from 21° Pisces to 20° Aries. Adaptable, persistent energy, calm authority, kindly and generous, but impatient of opposition. She has immense capacity for friendship and for love, but always on her own initiative.

---

[9] *Voyager Tarot* deck by James Wanless. Wanless does not use Court Cards but includes "Voyager Family Cards." They are Man, Woman, Sage, and Child, and here they are put with their closest corresponding Court Card. However, they are not the same.

[10] The four letters indicate the personality type according to the Myers-Briggs Type Indicator.

Eakins—*The Conduit.* A sense of being a sought-out leader, especially in matters of the spirit. Seeking quiet but consistent leadership that moves in accordance with nature's laws.

Fairfield—*A Mature Identity.* A high level of personal integrity, maturity, and self-respect. A feeling of self-sufficiency and confidence.

Greer—Love of happiness. Recognizes her personal power. Utilizes her creative energies and inspires them in others. Nurtures or stifles individuality.

Noble—Personal female power in action. A warm self-assurance and a fierce intensity of purpose. A charismatic personality, passionate, and generally glad to be alive.

Pollack—A Fire appreciation of life. Warm, passionate, honest, and sincere, seeing no purpose in deceit or nastiness. Sexuality. Offers advice, emotional support, and loves both life and people.

Sharman-Burke—Full of the love of life and can successfully run a home and family but still find time and energy to vigorously pursue her own interests. The 'Queen of hearth and home," who can have several projects going at one time yet never lets anything detract from the energy she puts into her home life. Well-liked and will help her friends enthusiastically.

Stewart—*Skilful.* A powerful mature woman, often of great sexual attraction. This energy may be routed into creative work such as art or music, into a career, or a lifetime dedication to bringing something of value into being.

Waite—A dark woman, countrywoman, friendly, chaste, loving, honourable. If the card beside her signifies a man, she is well disposed towards him; if a woman, she is interested in the Querent. Also, love of money, or a certain success in business. A good harvest.

Walker—*Hel.* Goddess and ruler of regeneration in the underworld where all the dead went to be purified, purged of their memories of former lives, and cleansed for a ritual rebirth. Fiery characteristics of warmth, illumination, benevolence, hot passion, and sharp wit.

Wanless—(Woman) *Sensor.* Master of Purity and Courage. Fiery sensitivity and spirit, finely honed to sense and detect.

Riley—*Introverted Intuition with Thinking* (INTJ). The Seer. Intensely individualistic and able to inspire individualism and confidence in others. Gifted with a keen intuitive innersight into the deeper meaning of things.

PRINCE OF WANDS

Arrien—*Spiritual Creativity.* A deep spiritual passion to release creativity and to express it in the world.

Cowie—*Putting Ideas into Action.* This person is pursuing his ideas, is under control, and is prepared to fight for the survival of his ideas.

Crowley—Air of Fire, with its faculty of expanding and volatilizing. Rules from 21° Cancer to 20° Leo. He is swift and strong, intensely noble and generous, romantic, and has an enormous capacity for work, which he exercises for its own sake "without lust of result."

Eakins—*Sun Warrior.* Aspiration of the inner spirit—like a flame reaching heavenward. Perception of great qualities of strength, swiftness, brilliance and agility, the sense of romantic revolution.

Fairfield—*Focusing on the Self.* Focusing intently on presenting a particular image to the world or putting energy into being with and discovering yourself, maybe to the point of self-centeredness.

Greer—Putting energy into self-growth, future prospects, and new directions. Inspired enthusiasm.

Noble—Power directed toward the service of life. A buoyant, energetic way of being in the world. The personality is alive and delights in amusing, entertaining, and attracting others.

Pollack—Eagerness, action, movement for its own sake, adventure, and travel. If aided by a sense of purpose and some Air-like influence of planning, can provide the energy and self-confidence for great achievement. Sometimes incomplete action and unformed plans from too much Fire. In reverse, can symbolize confusion, disrupted projects, breakdown, and disharmony.

Sharman-Burke—Splendid ideas and a fine sense of adventure. He makes a generous and warm friend or love, although he is unpredictable and hasty in judgement. Has a good sense of humor and will do anything for fun. If he stands for an event, it is usually a change of residence or a long journey, even immigration.

Stewart—*Perceptive.* A person from the early teens to late twenties with endless vitality, ceaseless activity, and ability. Intuitive insight which is spontaneous. Often a skilled facilitator who is able to see to the heart of any person or situation.

Waite—Suggests the precipitate mood, or things connected therewith. Departure, absence, flight, emigration. A dark young man, friendly. Change of residence. A bad card according to some readings, alienation.

Walker—*Dagon.* A shape-shifter God known in Christianity as a "devil" because he was opposed to the cult of Yahweh. All that is unexpected, startling, unpredictable, or unconventional. Often seeming irrational, but having a deep underlying consistency.

Wanless—(Sage) *Seer.* Mastery of Compassion and Integrity. The light of spirit's infinite radiance burning through to see the eternal truths. The light of the spirit.

Riley—*Extraverted Intuition with Feeling* (ENFP). The Carefree Spirit. Sudden inspirations with many possibilities which often result in a succession of new ideas or projects, not necessarily completing any of them.

PRINCESS OF WANDS

Arrien—*Spiritual Self-Liberation.* A major fear is being faced and overcome which is resulting in a vital new energy and a new self-awareness.

Cowie—*Contemplating New Thoughts.* This person has a new idea he is concentrating on. This could represent a new attitude which comes from new thought about a given situation.[11]

Crowley—Earth of Fire. Rules the Heavens for one quadrant of the portion around the North Pole. She is the fuel of fire, the irresistible chemical attraction of the combustible substance. Creates her own beauty by her essential vigour and force, her force of character imposing the impression of beauty upon the beholder.

---

[11]In some tarot decks, the Princess is perceived as male, hence the use of masculine pronoun.

Eakins—*The Spark/Free Spirit.* The acceptance of all change and movement with a balanced perspective. Moving with the will of the universe, favored by all universal forces. Being enthusiastic, self-confident, and eloquent.

Fairfield—*Taking Identity Risks.* Taking risks with presenting a part of yourself that was previously hidden, or recommitting to being the best you can be.

Greer—Open to new directions for self-growth and development. Messages and telephone calls. Uninhibited, frank, and forthright in speech.

Noble—The young-fiery part of the personality that manifests through dance and movement, joyful change, and growth. A natural joy within bursting free in some way.

Pollack—The start of projects, and in particular an announcement to the world, and to ourselves, that we are ready to begin either a project or a new phase of life. A messenger, message, or information. A faithful friend or lover. Or continued indecision from complexities and outright opposition caused by this person's basic qualities of simplicity and faithfulness.

Sharman-Burke—A quick, intuitive, enthusiastic personality with daring, energy, and optimism. Full of new life and vitality. As an event, may be a bearer of good news, glad tidings, a desire for growth and knowledge along with the opportunity to achieve this.

Stewart—*Diligent.* A child or young person full of potential, bursting with energy. Confident and willing to work very hard in an unassuming, efficient manner.

Waite—Dark young man, faithful, a lover, an envoy, a postman. Beside a man, he will bear favourable testimony concerning him. A dangerous rival, if followed by the Page of Cups. Has the chief qualities of his suit. May signify family intelligence.

Walker—*Atargatis.* The fish-tailed Goddess who gave rebirth to men by swallowing them. Associated with the Fishmother who swallowed the god Oannes, and Jonah's whale. A mysteriously dark, irresistible power with a great force which might be misused or misunderstood.

Wanless—(Child) *Seeker.* Mastery of Trust and Growth. The drive of the spirit to know itself.

Riley—*Introverted Intuition with Feeling* (INFJ). The Free Spirit. Restless with the desire to be free. Brings messages, telephone calls, news, information, a new acquaintance.

KING OF CUPS

Arrien—*The Optimist.* Issues of loyalty to family and relationships. "Ego-pride" has been mastered, or is needing to be dealt with. There is at this point the gift of giving totally and openly to others.

Cowie—*Projecting Ahead into Life.* This person has attained his position of authority by action and is looking ahead into life.

Crowley—The fiery part of Water. Rules the Heavens from 21° Aquarius to 20° Pisces. He is the swift passionate attack of rain and springs, the power of solution. Graceful, dilettante, placid, amiable in a passive way, and quick to respond to an attraction. Not very enduring, and lacks material depth in his character.

Eakins—*The Spirit of Water.* Listening to your conscience, trusting in your impulses, and being guided by your instincts and intuition. A gentle and sensitive period, like falling in love all over again.

Fairfield—*Releasing an Emotional Pattern.* Knowing that an emotion has run its course and is no longer operative in your life. Or becoming aware that an involvement with a psychic process has reached an end.

Greer—Established emotions or relationships. The ability to love. A counselor or care-giver. Creative and imaginative. Psychologist, priest.

Noble—Focus. Pulling all energies into facing the task at hand. Temporarily sacrificing the fleeting desires of personality for the higher goals of group work or spiritual purpose.

Pollack—Someone who has had to discipline and even suppress his dreams in order to achieve success. He has directed his creative powers into socially responsible achievements, believing responsibility comes before self-expression. Can use his creativity for his work, or in reverse, turn his talents to vice and corruption.

Sharman-Burke—A master of emotions. Has a lively imagination and can change his moods at will. Has the desire to be united with the unconscious world which does not come easy to him because he tends to pay lip-service to feelings rather than merging with them. In a spread, can suggest that it is time to get truly in touch with your feelings.

Stewart—*Jovial.* A mature male with considerable life experience who has not been hardened or embittered by his life. Good-natured, compassionate, and merciful, but does not let his kindly feelings control him or carry him away. Full of hidden depths and deep currents, seldom revealing his true strength and working through gentleness rather than overt acts of will.

Waite—Fair man, man of business, law, or divinity; responsible, disposed to oblige the Querent; also equity, art and science, including those who profess science, law and art; creative intelligence. Beware of ill-will on the part of a man of position, and of hypocrisy pretending to help.

Walker—*Dewi.* The ancient Lord of the Abyss. Also known as Bran the Blessed who became the Christianized Fisher King or Rich Fisher named Bron. A figure of ageless power and strength, reliably protective of the needy. A quality of irresistible force underlying a calm surface.

Wanless—*Surfer.* Mastery of Fear and Passion. Skillful negotiator of the emotional roller coaster of life.

Riley—*Extraverted Feeling with Sensing* (ESFJ). The Pleaser. Often has many people who love him but may be unaware of this. Manifests harmonious situations and feelings. An excellent diplomat.

QUEEN OF CUPS

Arrien—*The Emotional Reflector.* Empowers an individual to express feelings honestly and responsibly without blame or judgment. Can represent issues surrounding motherhood.

Cowie—*Too Much Imagination.* This person is imagining many things about her life but not doing anything about acquiring or solving them.

Crowley—Water of Water, with Water's power of reception and reflection. Rules from 21° Gemini to 20° Cancer. Dreamy, possessed of extreme purity and beauty, tranquil, patient, and often enough exceedingly popular. To see the truth of her is hardly possible, for she reflects the nature of her observer in great perfection.

Eakins—*The Keyhole.* Extreme purity and beauty in its most subtle form, the shimmering tranquility which results from the endurance of emotions over time. A feeling of maternal love and support which is stable and nurturing.

Fairfield—*Emotional or Intuitive Maturity.* Experiencing highly evolved and well-developed interpersonal interactions and emotions or psychic/intuitive abilities.

Greer—Love of love. Channels feelings, emotions, dreams, visions. Unusually empathetic and understanding but can be moody and fluctuating. Nurtures or stifles emotions.

Noble—Channels feelings and emotions, desires, dreams, and inner visions. The person who inspires from within. A time of inner musing, thoughts focused within, and the mind engulfed by the power of the imagination.

Pollack—The most successful and balanced of the cups. Joins consciousness to feeling. Knows what she wants and takes the necessary steps to get it, acting with an awareness of love. The possibility of blending imagination and action, creativity and social usefulness. Or loss of love resulting in deceit and dishonour.

Sharman-Burke—A person who has reached a degree of understanding of her own emotional depth and lives to a large extent in the realm of fantasy and imagination. Highly artistic and creative, even mystical or prophetic. She is often the object of the love of others. Deeply involved in her inner world so that it makes relationships of an everyday nature strangely difficult for her.

Stewart—*Loving.* A mature woman with deep sexual and fertility powers which may manifest as actual motherhood or through a creative line of work. Everything in her life is about nourishment, sexual exchange, giving and receiving, feeling, passion. Many Queens of Water become spiritually dedicated later in their lives, or become the mother of an extended family, the grandmother in a spiritual or physical sense.

Waite—Good, fair woman; honest, devoted woman who will do service to the Querent; loving intelligence, and hence the gift of vision. Success, happiness, pleasure; also wisdom, virtue; a perfect spouse and a good mother. Sometimes denotes a woman of equivocal character.

Walker—*Virginal.* Durga the Inaccessible who was inaccessible to males. Also Virginal the Ice Queen, a divine fairy of the high mountains, and the Christian Virgin Queen of Heaven. An ethereal, otherworldly person of the highest ideas, perhaps unattainably high.

Wanless—*Rejoicer.* Mastery of Equilibrium and Love. Feels and expresses the joy of life, allowing the love of life to flow through.

Riley—*Introverted Feeling with Sensing* (ISFP). The Listener. The effigy of water, having no need for recognition or ego-acknowledgment, she is the perfect screen for other people's projections.

PRINCE OF CUPS

Arrien—*The Lover.* An indication there is a great deal of passion and the desire to express feelings fervently.

Cowie—*Proceeding Slowly and Surely Ahead.* This person is pursuing his goal in life and will eventually achieve it, no matter what it is.

Crowley—Air of Water. Rules from 21° Libra to 20° Scorpio. Being Scorpio, he is extremely subtle, inclined to secret violence and craft, and intensely secret. An artist in all his ways, he appears susceptible to external influences but accepts them only to transmute them to the advantage of his secret designs. Cares intensely for power, wisdom, and his own aims.

Eakins—*Wings of Love.* Love giving wings to your spirit. Sensual and loving, tenuous and spiritual, an artist in all ways. Giving art to the world through love, imagination, grace, style, and deepest feelings.

Fairfield—*Emotional or Intuitive Focus.* Being completely involved in an emotional sensation, or focusing on psychic or spiritual awareness.

Greer—Following your dreams, visions, ideals, love. A romantic idealist. Can be moody and jealous.

Noble—The quiet, inner aspect of the male principle. Self-reflection and peaceful, meditative awareness. The mind turns to artistic visions or recognizes deep feelings.

Pollack—Pursuit of thoughts and fantasies deriving from the ego rather than the unconscious. He has not learned to direct the imagination into the world, therefore is dominated by dreams. Romantically, can represent a lover who does not wish to commit him or herself, who is perhaps attractive yet passive, withdrawn, or narcissistic.

Sharman-Burke—A refined, artistic, high-principled youth, an idealist and seeker of perfection. Quests for truth, beauty, and love, and nothing will deter him from this search. If he stands for an event, it is often a proposal of marriage, or a proposition in the field of art, or even a rival in love.

Stewart—*Idealistic.* A young man or woman filled with dreams, visions, and high expectations of life. Emotions are highly developed, and often an ideal will replace simple human love. With experience, such idealism is often modified, but is never completely lost or abandoned.

Waite—Higher graces of the imagination. A dreamer. Arrival, approach—sometimes that of a messenger. Advances, proposition, demeanour, invitation, incitement. A visit from a friend who will bring unexpected money to the Querent.

Walker—*Galahad.* The hero known as Lancelot, or Lancelot of the Lake, who quested for the Holy Grail (or Cauldron). Gallantry, gentleness, self-sacrifice, sensitivity, courtesy to women. A visionary well in touch with the "feminine" aspects of his own being.

Wanless—*Regenerator.* Master of Stagnation and Fulfillment. Finds joy, pleasure, fulfillment, and happiness in being alive.

Riley—*Extraverted Feeling with Intuition* (ENFJ). The Lover. Desiring your soulmate. Harmonious human contacts and enjoyment in the qualities and companionship of others. Likely to develop strong loyalties through projections.

PRINCESS OF CUPS

Arrien—*Emotional Detachment, Free of Jealousy.* The mastering of some possessiveness and feelings of jealousy. There is now an ability to love deeply in a loyal committed way, but with detachment.

Cowie—*Surprises in Life.* An unexpected event or surprise in life.

Crowley—Earth of Water. The faculty of crystallization. The power of Water to give substance to idea, to support life, and to form the basis of chemical combination. Her character is infinitely gracious, all voluptuousness, gentleness, kindness, and tenderness. Very dependent on others, but at the same time helpful to them.

Eakins—*Love Divine.* The power of the emotions and the unconscious to give sustenance to idea. Trusting your feelings and impressions. Being rapturous and gentle, kind and tender, full of romance, dreams, and loving vision.

Fairfield—*Emotional Risk-Taking.* Taking emotional risks in a public, up-front way or with psychic abilities. Committing to an emotional direction that may be a little scary.

Greer—Open to love and new relationships. Risks emotional dependency. Brings messages from dreams or intuition.

Noble—The playful, affectionate part of the personality that has a wonderful sense of humor and knows how to feel good. A time of experiencing feelings very strongly.

Pollack—A state or a time when contemplation and fantasy are very proper to a person. The imagination is its own justification. Stepping back to look at a situation. Can symbolize psychic talents and sensitivity, or show someone developing psychic abilities in a peaceful way. In reverse can mean to follow our inclinations, to act without thinking, to buy into something we do not need and do not even really want.

Sharman-Burke—A young, sensitive, kind natured, feeling person with strong artistic or even psychic talents. Sweet and gentle with a creative imagination. May bring news of a birth or indicate fragile new beginnings in starting to trust again.

Stewart—*Pleasant.* A young person or child, probably before the age of puberty. Responsive, easy, very attached to parents. A generally good-natured person who is able to easily make friends with others.

Waite—A fair young man, one impelled to render service and with whom the Querent will be connected; a studious, intent, contemplative youth. News, message; application, reflection, meditation; also these things directed to business. Good augury. A young man who is unfortunate in love.

Walker—*Elaine.* The Virgin Moon-goddess who was the keeper of the Grail in the Grail temple, where she wove the tapestries of life, death, and fate. "Dispenser of Joy" but also a source of hidden knowledge, mystical insight, and the gift of wisdom.

Wanless—*Feeler.* Mastery of Anger and Sorrow. Open to all feelings. Honest, non-premeditative, and authentic feelings.

Riley—*Introverted Feeling with Intuition* (INFP). The Dreamer. Learning to love or to be loved again, sometimes after hurt and withdrawal. Brings messages from the psychic realm, dreams, and emotions.

KING OF SWORDS

Arrien—*Passionate Thinking.* Passionate thoughts concerning the accomplishment of some goal the whole being is desiring at a deep level. Moving forward and succeeding at a particular task.

Cowie—*Defensive and Stubborn.* This person is restricted and defensive. A need to open to suggestions and to be more approachable.

Crowley—The fiery part of Air. Rules from 21° Taurus to 20° Gemini. The violent power of motion applied to an apparently manageable element. Active, skillful, subtle, clever, fierce, delicate, and courageous. Ideas can either absorb his entire life in concentrated aspiration, or he is incapable of decision or purpose, and any action taken is easily brushed aside by opposition.

Eakins—*The Will to Transcend.* An analytical period. The power of idea and motion, the spirit of the intellect. Highly analytical, exacting precision, brilliant, and highly rational.

Fairfield—*Releasing an Old Idea or Communication Pattern.* Trading in old philosophical ideas for a new point of view. Letting go of some old beliefs and values that no longer seem appropriate.

Greer—Established thought. The ability to communicate and be analytical. A writer, lawyer, diplomat, or philosopher (professional or otherwise). Sharp and quick.

Noble—Intellect, intelligence, and abstract thought. A strong blend of fiery emotions and powerful thought.

Pollack—Authority, power, and judgment. A person who possesses tough-minded common sense usually based on preconception and prejudice, rather than on observation of life. A narrow line between committed intellect and power for its own sake. In reverse, may simply mean some person in difficulty, a difficult relationship, or a failure to mature. By itself, however, symbolizes the arrogance of a powerful mind turned in on itself in its own desire for control.

Sharman-Burke—Firm moral conviction, inner strength, and deep commitment, both in friendship and in enmity. Not easily swayed by pleas for mercy or compassion; judges harshly but with scrupulous fairness. Often found in a position of authority and is much feared but always respected.

Stewart—*Severe.* A mature male through which the cutting power of the Sword of Air reaches its ultimate phase of creative control and will. Often involved with matters of justice, discipline, civic and personal order.

Waite—Whatsoever arises out of the idea of judgement and all its connexions—power, command, authority, militant intelligence, law, offices of the crown, and so forth. A lawyer, senator, doctor.

Walker—*Yama.* The bull-god who gave up his life to become king in the afterworld. A powerful judge, a godlike authority, an embodiment of discipline and order; can be dangerous, inhumane, or perverse.

Wanless—*Inventor.* Master of Creativity and Confusion. Sees new points of view, vents the mind, and brainstorms new thoughts.

Riley—*Extraverted Thinking with Sensing* (ESTJ). The Communicator. Intellectual and mental prowess without emotion. The lecturer, speaker, preacher, and teacher.

QUEEN OF SWORDS

Arrien—*Intellectual Thinking.* The desire to discard any roles, masks, or defenses that hide the true person, and to develop intellectual thinking. There may be a need to see a counselor at this time or to develop your own counseling ability.

Cowie—*Watch Out for Defensive Thoughts.* This person, although giving the outward appearance of love and kindness, is closing her heart inside.

Crowley—Water of Air, its elasticity and power of transmission. Rules from 21° Virgo to 20° Libra. A keen observer, subtle interpreter, and an intense individualist. Swift and accurate at recording ideas, in action confident, in spirit gracious and just, but the character, excellent in itself, cannot support interference.

Eakins—*The Eastern Threshold.* The completion of an intellectual process. A sense of resolution and commitment. Triumph, clarification, objectivity, and rationality.

Fairfield—*Intellectual Maturity.* Experiencing well-tuned mental faculties. Strong and effective communication resulting from depth of beliefs.

Greer—Love of ideas. Channels thought. Able to speak on the behalf of others. Intelligent and self-reliant. Usually fair but can be vindictive. Nurtures or stifles ideas.

Noble—The mind at work, a channeling of wisdom. A journey to the cool realms of intellect, a time-out from emotions in favor of a thoughtful, introspective period. Maybe feeling left out emotionally.

Pollack—The connection between sorrow and wisdom. Finding wisdom through accepting pain with courage, acceptance, and honesty. Or a person so forceful she expects everyone will do what she wants.

Sharman-Burke—A woman who has experienced sorrow, who may be alone through widowhood, divorce, or separation. She has loved and lost but will love again; she must bear her pain silently and with courage. Strong willed and determined, a woman who can bear whatever life presents her with.

Stewart—*Serious.* An older woman who is the feminine counterpart of the King of Swords in many ways. Critical of emotional outbursts and tends to use her mental discipline to balance emotions within herself.

Waite—Severity with chastenment, familiarity with sorrow. Widowhood, female sadness and embarrassment, absence, sterility, mourning, privation, separation.

Walker—*Kali.* The Destroyer Goddess who gave re-birth by bringing destruction. The culminating third of the original Holy Trinity of the Creating, Preserving, and Destroying Goddess. Deep comprehension of frightening truths, thinking the unthinkable, giving expression to the unspeakable.

Wanless—*Guardian.* Master of Equanimity and Negativity. Independent state of mental reflection. Clarity and focus amidst doubt and distraction.

Riley—*Introverted Thinking with Sensing* (ISTP). The Professional. Handles situations capably, quickly, and efficiently. Often the real strength behind the organization.

PRINCE OF SWORDS

Arrien—*The Creative Intuitive Thinker.* A need to release creative, intuitive thinking, to cut through anything that is limiting the ability to develop some *new* Aquarian thinking which is trying to break through.

Cowie—*Going Too Fast—Slow Down.* This person is going far too fast and must slow down if he is to succeed.

Crowley—Air of Air. 21° Capricornus to 20° Aquarius. Purely intellectual, full of ideas, intensely clever, and admirably rational—a perfect picture of the Mind. Reduces all ideas to unreality by removing them to an ideal world of ratiocination and formality, which, as such, is out of relation to any facts.

Eakins—*Warrior of Mind.* Feeling torn between two ideals which seem to be of equal weight or value. Being brave, dashing, domineering, clean, and full of courage, but if not committed, having no staying power.

Fairfield—*Focus on Communication.* Being deeply committed to acting out your philosophical ideals in your daily lifestyle. Putting incredible energy into supporting or examining particular beliefs.

Greer—Focused on making a point. Committed to ideas, thoughts, philosophy. Using mentality, communication. Speaks out, assertive and courageous, but headstrong and impatient.

Noble—Elementally all air, thus tending to be overly mental and out of touch with emotions. Approaching goals in an overly rational way.

Pollack—Brave, skillful, strong, tending toward wildness and fanaticism. Recognizes no limits. Directs all energy outwards, perhaps nervous of being alone with himself. Or extravagant, careless, excessive.

Sharman-Burke—An attractive, magnetic personality who easily draws attention and affection from others, but seems to have no need of them. Possesses a certain ruthless quality, a brilliant mind, and good business judgement. As an event, he represents a situation which is very swiftly started amid great excitement, and dies down almost as quickly, leaving a certain amount of chaos in its wake.

Stewart—*Combative.* A young man or woman in whom the originative Air is doubled, giving rise to a turbulent and changeable nature. Enthusiastic, highly active, rushing, often argumentative. May be buffeted to and from by the energy within, ready to fight and defend beliefs. This urge to combat may either be exteriorized or remain as an inner conflict.

Waite—Skill, bravery, capacity, defense, address, enmity, wrath, war, destruction, opposition, resistance, ruin. There is a sense in which this card signifies death, but it carries this meaning only in its proximity to other cards of fatality. A soldier, man of arms, satellite, stipendiary; heroic action predicted for soldier.

Walker—*Tyr.* The Norse god of battle, and *Mars*, the Roman god of war, who represented war, destruction, pestilence, daring, and death. A charismatic tyrant, inclined to dominate others, an impersonal force with great power to harm.

Wanless—*Knower.* Mastery of Synthesis and Delusion. Far-sighted point of view. Expansion into cosmic awareness.

Riley—*Extraverted Thinking with Intuition* (ENTJ). The Thinker. Total focus and absorption in something. Analytical and impersonal. Evolving a frame-of-reference on which to base his personal truths.

PRINCESS OF SWORDS

Arrien—*The Mood-Fighter.* The individual's moods are out of bounds and clouding mental clarity. May also be the individual who has the gift of being a *mood-fighter* and can help others learn how to strengthen their practical, common-sense thinking to control moodiness.

Cowie—*Defensive.* This person is very much on the defensive, may even be aggressive. Has feelings of hostility and negative emotions.

Crowley—Earth of Air, as such the fixation of the volatile. She is the materialization of Idea and the influence of Heaven upon Earth. Stern and revengeful, destructive logic, firm and aggressive, with great practical wisdom and subtlety in material things. Great adroitness at the management of practical affairs and in the settlement of controversial issues.

Eakins—*Truth.* The recognition of truth within. The stabilization of that which is volatile in the intellectual realm. Perhaps a feeling of engaging in a battle in which you are fighting against traditional notions or values.

Fairfield—*Risks in Thoughts or Communication.* Taking risks with your lifestyle or communication. Daring to commit to beliefs and attitudes that involve possible loss of comfort.

Greer—Open to justice and truth. Risks cutting through cloudy thought to get at the truth of the matter. Penetrating and cunning. Takes risks with communications.

Noble—The urge to action, impulsive and rash. A time of activity and starting new projects. The personality is impatient, maybe overeager, or even reckless.

Pollack—Solves conflicts and meets opposition by detachment, by simply getting "above it all". May spend a great deal of the time looking over his or her shoulder making sure that people or situations do not get too close. Unattached attitude, easygoing approach, observation, and aloofness. In reverse, can indicate paranoia and obsession with problems.

Sharman-Burke—A young person who may be very clever, but ruthless and unconcerned about the feelings of others. Extremely strong-willed and can be rather cold and calculating. In an event, may stand for situations complicated by rumour-spreading or gossip mongering.

Stewart—*Difficult.* A child or younger person who can have inner conflicts which will only be resolved with maturity and experience. A difficult nature which can manifest as obstinacy, a kind of inner strength, and willfulness. Can also be the intelligent child, perceptive beyond his or her years.

Waite—Alert and lithe. Authority, overseeing, secret service, vigilance, spying, examination, and the qualities thereto belonging. An indiscreet person will pry into the Querent's secrets.

Walker—*Skuld.* The leader of the Valkyries, a battle-maid who judged and received the souls of the dead. A sharp-minded woman of keen judgment and high spirit, stern and powerful and said to be a symbol of trouble and possible danger.

Wanless—*Learner.* Mastery of Narrowness and Dullness. The curious mind which investigates and explores the possibilities.

Riley—*Introverted Thinking with Intuition* (IN_T_P). The Initiator. Brings changes or knowledge through the spoken or written word.

KING OF DISCS

Arrien—*The Physical Doctor, the Healer.* A concern for the body and good health. Interest in health care and the ability to be a leader and a guide to others concerning health care issues.

Cowie—*Material Attainment.* This person has achieved material success and will fight to maintain it.

Crowley—The fiery part of Earth. Rules in the zodiac from 21° Leo to 20° Virgo. Refers in particular to mountains, earthquakes, and gravitation, but also represents Earth as the producer of life. Laborious and patient, concerned with material things, and stolid, but little intellectual grasp even of matters which concern him most closely.

Eakins—*The Spirit of Fertilization.* A sense of joyous practicality which is reflected in daily life. Mastering potential though self-knowledge. Steadiness, reliability, accomplishment, the epitome of material success.

Fairfield—*Releasing Something Physical.* An end to a physical, material, financial, or security pattern that is no longer working.

Greer—Established work. The ability to produce and be practical. A manager, financier, or craftsperson. Concerned with security and quality.

Noble—The person who has learned to work on the physical plane in such a way as to succeed at whatever he does. Knowing where to go and how to get there.

Pollack—Generous, even courageous, not especially given to adventure. Ordinary activity, accomplishments, social position, and success that is relaxed and enjoyed.

Sharman-Burke—A man who loves money and riches and is happy to amass as much as possible. Very clever in business matters, a bit of a financial wizard. He is not corrupt in his love for riches and earns his money through hard, patient effort. Generous with what he has and gladly shares the fruits of his labor with others.

Stewart—*Reliable.* A mature, dependable, and wise male, one upon whom others can, and often do, lay their burdens. The primal male ancestor of Earth who holds up the Mirror of the Elements and teaches that we must all learn balance and strength from within ourselves. The older man whom others instinctively trust, rely upon, and ask for help and advice.

Waite—A rather dark man, courageous, but somewhat lethargic in tendency. Valour, realizing intelligence, business and normal intellectual aptitude, sometimes mathematical gifts and attainments of this kind; success in these paths.

Walker—*Baal.* The mountain god who handed down the laws from sacred mountaintops to the men who climbed to the summit of his mountain throne to receive them. Stern, rocklike, authoritarian, heavy, tenacious, reliable, practical, and stable.

Wanless—*Achiever.* Mastery of Synergy and Reward. The drive to succeed and reach goals; achievements, manifestation, and producing.

Riley—*Extraverted Sensing with Thinking* (ESTP). The Producer. Ordering up, taking charge, manifesting, and releasing earthly things. A good financial provider because he likes to work and values material security.

QUEEN OF DISCS

Arrien—*The Physical Nutritionist.* The beautifying of the body and healthy nutrition is an issue. This might be the shedding of old unhealthy eating habits, beginning a new diet, or buying new clothes.

Cowie—*Aware of Limitations.* This person is aware of what is around her, how much she can do, and her limitations. What she can do, she does well, and it will be fruitful.

Crowley—Water of Earth. 21° Sagittarius to 20° Capricornus. The function of Earth as Mother. Passivity, usually in its highest aspect. Possesses immense funds of affection, kindness, greatness of heart; quiet, hard-working, sensible, and practical. Often has great difficulty rising above the material, and not particularly intelligent.

Eakins—*Threshold to Birth.* Experiencing a high level of compassion. Loving and nurturing the Earth, rejoicing in life, loving the physical plane and the opportunities to manifest spirit in physical form. Knowing that all forms of manifestation have the same source.

Fairfield—*Physical or Practical Competence.* Experiencing a high level of competence. Knowing how to create and maintain personal security.

Greer—Love of the world, earth, and life. Channels sensory information and practical knowledge. Inspires trust and provides security. Nurtures or stifles physical well-being.

Noble—The procreative and nurturing aspects of physical mothering. A personality grounded in the physical world, in harmony with Mother Nature. Health.

Pollack—A love and unity with the world. Knowing and believing in your self and in the magic of life. Allowing the hidden forces of the world to flow through you into your daily life. Or not trusting yourself in some specific situation.

Sharman-Burke— Practical and materialistic. She loves the good things in life and having acquired them, is then easily content to spend her life enjoying them. Knows what she wants and is satisfied when she gets it. Often rich because she works hard for material gain and is generous with her good fortune.

Stewart— *Practical.* A mature woman who is able to make specific forms out of potential substance, able to both nourish and define. Her power is that of practical wisdom on the human level, and on the inner level, applied wisdom of spiritual reflection.

Waite—A dark woman with greatness of soul and serious cast of intelligence. Opulence, generosity, magnificence, security, liberty. Augments presents from a rich relative; a rich and happy marriage for a young man.

Walker—*Erda.* The Mother Earth, the Teutonic Erda, who was worshiped by all primitive peoples as the universal life-giver and primary Muse. Generous, opulent, overflowing fertility, compassionate, comfortable, supporting, and abundant. A warm, nurturing personality.

Wanless—*Preserver.* Mastery of Reflection and Nurturing. Protecting and preserving by multiplying. Giving birth and nurturing creation.

Riley—*Introverted Sensing with Thinking* (IS̲TJ). The Provider. Because this Queen possesses inner security, she is able to provide it for others, and thus on an event level, this card has traditionally been called "the answer to prayers."

PRINCE OF DISCS

Arrien—*The Physical Architect.* Issues concerning physical activity, building, sports, good muscle tone. A steel-like determination to move forward with less blocks or obstacles. Also the gift of practical thinking.

Cowie—*Sitting Still, While Surveying Where He Wants to Go.* This person is not moving. He has the correct ideas, but so far lacks the motivation.

Crowley—Air of Earth. Rules from 21° Aries to 20° Taurus. The fluorescence and fructification of Air and Earth. Capable and enduring, steadfast and persevering, with great energy brought to bear upon the most solid of practical matters. Lacking almost entirely in emotion and makes no effort to understand ideas which are beyond his scope.

Eakins—*Moving Meditation.* Accomplishment through thoughtful meditation. Experiencing personal equilibrium and productivity. Being a master at growing the vegetation that sustains the spirit.

Fairfield—*Focused in the Material World.* Focusing intensely on establishing security. Putting all your attention into feeling safe, secure, and centered.

Greer—Doing or teaching your accomplishments. Using your knowledge. Committed to security. Stable and reliable but sometimes stubborn.

Noble—The life force expressed through the body and the senses. A builder. Working steadily toward goals, knowing what is wanted, and being singly focused on getting it.

Pollack—Responsible, hardworking, uncomplaining. In his best sense he is deeply rooted to the outer world and to simplicity. He is dedicated to purely practical matters, cutting himself off from the deeper things in Earth.

Sharman-Burke—Kind and trustworthy and will carry out a task to completion, no matter how long it takes. Reaches his goal because he never gives up and sets his sights on achievable rewards. Kind to animals and children and loves all nature. As an event, he stands for the eventual positive outcome of a situation which has dragged on for a long while or which has appeared fruitless.

Stewart—*Ambitious.* A young man or woman who seeks to benefit from changing his or her circumstances. Often a corresponding drive to work hard and will toil and strive for a chosen ambition. Ambitions range from the most banal to the most extreme, depending upon the factors of imagination, discretion, or judgement.

Waite—A slow, enduring, heavy man. Utility, serviceableness, interest, responsibility, rectitude—all on the normal and external plane. A useful man; useful discoveries.

Walker—*Merlin.* The mysterious figure in the Arthurian cycle of legends who prophesied the death of Vortigern at the hands of the Britons and is said to have completed the building of the temple which became Stonehenge. The defense of free expression, truth, honor, patience, and determination. Implies investigation of origins into things and a fearless following of clues, regardless of possible dangers.

Wanless—*Master.* Mastery of Change and Harvest. Productive power that has knowledge, responsibility, and discipline.

Riley—*Extraverted Sensing with Feeling* (E<u>S</u>FP). The Builder. Learns well and realistically from physical experiences and life. Concerned with building a strong financial future.

PRINCESS OF DISCS

Arrien—*The Pregnant One.* Issues of motherhood and pregnancy. May also be a birth of ideas, projects, identity, and aspects of oneself.

Cowie—*Too Absorbed in One Thing.* This person is too absorbed in an idea, situation, or emotion, so he is not enjoying what is around him.

Crowley—Earth of Earth. The brink of transfiguration. Strong and beautiful. Womanhood in its ultimate projection, containing all the characteristics of woman, and it depends entirely upon the influences to which she is subjected whether one or another becomes manifest.

Eakins— *Revelation.* Complete balance and total success. The brink of transformation. Something new is coming from the completion of a cycle, and the present is pregnant with the secret of the future.

Fairfield—*Security Risks.* Making a renewed commitment to a security base that was stagnating, or taking risks with some things that have been safe and secure in the past.

Greer—Open to knowledge, experience, and new skills. Vision quest. Seeks guidance from the earth. Examines values.

Noble—Pure elemental earth energy—the personality seeking its own name through solitary prayer and fasting. A time of solitude and learning to trust the wisdom of the body and instincts.

Pollack—The student lost in studies, feeling little concern for anything outside them. Actual work, study, and scholarship. Someone approaching any activity with these qualities of involvement and fascination.

Sharman-Burke—A child or young person who has respect for material things and takes the learning of new ideas seriously. Careful, hard-working, and diligent, though sometimes rather solemn. As an event, often signifies an opportunity to make money, usually starting from the bottom but with plenty of promise for the future.

Stewart—*Amenable.* A child or younger person who may be shaped or developed. Direct, uncomplicated children, mirroring their circumstances and other people around them. A being of tremendous potential as a result of impressionability of the mind and soul, and thus will be of great influence when he or she emerges into Spring.

Waite—A dark youth; a young officer or soldier; a child. Application, study, scholarship, reflection; news, messages, and the bringer thereof; also rule, management.

Walker—*Nimue.* Nemesis and consort of Merlin. A deity of Druidesses from whom, according to the oldest myths, Merlin is said to have learned his magic. Concentration, desire to learn, and application to scholarly pursuits.

Wanless—*Player.* Mastery of Commencement and Setback. The inner child's playfulness which creates with fantasy, imagination, and daydreams.

Riley—*Introverted Sensing with Feeling* (ISFJ). The Learner. The need to establish security, perhaps through study and introspection. Brings messages concerning health, money, work, or study.

NOTES

Chapter

5

CORRESPONDENCES

The Magician

Moreover, we note that the meaning of any symbol can be enriched by the application of the law of correspondences and its corollaries. In other words, objects possessing "common rhythm" barter some of their properties. . . . But we must also recall that the Scylla and Charybdis of symbolism are (firstly) devitalization through allegorical over-simplication, and (secondly) ambiguity arising from exaggeration of either its meaning or its ultimate implications; for in truth, its deepest meaning is unequivocal since, in the infinite, the apparent diversity of meaning merges into Oneness.

—J. E. Cirlot

A correspondence is something that is like something else. It is two or more objects, beings, or symmetries which possess grounds for commonality. It is, in a manner of speaking, an archetype coming eyeball to eyeball with itself and blinking.

Correspondences are rewarding and necessary companions in life, and in the tarot, because it is from seeing and recognizing them that we derive conscious knowledge. Some may claim correspondences have little to do with the art and skill of reading cards, yet it is correspondences which form the very basis and infrastructure of the tarot. Actually, not only of the tarot but of everything, but the tarot is a particularly susceptible form of recognizing them because of the cosmological nature of its symbology. The human *conscious* mind functions *solely* through association, or correspondences, in everything it thinks and learns. There is nothing that we are able to take in, feel, think, hear, touch, taste or see without associating it to something else. We are able to read the words on this page only because we were taught the alphabet and learned to make the letters of the alphabet into words. Then with equally formidable effort, we learned to make words into sentences and sentences into ideas. All of these symbols—letters, words, sentences, and ideas—were stored in our subconscious so magically and wholly that we no longer have to—or are even able to—remember how it was all originally done in the first place, nor do we have the least idea how we are doing it now at this very moment. It is impossible for us to go back and remember that before we could think we had to learn associations. The conscious mind functions only because of the automatic rote learning and memory of its subconscious, and in such a way are all words and symbols and everything our five senses perceive interpreted.

Correspondences are not linear, but circular. They spiral, and when we perceive them, if we perceive them at all, it is because we are recognizing in them one or more of our own personal angles on something. For instance, the Emperor does not correspond to certain stones, or gems, merely by the color of the stones, but also by their chemical composition, hardness, clarity, and shape. The Emperor corresponds to iron by chemical composition; to diamonds by resilience; to opaque stones by clarity; and to garnets, rubies, rhodonite, and all red-hued stones by color. The Emperor shares common ground with all of these minerals according to his *and* their innate attributes.

Color also corresponds to the tarot by any number of its various attributes. Color has four scales—that of the King, Queen, Prince, and Princess. Color can be either pigment or light. In pigment, the three primary colors are red, yellow, and blue, whereas in light, the three primary colors are red, green, and violet.

Correspondences are not clear-cut, nor are they ever separations of form and motion. Just as all colors are in actuality only one color—white—because white is the reflection of all colors, so does every person, regardless of any personal tarot image, correspond to all the other tarot images. The lower self of Huna is just as much in a Taurus as it is in a Pisces because we are all a perfect combination of all three selves. On the color wheel on page 203, correspondences are drawn among Huna, chakras, astrology, color, the calendar, and the tarot. None of these systems correspond *only* to those indicated. Rather, they are different angles of perception which interrelate in a circular, holographic integrity which, in reality, is completely equal.

The correspondences employed in this chapter are hopefully those which are most easily recognized. Correspondences with stones are done by color because the color of a stone is its most readily distinguishable feature to the average person. Correspondences to color are based on the King scale in the light spectrum because the King scale is closest to the primary colors, and the light spectrum is closer to the Source than physical pigment, thus more true to its origin.

Because every yin has its yang, every trump in the Major Arcana has a companion card. The tarot represents archetypes, and archetypes are perceived by us to be *symmetries of like-form and motion.* Normally, we either perceive something as motion or form, and rarely do we perceive something to be both simultaneously. In the Major Arcana one card represents the archetype's *form* while the other card represents the archetype's *motion.*

The correspondences offered here come from many sources. Most have been compiled over many years of research and observation. Fortunately, there are many genuine scholars in various fields of scientific and divinatory endeavor, and it is not difficult to find a general consensus. The only section explained at any length is "Word Archetypes," and this is because that is its nature. The reader may notice in "Word Archetypes" that occasionally a holiday is a week or more off from the astrological dates given. Because of the precession of the equinoxes, modern mankind's inability to make and maintain a calendar that works accurately over the ages, and because the original intent of most holidays has been forgotten or obscured, some dates have shifted; but even so, modern dates remain uncannily close to their origin. By "origin," is not meant a real honest-to-goodness beginning, but merely as close as historians are able to ascertain. The oldest written records archeologists have found thus far are Sumerian, dated about 6,000 years ago, and since it is apparent that such a great civilization as Sumeria did not simply spring up out of nowhere overnight, and also because of other archeological discoveries, we realize that civilizations are much older. The deluge, or biblical flood, is supposed to have occurred approximately 12,000 years ago. That civilizations existed prior to the deluge is presumable because nearly every culture has a legend of an ark being built by wise men in order to save human beings and animals from the great flood. It would have taken a lot of technological savvy and engineering skill to build huge seaworthy vessels, not to mention all the other particulars that had to be involved to save a few in each land. And we can propose that these legends have some basis in truth, which implies civilization is very, very old. So anything that is said to be "original" or "the beginning" is relative to our present extent of knowledge.

While compiling this information, I was struck by the synchronicities and hundreds of amazing unseen ways that life is attracted to itself. Each time I edited this chapter, I would see another synchronicity that I had not noticed before. Although there are few people who would claim any divinatory system—or any mortal system whatsoever—is perfect, these correspondences demonstrate that the roots go deep in divination. Life is timeless and spaceless. Life is infinite (spaceless) and eternal (timeless), which makes correspondences, or archetypes' likenesses to the original Archetype, in actuality, everything forever.

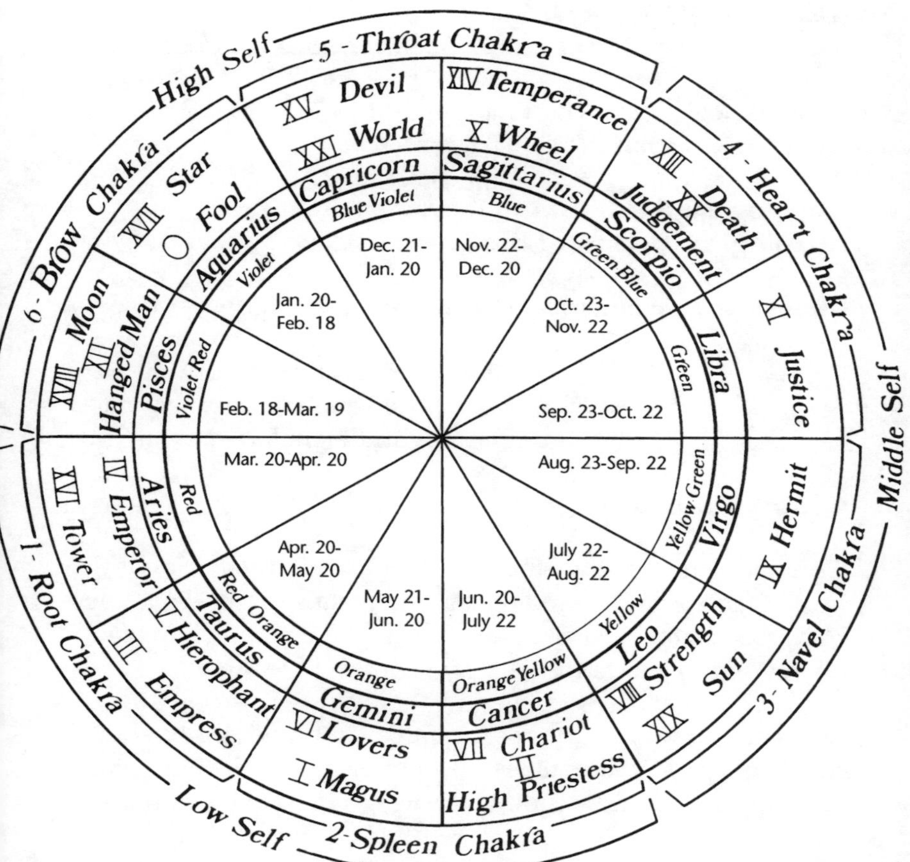

Wheel of Correspondences (Drawing by Jenny Lee Oldis).

IV—THE EMPEROR
XVI—THE TOWER

Astrological Sign: The Emperor—Aries
Astrological Planet: The Tower—Mars

Astrological Form[1] of the Emperor: I am.
Astrological Motion of the Tower: I seek myself.

Runestones: Emperor—*Teiwaz*, the rune of warrior energy, victory in battle, courage; *Tiw*, Old English God of War.
Tower—*Hagalaz*, the rune of disruptive natural forces and elemental power.

Colors: RED;[2] rose, pink

Chakra: First chakra—the Root Chakra. *Instincts.* Survival, health, genes and heredity, habits, matter, grounding, the body, sensuality, fear of bodily harm. The chakra where vital energy enters the body. The *Life Force.*

Stones: Ruby, garnet, rose quartz, red and pink coral, rubellite (pink tourmaline), watermelon tourmaline, pink kunzite, rhodonite, rhodochrosite, red beryl, cinnabar, barite, lepidolite, tigereye, all red hues of chalcedony.[3]

Notes: Emperor: C
Tower: C

---

[1]Form is the symmetry of motion.
[2]Color in caps is the primary color. Lower case indicates secondary and tertiary colors of the primary.
[3]Chalcedony is microcrystalline quartz which includes all agates, jaspers, carnelian, chrysophase, sard, onyx, sardonyx, plasma, and bloodstone. A stone which the Earth creates abundantly in a full spectrum of colors, chalcedony is applicable to everyone according to their own personal corresponding color to it.

Qaballah: Emperor: Simple Letter—Sight
Path—*Heh*, the Constituting Intelligence
Meaning—Window
Tower: Double Letter—Grace-Indignation
Path—*Peh*, the Exciting Intelligence
Meaning—Mouth

Plant Essences:[4] The Emperor—Ginger, Petitgrain, Bay
The Tower—Black Pepper, Pine, Sassafras

Psychic Energy: Instincts—the ability to "know" the correct thing to do at the exact moment it occurs. Because the Emperor is physical, he can't be relied on to know what to do in advance, but no one excels more than he at actions being correct, instant, and courageous at the exact moment they are needed.

Huna: In the ancient science/religion of Huna, people are said to consist of three selves: the low self, the middle self, and the High Self. The Emperor and the Tower correspond to the low self. The low self is that part of us which is our emotions, physical energy, survival instincts, memory, and the body's vital functions. Altogether, the low self corresponds to the first four houses, signs, and planets of the zodiac, the first two chakras, and with the Emperor, Tower, Hierophant, Empress, Lovers, Magician, Chariot, and High Priestess.

---

[4] Plant essences are contributed by Mary Greer from her book *The Essence of Magic: Tarot, Ritual, and Aromatherapy* (N. Hollywood, CA: Newcastle, 1993). She has drawn them from astrological affinities described by Paracelsus in the 16th century, the herbalist Culpeper in the 18th century, and the 19th century Hermetic Order of the Golden Dawn, and then checked them against modern studies of the psychological and physiological influences of plant essences.

Word Archetype: The Emperor

The word Emperor derives from the Latin *imperator*, meaning "commander," and the French *in + parare*, meaning "to prepare, to order." Archetypal words are: empress, empire, empathy, empower, power, import, important, impertinent, imperative, produce, and prepare.

The Emperor is the Father, *in-parare*, the parent, pa, papa, pop, padre, paternal, patriot, patron, pattern, patriarch, pater, person, pastor, St. Patrick (*Pa*tron Saint), and St. Peter (the rock on which the church was built). The Catholic church is seen in its socially acquired role of the Father by its affiliated titles: Father, papacy, pope, papal, papistry, and pontifex. In Sanskrit, the "Celestial Father" was Dyaus, and in Greek he was Zeu Pater.

Word Archetype: The Tower

The word Tower comes from the Middle English *tour*, *tor*, Old English *torr*, and Old French, *tor* and *tur*. Archetypal words are: torrent, torrid, tour, turbulent, turf, torn, tyrant, Tory, tear, terrible, and terrific.

The Day of Tuesday is named after Mars. The Old English God of War was known as *Tiw*, and the Norse called their God of War, *Tyr*, from whence comes the day sacred to Tyr, *Tyr's Day*, or Tuesday. The Romans also celebrated Tuesday as the Day of Mars, in Latin called *Dies Martis*. The Italians call it *Martedi*, and in French, Tuesday is *Mardi*. In Germanic lore, Mars was called *Mars Thincsus*.

March was named for Mars. During the Age of the Ram (circa 2,130 B.C.–A.D. 30) and up until the 16th century, March, rather than January, was the first month of the calendar year. That's why the word September derives from *septem*, meaning seven, because September was the seventh month of the year; October from *octo*, eight; November from *novem*, nine; and December from *decem*, ten. This changed in 1582 when Pope Gregory XIII adopted the Gregorian calendar to replace the Julian calendar and declared January 1 to be the beginning of the year. During the Age of the Ram, Aries was also the first sign of the zodiac and is still treated as such by most astrologers. Aries' color, red, is the first color on the color wheel because of all the colors red has the longest and slowest wave length, making red the most rudimentary. Aries' chakra is the first, or base, chakra, and Spring (Aries—March 20th-April 20th) is still considered the first season of the year.

Mars, as the primal beginning, remains one word that can still be easily spotted archetypally. The word March can be divided into *Mar*/ch (*Mar*s); M/*ar*/ch (*Ar*ies); and M/*arch*, (*arch*-e-type). The first three letters of March backwards spell *ram*, and the ram is the astrological animal of Aries and the Emperor. Mars comes from the Old Norse word *ar*, meaning "ye*ar*," and "god." Both Mars and Aries were the Warrior God known as *Ar*, which is found in the words M*ar*ch, M*ar*s, *Ar*ies, w*ar*, ye*ar*, and the first race of w*ar*riors, the *Ar*yans, and w*ar*rior words, such as *mar*tial, milit*ar*y, m*ar*ines, and *ar*my.

As the primal beginning it is also interesting that Arcanum XVI, the Tower, is sometimes called "The Lightning-Struck Tower," and the Emperor is referred to as "manifestation" because in the Qaballah's Tree of Life it is said that the world of matter is initially energized by the grounding of a "lightning flash" from above, and it is from this original transmission that the Divine becomes manifest and permeates all living things without exception.

V—THE HIEROPHANT
III—THE EMPRESS

Astrological Sign: The Hierophant—Taurus
Astrological Planet: The Empress—Venus

Astrological Form of the Hierophant: I have.
Astrological Motion of the Empress: I seek myself through what I have.

Runestones: Hierophant—*Fehu*, the stone of ambition, fulfillment, possessions, and cattle.
Empress—*Berkana*, the rune of growth, fertility, and new life.

Colors: RED-ORANGE; brown, peach

Chakra: First chakra—the Root Chakra. *Instincts.* Survival, health, genes and heredity, habits, matter, grounding, the body, sensuality, fear of bodily harm. The chakra where vital energy enters the body. The *Life Force.*

Stones: Dravite (brown, orange tourmaline), uvite (dark brown, green tourmaline); buergerite (iridescent dark brown tourmaline), tsilaisite (yellow, brown tourmaline), petrified wood, lodestone, meteorite, staurolite, tigereye, barite, red-orange and brown chalcedony.

Notes: Hierophant—C#
Empress—F#

Qaballah: Hierophant: Simple Letter—Hearing
Path—*Vah*, The Triumphal or Eternal Intelligence
Meaning—Nail or Hook

Empress: Double Letter—Wisdom-Folly
Path—*Daleth*, the Illuminating Intelligence
Meaning—Door

Plant Essences: The Hierophant—Thyme, Cardamom, Bois de Rose
The Empress—Ylang-ylang, Vanilla, Rose

Psychic Energy: Artists and Artisans—the ability to put into a manifested physical medium what is perceived on the inner planes. This medium can take any physical form, such as painting, drawing, decorating, hosting, cooking, fashion, mechanics, carpentry, but it is always an artistic and harmonious outer expression of inner vision.

Huna: The Hierophant and the Empress correspond to the low self, that part of us which provides all our emotions, physical energy, survival instincts, memory, and maintains the body's vital functions. In humanistic psychology the three selves of Huna correspond to the subconscious (low self), conscious (middle self), and superconscious (High Self).

Word Archetype: The Hierophant

The word Hierophant is a combination of two Greek words, *hiero* meaning "sacred" or "holy," and *phainein* meaning "to bring to light." Hierophant is synonymous to High Priest, and High Priest remains the title of the card in many decks. Archetypal words are: higher, height, heir, heifer, heist, hierarchy, and hieroglyphics.

The Hierophant is Taurus and the month of April (April 20-May 20). April is named after the sacred Egyptian bull, *Apis*, who carried the Sun and Moon on its back. Millennia later, when the Greeks changed the calendar, they must have been happy enough with April's original Egyptian name, which was, not coincidentally, a synonym for their Greek Goddess of Beauty, *Aphrodite*.

Although at first glance it seems the Hierophant, or High Priest, should be paired with the High Priestess, not with the Empress, this mating is actually entirely appropriate. In ancient cultures such as Egypt and Sumeria, the High Priest and the King were sometimes the same person, as often was the Empress and High Priestess. And if they weren't the same person, they were nearly always of the same family. It was sacred law, in order to maintain both the purity of blood line and the transmission of sacred knowledge, that royalty and the priesthood marry within the family. This is also why we see similarities in the etymological root of "The Emperor" with "The Hierophant," both being the parent, padre, and papacy. The blending of state and religion is as old as the institutions which maintain them and is still seen today in many forms. For example, the Catholic Church is tax-exempt from the government, it's the largest landowner of any organization in the world, and its power is subservient to none, except perhaps government's.

Word Archetype: The Empress

The Empress is from the Latin word base *imperare*, which means "to command," the Middle English *emperesse*, and the Old French feminine form of *empereor*, meaning "to empower." Archetypal words are similar to those of the Emperor: empire, empower, power, prowess, import, important, impertinent, and imperative.

The god-goddess called *Apis* in early Egypt, and *Aphrodite* in Greece, was known as *Venus* to the later Romans. Venus was often called "The Great Cow Who Gives Birth to the Sun." Like Apis and Aphrodite, Venus is associated with love, passion, and sex, thus from her originated the English word for diseases associated with sex, "venereal disease."

To the Romans, Friday was *Dies Veneris* (day of Venus). In French, Friday is *Vendredi*, and in Italian it is *Venerdi.* But it is to the Norse that we owe the present English name of our day Friday, *Freya's Day*, in honor of the Norse Sea-Goddess of Love and Beauty, *Freya*. Because *Freya* was a sea-goddess, the Norse ate fish on Friday to arouse Freya's passion and love, from whence originally came the Catholic decree of eating only fish on Friday.

This goddess has also been known by the names of Artha, Hretha, Urtha, Erda, Ertha, Heartha, Astarte, Astoreth, Ishtar, Eostre, Hestia, Esther, Earth and Easter. The holiday of *Easter* is still celebrated on its original date, the first Sunday after the first full moon after the vernal equinox. The vernal equinox is the day when the Sun's light and the Moon's light are of equal duration, offering equitable entry into both the underworld and the upper worlds at which time the gods and goddesses could come and go. At one time Easter was the *Holiday* (HolyDay or Whole Day) that ancient cultures celebrated to honor all goddesses who visited the underworld and returned. In Christianity, it was Jesus, after his crucifixion, who visited the underworld for three days and returned.

The Old English name for the month of April was *Ostermonath*, or *Easter-monath* because it was sacred to *Eastre*, the Empress—Goddess of Spring. In Germany, April is still called *Ostermonath.*

The Empress is the Mother, ma, mama, mommy, matriarch, matron, maternal, matrimony, matrix, money, monetary, matter, and the material. She is De-meter, the Earth Goddess. The giving and nurturing of the Goddess is where we get the expression, "Thank Goodness!" or "Thank Goddess!"

VI—THE LOVERS
I—THE MAGICIAN

Astrological Sign: The Lovers—Gemini
Astrological Planet: The Magician—Mercury

Astrological Form of the Lovers: I think.
Astrological Motion of the Magician: I seek myself through what I think.

Runestones: Lovers—*Gebo,* the stone of partnership; a gift.

Magician—*Ansuz,* the messenger rune; the mouth which is the source of divine utterance.

Colors: ORANGE; copper

Chakra: Second chakra—the Spleen Chakra. *Emotions.* Movement, pleasure, polarities, instinct to nurture and to be nurtured, socialization, sexuality, choices, pride, fear of being left out. The chakra which provides our *life energy and vitality.*

Stones: Copper ore, barite, dravite tourmaline, citrine, topaz, orange coral, all orange chalcedony.

Notes: Lovers—D
Magician—E

Qaballah: Lovers: Simple Letter—Smell
Path—*Zain,* The Disposing Intelligence
Meaning—Sword or Armor
Magician: Double Letter—Life-Death
Path—*Beth,* The Intelligence of Transparency
Meaning—House

Plant Essences: The Lovers—Lavender, Geranium, Peppermint
The Magician—Dill, Lemongrass, Storax or Benzoin

Psychic Energy: Active Magic and Synchronicity—the ability to magnetize and materialize coincidences, omens, images, and messages into one's life.

Huna: The low self. That part of us which provides all our emotions, physical energy, survival instincts, memory, and maintains the body's vital functions. In behavioral psychology, the low self corresponds to the id, and the middle self to the ego, but the High Self does not correspond to the superego.

Word Archetype: The Lovers

Lovers (or the word love) comes from the Aryan *libet*, *lubido*, and *luff-luf*; from the Sanskrit *lobha* and *lubh* meaning "to desire"; and from the Old English *lufu*, meaning "to free," or "to please." Word archetypes of love are: liberty, libel, liberal, library, libido, Libra, laugh, luck, lovely, lobe, lust, liaison, life, and live.

The Lovers is the astrological equivalent of Gemini (May 21-June 20). The month of June is named after the Roman Goddess, *Juno*. Juno was the wife of Jupiter, sometimes called *Juno Lucina*. She was the Goddess of Marriage, and it was said that wherever she went she was followed by her messenger, Isis, who was so brilliant that she could always be seen in the skies above Juno. This connection can be seen in the Lovers card today when an angel (or Cupid) is hovering in the sky over the Lovers. In olden lore it was thought to be lucky to marry in June and unlucky to marry in May. The Lovers is also connected to other celestial twins, such as the Norse God Loki and his twin brother, Baldur;

Phrixis and Helle; Apollo and Aramis; Remus and Romulus; and possibly Jesus and a twin brother, Thomas.[5]

The expression "Good luck," comes from the original farewell aphorism of: "God loves you," or "God loves."

Word Archetype: The Magician

The word Magician comes from the Middle English *magik*, the Middle French *magique*, and the Latin *magus*, meaning "mage" or "seer." Word archetypes are: magic, magi, image, imagination, messenger, motion, memory, magistrate, magnet, magnificent, magnify, magpie, majestic, majesty, magnanimous, Magna Carta, magna cum laude, and Mercury.

The Magician is associated with the arcana of both the Lovers and the Hermit. For archetypes associated with the Magician, see the Hermit.

---

[5] There is evidence that the figure of Jesus was a twin. See *The Messianic Legacy* by Baigent, Leigh, and Lincoln. Also *The Nag Hammadi Library*; The Gospel of Thomas (II, 2); The Book of Thomas the Contender (II, 7). In Hebrew, *Thomas* means "twin."

VII—THE CHARIOT
II—THE HIGH PRIESTESS

Astrological Sign: The Chariot—Cancer
Astrological Planet: The High Priestess—Moon

Astrological Form of the Chariot: I feel.
Astrological Motion of the Moon: I seek myself through what I feel.

Runestones: Chariot—*Ehwaz*, the rune of movement, gradual progress, dwelling places, and horses.
High Priestess—*Othila*, the rune of retreat, separation, inheritance, and the home.

Colors: ORANGE-YELLOW; gold. Also white and silver[6]

Chakra: Second chakra—the Spleen Chakra. *Emotions.* Movement, pleasure, polarities, instinct to nurture and to be nurtured, socialization, sexuality, choices, pride, fear of being left out. The chakra which provides our *life energy and vitality.*

Stones: Gold, silver, and platinum. Amber, pyrite, golden beryl (topaz), citrine, all orange-yellow chalcedony. Also clear quartz crystal, diamond, moonstone, pearl, spinel, white coral, opal, zircon, and gray or white fluorites and chalcedony.

Notes: Chariot—D#
High Priestess—G#

---

[6]The Chariot and the High Priestess (and astrologically, Cancer, the Moon, and the 4th house) are said to be the exit from the physical world into the higher worlds, so they also have white and silver as their colors.

Qaballah: Chariot: Simple Letter—Speech
Path—*Cheth*, the House of Influence
Meaning—Fence, Enclosure
High Priestess: Double Letter—War—Peace
Path—*Gimel*, the Uniting Intelligence
Meaning—Camel

Plant Essences: The Chariot—Coriander, Carrot, Labdanum, Roman Camomile
The High Priestess—Camphor, Lemon, Jasmine

Psychic Energy: Clairsentience—means "clear feeling." The ability to "feel" other people's emotions. This feeling is not always received consciously, but many times is felt as a subconscious emotional transference, so the clairsentient often feels moody or disturbed without knowing why.

Huna: The low self. The self which is our emotions, physical energy, survival instincts, memory, and maintains the body's vital functions. Collectively, the three selves of Huna correspond to: low self (animals); middle self (people); and High Self (Angels). Individually, they correspond to: low self (the anima-animus in the psyche); middle self (the individual); and High Self (one's own personal Guardian Angel).

Word Archetype: The Chariot

The word Chariot comes from the Old French *char* and the Latin *carrus*, meaning "cart," and is equivalent to car. Archetypal words are: carriage, charley horse, chauffeur, carry, char, charity, charwoman, character, charade, charge, charisma, care, charlatan, charm, chart, chase, chaste, chastity, chateau, carton, and chasm.

The Chariot is strongly associated with the chasm. In the Qaballah, on the Qaballistic Tree of Life, the Moon and the Chariot are the paths which cross Daath, the Abyss, the Great Gulf between the Supernal Triangle and all beneath. The Abyss is understood to be the condition of no-thing because it is every-thing.

In astrology, the Chariot is the 4th house of Cancer and the Moon, which symbolizes the exit from the physical world into the higher realms. When the Chariot is solar, it is driven by solar and spiritual animals, such as white or golden swans, dogs, horses, or gryphons. When the Chariot is lunar, it is driven by lunate and magical animals, such as white or silver lions, deer, or doves. The Roman Sun God, Apollo, drove a golden chariot, and in Christianity, Elijah was taken to heaven in a flaming chariot of fire. In Scandinavian lore, Freya's lunar chariot was drawn by moon cats. In Mithra, Luna is depicted in a one-horse chariot with Luna on the left and Sol on the right. Nearly all former religions symbolized their gods with or as animals. The charioteer may represent the conscious mind (person), either being led, driven, or in partnership with the subconscious (animal). A peaceful union took them both to the Sun (Angel), which represented the divine unity of the trinity.

Word Archetype: The High Priestess

High means "hill" or "lofty." The word *Priestess* comes from the Old English *preost* and the Middle English *priest*, meaning "old" and "elder." Word archetypes are: high, height, preach, priest, prier (an inquisitive person), pristine, private, prim, princess, prioress, and preordain.

The High Priestess is associated with the Moon. The Latin for Moon is *luna*, which is why the Moon is said to be "lunar." Folklore has it that people tend to get a little "loony," or "lunatical" around a Full Moon and this may be true, or it may be a corruption of astrological lore that says people get a little more like whatever it is they already are around the phase of the Moon under which they are born.

For the Romans, Monday was *Dies Lunae*, Day of the Moon. For us, the Moon's day is Moonday, or Monday. The Moon is also where we derive the name of *month*, or "moonth." Twenty-nine and one-half days is the period that divides two new Moons, and four weeks (4 × 7) are the four quarters of the Moon.

The High Priestess and the Empress both represent the feminine principle, which sometimes results in confusion between the two arcana. The Empress is the feminine principle on the conscious level, while the High Priestess is the feminine principle on the subconscious level. The Empress is the obtainable physical mother—the mama and mom, while the High Priestess is the unobtainable celestial mother—Mary, Maya, and the Mona Lisa. The High Priestess and the Moon are found in nearly all religions, and also in the name of our month of *May*, named after *Maia*, a Greek and Roman Goddess. *Miriam* was a Canaanite goddess, *Mariamma*, a Hindu goddess, and *Morgana* was the High Priestess of the Druids. *Minerva* was the Roman Goddess of Wisdom, and *Maya* was the Buddhist virgin of God, mother of Buddha. *Mary* was the Christian virgin-mother of Jesus, *Mary of Bethany* was the name of the sister of Lazarus and Martha, and *Mary the Magdalen*, according to recently discovered buried texts, was the consort and 13th disciple of Jesus.

VIII—STRENGTH
XIX—THE SUN

Astrological Sign: Strength—Leo
Astrological Planet: The Sun—Sun

Astrological Form of Strength: I will.
Astrological Motion of the Sun: I seek myself through what I create.

Runestones: Strength—*Uruz*, the run of strength, sacrificial animals, and physical endurance.
The Sun—*Sowelu*, the rune of wholeness and the life forces; means "the Sun."

Colors: YELLOW; mustard

Chakra: Third chakra—the Navel Chakra (solar plexus). *Will/power.* Power, will, wishes, metabolism, humor, wisdom, ego, attitudes, prejudices, reactions, ideas, intellectual analysis, thinking, fear of rejection. The chakra of the *intellect.*

Stones: Topaz, amber, citrine, tsilaisite tourmaline, yellow fluorites, yellow chalcedony.

Notes: Strength—E#
Sun—D

Qaballah: Strength: Simple Letter—Taste
Path—*Teth*, The Intelligence of all the Activities of the Spiritual Beings
Meaning—Snake
Sun: Double Letter—Fertility—Barrenness
Path—*Resh*, The Collecting Intelligence
Meaning—Head

Plant Essences: Strength—Rosemary, Juniper Berry, Orange
The Sun—Cinnamon, Mandarin or Tangerine, Frankincense

Psychic Energy: Passive Magic. The ability to create magic by trusting the plan of operation to God. The most potent kind of magic that comes with release from personal desire for one's own ends, patience through faith, and power through acceptance.

Huna: The middle self. That part of each of us that has the ability to reason, plan, analyze, learn, and use logic. It is also that part of us which draws opinions and makes judgments. It corresponds to the third and fourth chakras, the astrological houses Leo through Scorpio, and the eight Arcana of Strength, the Sun, Hermit, Magician, Justice, Empress, Death, and Judgment.

Word Archetype: Strength

The word Strength comes from the Old English *strenghu*, Old High Greek *strengi*, and the Latin *stringere*, means "severe, strict," and "stringent." *Stanae* is Latin for "omens," and the Roman Goddess of Strength and Optimism was *Stenia*. Word archetypes are: strong, strong-minded, strong-willed, stroke, strenuous, strike, and string. In mythology, and in actual practice, the word *string* implies joining, binding, and union.

Strength and the Sun rule July which corresponds to the astrological sign of Leo (July 22-August 22). July is named after G. Julius Caesar, a Roman general and statesman born in July, 100 B.C.

In early Dynasty Egypt, July was dedicated to the star *Sirius*. Sirius, the brightest star in the sky, is located in the constellation of *Canis Major*, the Big Dog, and is commonly called the Dog Star. Thousands of years ago Sirius began its helical rising with the Sun and for a few minutes each morning cast brilliant red rays across the land. Sirius shone brightest the last days of July, all of August, and part of September. The procession of the equinoxes has now carried Sirius' helical rising to July 3rd through August 11th, and it no longer casts brilliant red rays for us to see, but we still call the latter part of summer, "the Dog Days of Summer."

The Strength card depicts a person either fighting or at peace with an animal, usually a lion. In the Tao, the Void is called the "lion ball," denoting emptiness, withdrawal of the mind. This card may hearken back to the Age of the Sun—to a time, according to the ancients, when people did not eat animals.[7] The word animal derives from the Latin *animalus*, meaning literally "breathing, living."

Word Archetype: The Sun

The word sun comes from the Latin root of *sol.* Word archetypes are: the runestone Sowelu, son, soul, solar, song, sung, sunny, solace, soldier, sole, solemn, solicit, solicitous, solid, solstice, solo, solution, and solve.

The Latin for Sunday was *Dies Solis*, meaning "Day of the Sun." We call the Sun's day, Sunday. The Sun is associated with the Sun Gods of Adonis, Apollo, Adin, Odin, Amun, and Adamas. Before Paradise was called the Garden of Eden with the advent of Christianity, it was known as the Garden of Adonis, Amun, and Odin. In all Gardens of Paradise there are two trees—the Tree of Life and the Tree of Knowledge. Eden is called Paradise, or Paradise Lost, because it is supposed to be where angels, mankind, animals, and nature lived in perfect accord together before the Fall. According to the *Book of Enoch*, the Fall may have been caused because we began to kill trees, animals, and one another.

---

[7]See Bibliography. *Man into Wolf* by Robert Eisler; *Cults of the Dog* by M.O. Howie; and *The Beast Within* by Adam Douglas, p. 25. Also *The Koran*, VI, p. 92; *King James Bible*, Genesis 1: 29-30; Ecclesiastes 3:18-19; *Book of Isaiah*, lxvi: 3; *The Bhagavad Gita*; *The Book of Enoch*, ch. 7; *The Book of the Secrets of Enoch*, ch. 58, 59.

It happened after the sons of men had multiplied in those days, that daughters were born to them, elegant and beautiful.

And when the angels, the sons of heaven, beheld them, they became enamoured of them, saying to each other, Come, let us select for ourselves wives from the progeny of men, and let us beget children . . .

. . . Then they took wives, each choosing for himself; whom they began to approach, and with whom they cohabited; teaching them sorcery, incantations, and the dividing of roots and trees.

And the women conceiving brought forth giants,

Whose stature was each three hundred cubits. These devoured all which the labour of men produced; until it became impossible to feed them;

When they turned themselves against men, in order to devour them;

And began to injure birds, beasts, reptiles, and fishes, to eat their flesh one after another, and to drink their blood.

Then the earth reproved the unrighteous.[8]

[8]Elizabeth Clare Prophet, *Forbidden Mysteries of Enoch* (Livingston, MT: Summit University Press, 1983), ch. 7.

IX—THE HERMIT
I—THE MAGICIAN

Astrological Sign: Virgo
Astrological Planet: Mercury

In astrology, Mercury rules both Gemini and Virgo. In tarot, he is associated with both the Lovers and the Hermit.

Astrological Form of the Hermit: I learn.
Astrological Motion of the Magician: I seek myself through what I serve.

Runestones: Hermit—*Jera,* the runestone of harvest, beneficial outcomes, and the span of one year.
—*Algiz,* the rune of protection, the spiritual warrior; the one whose battle is with himself.

Colors: YELLOW-GREEN (lime green)

Chakra: Third chakra—the Navel Chakra (solar plexus). *Will/power.* Power, will, wishes, metabolism, humor, wisdom, ego, attitudes, prejudices, reactions, ideas, intellectual analysis, thinking, fear of rejection. The chakra of the *intellect.*

Stones: Peridot, moldavite, jade, jadeite, aventurine, green kunzite, the green-containing tourmalines of uvite, feridravite, verdelite, and watermelon; yellow-green fluorites and chalcedony.

Notes: Hermit—F
Magician—E

Qaballah: Hermit: Simple Letter—Sexual Love
Path—*Yod*, The Intelligence of Will
Meaning—Hand
Magician: Double Letter—Life-Death
Path—*Beth*, the Intelligence of Transparency
Meaning—House

Plant Essences: The Hermit—Sage, Wintergreen, Caraway
The Magician—Dill, Lemongrass, Storax, or Benzoin

Psychic Energy: Meditation—the ability to surrender the conscious mind to the superconscious, the human key which unlocks exploration and knowledge of the whole self.

Huna: The middle self. That part of us that reasons, plans, analyzes, learns, uses logic, draws opinions, and makes judgments. It makes laws, believes it can decide justice, and lives in time and space. In humanistic psychology, it corresponds to the *conscious*, or *conscious mind.*

Word Archetype: The Hermit

The word Hermit comes from the Middle English *eremite* and the Old French *eremita*, meaning "recluse, solitary," and "living in the desert." Word archetypes are: the runestone Jera,[9] hermaphrodite, hermetic, Hermes, hematite, hemoglobin, hemisphere, errand, heretic, heron, heriot, heal, and hermetically sealed (impervious to external influence).

The Hermit is associated with *Hermes Trismegistus*, whose name means "Hermes thrice Greatest." Hermes the

[9]Prior to the 17th century there was no "J" in most languages. Words that now begin with J derive from words that once began with other letters, commonly H, I, K and L, i.e., Jerasalam was once Hera-salam, and Jera was Hera.

megistus, or the magician, was the legendary god-savior, king, healer, teacher, astrologer, astronomer, priest, architect, alchemist, and prolific writer-scholar. The Greeks called him Hermes, the Romans called him Mercury, and to the Egyptians he was their god Thoth, or Thot (sic, thought). He was supposed to have written hundreds of books in his lifetime which are believed to have been mostly destroyed by the Christians during the sacking and burning of Alexandria in 30 B.C. and again in A.D. 411. He taught agriculture and numbers, originated the seven liberal arts and the 10,000 names of God in *Tao*. (One can see why the Romans put wings on this guy's feet.)

The Hermit is associated with the month of August and the sign of Virgo (August 23–September 22). Before it was called August, this month was called *Sextilis*, the sixth month. The Romans re-named it after Augustus Caesar, the first Roman Emperor, who came to power in A.D. 14. But the name Augustus derives from the Latin *augur*, meaning "to increase by foretelling events by omens," a form of magic attributed to Mercury, Hermes, and the Magician.

Word Archetype: The Magician

The word Magician comes from the Middle English *magik*, the Middle French *magique*, and the Latin *magice*, meaning "mage" or "seer." Word archetypes are: magic, magus, magi, image, imagination, messenger, motion, memory, magistrate, magnet, magnificent, magnify, magpie, majestic, majesty, magnanimous, Magna Carta, magna cum laude, and Mercury.

The Magician is associated with the Hebrew Magen David (maghen Davidh), two superimposed triangles drawn in the shape of a six-pointed star. It is also called the Shield of David, the Seal (or Signet) of Solomon, and the Star of Zion.

Hermes has been associated with nearly every religion that has ever existed, and it was maintained by Sir William

Jones, and Thomas Maurice writing in 1801, that this is demonstrated by similitude of rites, symbols, and the assignation of Wednesday to Hermes in most cultures, and that Hermes was in fact "the elder Buddha of India."[10]

In India Wednesday is assigned to Buddha and is called *Boodh* or *Buddawar.*

In Rome, Wednesday was *Dies mercurii,* the Day of Mercury.

In Italy, Wednesday is *Mercoledi,* meaning Day of Mercury.

In Northern Europe, the Norse Mercury was Odin, or *Woden,* the God of Memory and Thought, after which we get Wednesday—from *Wodnes-daeg,* or *Woden's Day.*

---

[10]M.O. Howie, *The Cults of the Dog* (Saffron Walden, England: C. W. Daniel Company, 1972), p. 92.

XI—JUSTICE
III—EMPRESS

Astrological Sign: Justice—Libra
Astrological Planet: The Empress—Venus
In astrology, Venus rules both Taurus and Libra. In tarot, she is associated with both Justice and the Hierophant.

Astrological Form of Justice: I weigh (balance).
Astrological Motion of the Empress: I seek myself through what I unite.

Runestones: Justice—*Thurisaz*, the rune of the gateway, the place of non-action.
—*Eihwaz*, the rune of defense; a yew-tree, rune magic, runic avertive powers.

Colors: GREEN; emerald green, dark-green

Chakra: Fourth Chakra—the Heart Chakra. *Change.* Breath, balance, relationship, truth, compassion, empathy, hope, brotherhood, healing, sense of time, changes, evolution, growth, self-security, possessiveness, fear of loss. The Heart Chakra is the chakra of *harmony/ sympathy* and is the center of the self.

Stones: Emerald, jade, green tourmaline, chromdravite (dark green tourmaline), malachite, green and dark green chalcedonies and fluorites.

Notes: Justice—F#
Empress—F#

Qaballah: Justice: Simple Letter—Work
Path—*Lamed*, The Faithful Intelligence
Meaning—Ox Goad
Empress: Double Letter—Wisdom-Folly
Path—*Daleth*, The Illuminating Intelligence
Meaning—Door

Plant Essences: Justice—Myrtle, Palmarosa, Spearmint
The Empress—Ylang-ylang, Vanilla, Rose

Psychic Energy: Magnetism, charisma—the ability to draw resources, people, and situations that one needs or wants. This gift is sometimes not recognized by the person possessing it, but others see it.

Huna: The middle self. The self which reasons, plans, analyzes, learns, uses logic, draws opinions, and makes judgments. The three selves correspond to three kinds of love:

Low Self	Subconscious	Eros (erotic, or physical and emotional, love);
Middle Self	Conscious	Philia (brotherly love, or love of one's own kind);
High Self	Superconscious	Agape (love of all things equally).

Word Archetype: Justice

The word Justice derives from the Latin *justus* and the French *jus*, meaning "right." Word archetypes are: jury, Judaism, Judas, jurisprudence, judge, jurisdiction, just, justify, and juxtapose (to place side by side).

Justice rules from September 23 to October 22nd, and corresponds with the Goddesses of balance and truth in which the balance of yin is weighed against yang. A very old Sanskrit title for Justice was the Goddess of the Primordial

Abyss, *Kala-Nath*. As an underworld goddess of the Egyptians, Justice was called *Am-Mut*, "devourer of hearts." Before she became the Great Goddess *Devi* of the Hindus, they knew her as *Kali Ma*, the Creating, Preserving, and Destroying Goddess, married to the God, Shiva. To the Scandinavians, she was *Kalma*, the haunter of cemeteries. In these images and names, we see her relationship with both the creator-destroyer aspect of Justice (Kal) and with the Empress (*Ma*). Like Justice, these goddesses are often depicted with a sword in one hand, and a cup or article of peace and beauty in the other hand. The name *Kal* is archetypal with *Ka*, the Egyptian word for "soul," and the word *kalends*, meaning calendar, perhaps because the soul is caught in time and space, and it is timespace through which the soul learns, and is always eventually decreed justice accordingly.

Word Archetype: The Empress

The Empress is from the Latin word base *imperare*, which means "to command," the Middle English *emperesse*, and the Old French feminine form of *empereor*, meaning "to empower." Archetypal words are: empire, empower, power, prowess, import, important, impertinent, and imperative. For archetypes, see V-The Hierophant and III-The Empress.

XIII—DEATH
XX—JUDGMENT

Astrological Sign: Death—Scorpio
Astrological Planet: Judgment—Pluto

Astrological Form of Death: I need.
Astrological Motion of Judgment: I seek myself through what I need.

Runestones: Death—*Dagaz*, the rune of breakthrough, transformation, and day. The rune of "God's Light."
Judgment—*Kano*, the rune of opening; fire, torch, dispelling darkness.

Colors: GREEN-BLUE; turquoise.

Chakra: Fourth chakra—the Heart Chakra. *Change.* Breath, balance, relationship, truth, compassion, empathy, hope, brotherhood, healing, sense of time, changes, evolution, growth, self-security, possessiveness, fear of loss. The Heart Chakra is the chakra of *harmony/sympathy* and center of the self.

Stones: Turquoise, aquamarine, blue topaz, amazonite, blue coral, indicolite (blue-green tourmaline), abalone, green-blue fluorites and chalcedonies.

Notes: Death—G
Judgment—C

Qaballah: Death: Simple Letter—Movement
Path—*Num*, The Imaginative Intelligence
Meaning—Fish
Judgment: Maternal Letter—Fire
Path—*Shin*, The Perpetual Intelligence
Meaning—Tooth

Plant Essences: Death—Cypress, Rue, Opoponax
Judgment—Basil, Pennyroyal, Anise

Psychic Energy: Healing—the ability to heal on one or more levels—the physical, emotional, mental, or spiritual. Doctors and people in the medical profession are often born under the sign of Scorpio. Also *deja vu* (French for "already seen")—the feeling of having previously experienced something actually being encountered for the first time.

Huna: The middle self. The self which reasons, plans, analyzes, learns, uses logic, draws opinions, and makes judgments. Life possesses three selves. The middle self is that part of any consciousness which is conscious to the perceiver as opposed to the part which is unconscious.

Word Archetype: Death

The word death comes from the middle English, *deeth*, akin to the Old Norse *dauthi* and *deyja*, "to die." Word archetypes are: the runestone Dagaz, teeth, daunt, dear, dearth, deity, devil, deva, destiny, desire, destination, determine, deal, deep, deem, dead, die, deacon, and *deja vu*.

Death was the old Norse God of the Underworld, *Daath*. Daath is also the name of the "Invisible Sephira" on the Qaballistic Tree of Life. In Qaballistic doctrine the level of Daath is as far as the High Self can rise, the High Self, or Holy Spirit, being that multiple-spirit-in-one who guides and directs the personality through various incarnations. When complete integration of the soul-personality-spirit is achieved, or when all parts of our Self unite with our one Oversoul, then Daath, or the Abyss, is crossed to the Divine Essence of Kether.

Word Archetype: Judgment

The word judgment comes from the Latin *judicare,* and the Middle English *juggen,* meaning "to decide." Word archetypes are: Judeo, Judaism, Judah, Judas, Jude, judicial, jury, judge, juggler, juggernaut, and jugular.

Death and Judgment rule from October 23 to November 22. October derives from *octo,* which means eight, originating when the calendar started at the Vernal Equinox (then called March lst), and October was the eighth month of the year.

It is on the last day of October that the holiday, Hallowe'en, is celebrated. Hallowe'en is the eve, or *een,* of All Hallow's Day, November 1st. Over 2000 years ago, the Celtic order of priestly Druids celebrated the eve of *Samhain,* the Celtic Lord of the Dead, every October 31st. After the Romans invaded England, the Catholic Church forbade the observance of Samhain, but in spite of systematically persecuting and slaughtering Druids, the people continued to find ways to celebrate the holiday, so in the 5th century A.D. Pope Gregory declared November 1st to be All Saint's Day, hoping thereby to obscure pagan rites into Christian affiliation. Hallowe'en and All Hallow's Day, congruent to respective culture and time, have also been known as All Hallowmass, All Soul's Day, Mallowmas, the Druidic Feast of the Spirits of the Air, the Day of the Dead (Mexico and South America), Rite of Hella (Scandinavia), and the Isia or Helaria (Egyptian recovery from death and rebirth of Osiris). It is the day of the year when the veil between the living and the dead is the thinnest, thus a time when the dead can talk to the living. There is some evidence that originally it was in remembrance of a great cataclysm that occurred millennia ago, thus another correspondence to Death, Judgment Day, souls, and communicating with the dead.

The Celts honored "The Apple Woman" on this day, who was the goddess of both life and death. She gave away magical apples which were laced either with a benevolent enchantment or a malevolent poison. From this may have evolved our tradition of Trick or Treat.[11] It is interesting, if sad, that Halloween treats have once again come around to the danger of containing poison or death in modern times. The Apple Woman lived in a beautiful secluded forest by a holy river, and this may also be whence we derive the apple as the forbidden fruit which bestows life or death, for nowhere in the Bible is the apple mentioned as being the food of which Adam and Eve ate.

---

[11]W. Y. Evans-Wentz mentions that it was an original Celtic belief that part of all harvest was to be given to the Fairy World. "On November Eve [formerly November 11th] it is not right to gather blackberries or sloes, nor after that time as long as they last. On November Eve the fairies pass over all such things and make them unfit to eat. If one dares to eat them afterwards one will have serious illness." *The Fairy Faith in Celtic Countries* (New York: University Books, 1966), pp. 38–39.

XIV—TEMPERANCE
X—WHEEL OF FORTUNE

Astrological Sign: Temperance—Sagittarius
Astrological Planet: Wheel of Fortune—Jupiter

Astrological Form of Temperance: I perceive.
Astrological Motion of the Wheel of Fortune: I seek, therefore I am.

Runestones: Temperance—*Raido*, the rune concerned with communication, union, reunion, and journeys; means "to read, to interpret."
Wheel of Fortune—*Inguz*, the rune of completion, release, and sharing; the hero.

Colors: BLUE; royal blue, deep blue, bright blue, powder blue, sky blue

Chakra: Fifth chakra—the Throat Chakra. *Expression.* Communication, creativity, mantras, media, inspiration, self-expression, speech, sound, devotion, spiritual understanding, faith and devotion, ideals, feeling, fear of change. The Throat Chakra symbolizes *religious inspiration.*

Stones: Sapphire, sodalite, lapis lazuli, bornite (peacock copper), abalone, blue fluorites and chalcedonies.

Notes: Temperance—G#
Wheel of Fortune—A#

Qaballah: Temperance: Simple Letter—Anger
Path—*Samekh*, The Intelligence of Probation
Meaning—Prop

Wheel of Fortune: Double Letter—Riches-Poverty
Path—*Kaph*, The Intelligence of Conciliation
Meaning—Fist

Plant Essences: Temperance—Hyssop, Bergamot, Angelica
Wheel of Fortune—Cedar, Nutmeg, Clove

Psychic Energy: Telepathy—the ability to communicate across time and space without use of the normal five senses. Also, *presque vu*, the feeling of sensing something which has not yet happened, but will. *Presque vu* is the opposite time-frame of *deja vu* in that *deja vu* is a feeling that the event is being re-experienced, *presque vu* that the event has not yet been experienced.

Huna: The High Self. That part of us which is spirit, grace, our connection to God, and our soul's (or low self's) mate. The fifth and sixth chakras, the astrological signs Sagittarius through Pisces, and the major trumps Temperance, Wheel of Fortune, Devil, World, Star, Fool, Moon, and Hanged Man all represent the High Self. This does not mean that people born under these signs are more evolved. In Huna all life consists of three parts which are equal and comprise the *Whole Self*; in Christianity, this is called the Holy Spirit.

Word Archetype: Temperance

The word Temperance comes from the Middle English and Latin *temperantia*, meaning "moderate, not excessive." Word archetypes are: temporary, temperament, temptation, temporal, tempest, template, temple, and the Knights Templar.

Temperance is our personal Guardian Angel, High Self, the Watcher of our Soul, Inner Guide, superconscious, the Guardian of our Journey. Corresponding to the relationship between the anima and animus in humanistic psychology, she stands with one foot on land and one foot in the water. According to C. G. Jung, spirit is likely to appear feminine for a man; and a woman's spirit appears masculine.[12] Temperance is often depicted as the alchemist combining elements—the homeopathist—conjunction, healing, transformation, and wholeness brought about because of sympathy and/or antipathy. In this respect, Temperance pours the liquid of life from the silver urn into the golden urn, never losing a drop of life in the transition from life to death, in the transition of soul to its spirit.

Word Archetype: Wheel of Fortune

The word wheel comes from the Greek *kyklos*,[13] meaning "cycle" and "wheel," and from the Middle English *cercle*, meaning "circle." Word archetypes are: circus, circuit, circular, cereal, cerebral, ceremony, Ceres, certain, cervix, Cyclops, cyclone, and cylinder. The word fortune comes from the Latin *fortuna*, meaning "chance, luck, destiny, and fate." Word archetypes to fortune are: forte (one's strong point), fortitude, fortress, fortnight, fortissimo, fortuitous (fore-tuit—to see before).

The Wheel of Fortune is from November 22nd to December 20th. The temples of Temperance were built in circles and spirals because it was known then that all life is in the shape of a spiral, something modern scientists have

[12]"Wholeness consists in the union of the conscious and the unconscious personality. Just as every individual derives from masculine and feminine genes, and the sex is determined by the predominance of the corresponding genes, so in the psyche it is only the conscious mind, in a man, that has the masculine sign, while the unconscious is by nature feminine. The reverse is true in the case of a woman . . . as a rule the feminine unconscious of a man is projected upon a feminine partner, and the masculine unconscious of a woman is projected upon a man." (C. G. Jung, *The Archetypes & the Collective Unconscious*, pp. 175, 177.)

[13]The letter "C" was at one time pronounced as a "K," as in *cat*. It now has both pronunciations, as in Cain, circles, cycles, clowns, customs, and cells.

only recently been re-discovering. The Northern peoples of Europe celebrated a holiday in December called *Yule* in honor of the cycles, circles, and spirals of life. Yule comes from the Gaelic "gule," meaning a *wheel*. At one time in England and Germany it was the custom to set fire to a huge wooden wheel or log wrapped in straw and send it rolling down a hill. The Yule Log was oak, also the Cosmic Tree of the Druids. In other cultures it was the pine of Attis and Dionysus, and for the Norse it was the Ash of Woden. The holiday of Yule eventually became intertwined with Christmas, from which we now have the seasonal words, *Yuletide* and *Yulelog*. Traditionally a time of wild merry-making, noise, pranks, costumes, masks, jokes, dancing, orgies, drink, and games, the wheel, or English *cercle,* is also where our modern *clowns* in our two- and three-ringed *circuses* derive.

Jupiter corresponds to both Temperance and the Wheel of Fortune. Jupiter was the Roman's chief god who reigned over all the lesser gods and goddesses. He was a jovial god of benevolence, good fortune, glad tidings, abundance, and all the good and happy things that can possibly happen to a person. In general, he ruled or had his finger in just about every pie there was. Jupiter, under one name or another, has remained the main god of most civilizations on into our modern era, which is hardly surprising, considering what a great, all-around type guy he was. To the Romans, he was *Jupiter*, or *Jove*; to the Greeks, *Zeus* or *Iesus*. To the Celts, he was *Esus*, a Celtic god known as "the Son of Light" who lived three centuries before the time of Jesus. To the Hebrews, he became *Jehovah* or *Yehweh*; to the Spanish, *Jezeus*; and to the English, *Jesus*.

Thursday is the day sacred to Jupiter. In Italian Thursday is *Giovedi*. In French, it is *Jeudi*. To the Norse Jupiter was *Thor*, the God of Thunder and the Sky, and thus in English *Thor's Day* became Thursday.

XV—THE DEVIL
XXI—THE WORLD

Astrological Sign: The Devil—Capricorn
Astrological Planet: The World—Saturn

Astrological Form of the Devil: I structure.
Astrological Motion of the World: I seek myself through what I use.

Runestones: Devil—*Nauthiz,* the rune of constraint, necessity, and pain.
World—*Wunjo,* the rune of joy and light, the absence of sorrow and suffering.

Colors: BLUE-VIOLET (indigo); navy-blue. Also black[14]

Chakra: Fifth chakra—the Throat Chakra. Expression. Communication, creativity, media, inspiration, self-expression, speech, mantras, sound, devotion, spiritual understanding, faith and devotion, ideals, feeling, fear of change. The Throat Chakra represents *religious inspiration.*

Stones: Sapphire, sodalite, lapis lazuli, tanzanite, blue-violet fluorites and chalcedonies. Hematite, smoky quartz, onyx, jet, coal, and all black stones.

Notes: Devil—A
World—A

Qaballah: Devil: Simple Letter—Mirth
Path—*Ayin,* The Renovating Intelligence
Meaning—Eye

[14]The Devil and the World are the entrance into the physical world from the higher worlds, so they also use black as a color. Black is not an absence of color, as is sometimes believed, but rather it is the absorption of all color, as opposed to white, which is the reflection of all color.

World: Double Letter—Power-Servitude
Path—*Tau*, The Administrative Intelligence
Meaning—Tau Cross, Equal-Armed Cross

Plant Essences: The Devil—Clary Sage, Patchouli
The World—Vetivert, Oakmoss, Myrtle

Psychic Energy: Clairaudience—means "clear hearing." The ability to "hear" without regard to time and space or the physical ears.

Huna: The High Self. The self which is spirit, grace, our connection to God, the mate of the subconscious. In humanistic psychology, it is called the *superconscious* and forms the third part in the human psyche of subconscious, conscious, and superconscious.

Word Archetype: The Devil

The word devil derives from the Greek *diabolos*; *di* meaning "to divide," or "two," and *abolos* meaning "to abolish." Word archetypes are: evil (live spelled backwards), lived (devil spelled backwards), deus (two), divide, diverse, die, deva, dervish, deviate, devious, diabolic, and diablerie (black magic).

The Devil is associated with Saturn. The name of our day of Saturday comes from the Latin *Dies Saturni*, meaning "Day of Saturn." Saturn is the other most well-known god, along with Jupiter, who has developed into one of the two main protagonists of most modern civilizations. To the Greeks he was known as *Kronos* or *Cronus*, from which is derived the word *chronic*. To the Egyptians he was *Set*; in Hinduism, he is *Shiva, the Destroyer*, and in Christianity, he is *Satan*. Saturn is typically associated with the serpent, or snake, although in antiquity the snake was considered a holy animal, as once was Saturn's Day revered as a holy day.

Originally, Saturday was the seventh day of the week, with Sunday being the first, and we still retain seven, Saturn's number as the seventh planet, as holy. It is only fitting that *s* is the letter in the Latin-based alphabet that most closely resembles a snake.

The chief festival extolled by the Romans was the *Saturnalia*, celebrated on December 17th in honor of Saturn, who was the Father of Jupiter. Saturn, or Satan, is associated with Capricorn and Pan. Capricorn is *Cornucopia*, the "Horn of Plenty," and *Capricornus* is the fish-tailed goat. *Caper* is Latin for "goat" and in English means "to dance around," which, if you've ever seen a goat dance, is unequivocally a dance of bursting joy and love of life. Pan was connected with the Dionysian mysteries of the Greek God of Wine, Dionysos, and drunkenness, and Saturday is still the day in modern western culture when we celebrate drunkenness. Due to his association to wine, Pan was originally called the "grapegoat," who has now become the "scapegoat" (see the Fool).

Word Archetype: The World

The word World comes from the Old English *weorold* or *woruld*, the Danish *werld*, and Old High German *weralt*, meaning "human existence, age." Word archetypes are: the runestone Wunjo, wreathe, wealth, weal, woe, work, worry, worse, worship, were, weasel, weaver, weather, we, week, weak, woman, womb, word, and eat.

The World is also associated with Saturn and Capricorn (December 21-January 20), in which falls our most festive and well-known holiday—Christmas. Millennia before Christians celebrated Christmas as the birth of the *Son*, Christmas was celebrated as the birth of the *Sun*. December 24th is the commemoration of the first day of Winter—the Winter Solstice—the day of the year when the Sun's rays are furthest away from Earth, and the day in which Earth receives the least amount of the Sun's light. Christmas Day is when the Sun begins to rise again from its deepest descent; when the Sun, or Son, is born again. Gods and goddesses born at Christmas were: Buddha, Tammuz, Mithra, Quetzalcoatl, Frey and Freya, Attis, Saturn, Adonis, Herne, Pryderi, Peresphone, Baalim, Dionysus, Osiris, Horus, and Jesus.

Many of the traditions and customs observed at Christmas originated from cultures commemorating the Winter Solstice. Northern Europeans celebrated the Winter Solstice by Candle Mass, the lighting of candles to honor the birth of the Sun's light, an ancient custom still observed in many Christian churches on Christmas Eve. Another Winter Solstice tradition is mistletoe. The Celtic Druids held that Mistletoe was sacred because the missel thrush brought the green holly to Earth from the heavens, carrying it in his toes. Over time, "missel thrush's toe," became mistletoe. The custom of kissing under the "missel thrush's toe" comes from the Norse legend of Balder, the God of Sun and Light, and Frigga, the Goddess of Love. Balder was accidentally shot and killed with an arrow poisoned with mistletoe by his blind brother god, Hoder. After Balder's light had been out for three days, Frigga succeeded in bringing him back to life with her love and her kisses.

But perhaps it is the tree which remains one of the very oldest religious traditions we still have with us today at Christmas. Trees were once considered the most scared of all flora—they were believed to be the High Self of the botanical kingdom—the intelligent friend and keeper of the Earth on which all life depended. The Mayans believed that flora possessed sentient intelligence and feelings, and there is a traditional Mayan teaching that says "with the death of the last tree, comes death to the last human.[15] Ecologically speaking, this is true, of course, because trees cause it to rain and maintain the ecobalance of the entire planet. Also

---

[15]Hunbatz Men, *Secrets of Mayan Science—Religion.* (Santa Fe, NM: Bear & Company, 1990), p. 84.

it was believed that it was *only* the fruits and seeds of trees and plants (not the trees and plants themselves) of which humanity was to eat, and there is a possible reference to this in the Bible.

"And God said, Behold I have given you every herb bearing seed, which is upon the face of all the earth, and every tree, in the which is the fruit of a tree yielding seed: to you it shall be for meat" (Genesis 1:28).

The tree bears the spiral shape of life in its trunk's inner rings and in all of its spherical outer shapes. It also combines the Holy Trinity—growing from the nether world through the world of the physical unto the realms of the light. For these holy reasons and more, humanity has long decorated trees with lights at the time when the Sun's light is re-born, especially the evergreen. Because evergreens do not ever lose their leaves, they are often considered the supreme floral representative of everlasting life. In like manner, the evergreen is one of the few trees that still exists today from the Prehistoric Age.

XVII—THE STAR
O—THE FOOL

Astrological Sign: The Star—Aquarius
Astrological Planet: The Fool—Uranus

Astrological Form of the Star: I know.
Astrological Motion of the Fool: I seek myself through what I don't know.

Runestones: Star—*Lagaz*, the water stone that flows and conducts.
Fool—The Fool has two runestones. One is *Mannaz*, the rune of mankind, the human race, and the self. The other is the *blank* rune, called "the unknowable," the rune of destiny. As in the tarot where the Fool can either be placed at the beginning or the end of a tarot deck, so in runeology *Mannaz* is the first rune, and the *blank* rune is the last rune.

Colors: VIOLET; purple, lavender

Chakra: Sixth chakra—the Brow Chakra. *Intuition.* Light, color, seeing, thought, information, meditation (inner and outer), visualization, imagination, spiritual perception, dreams, fantasies, spaciness, fear of faith (doubt). The chakra of *purpose* and *patience.*

Stones: Amethyst, sugalite, charoite, siberite (violet tourmaline), chalcedonies and fluorites of violet hues.

Notes: Star—A#
Fool—E

Qaballah: Star: Simple Letter—Imagination
Path—*Tzaddi*, The Natural Intelligence
Meaning—Fish Hook
Fool: Maternal Letter—Air
Path—*Aleph*, The Scintillating Intelligence
Meaning—Ox

Plant Essences: The Star—Eucalyptus, Fir, Lime, Blue Camomile
The Fool—Fennel, Niaouli

Psychic Energy: Precognition—means "pre-knowledge." The ability to "know" the future ahead of time. Also retrocognition—the ability to know the past and/or past lives.

Huna: The High Self. The self which is spirit, grace, our connection to God, our soul's mate. In early Gnostic-Christian theology, the Holy Trinity consisted of Father, Mother, and Son which correspond to low self (Mother); middle self (Son), and High Self (Father). The Catholic Church later changed this to Father, Son, and Holy Ghost which is now generally thought of as being all masculine, but in ancient texts the Holy Ghost was feminine and called *Sophia*, the Mother and Beloved of the Father.

Word Archetype: The Star

The word "star" comes from the Latin *stella* and the Greek *aster* and *astron*. Word archetypes are: astrology, astronomy, asteroid, astronaut, astrophysics, astral, and disaster (*dis* is Latin for "apart." *Dis-aster* is "being apart from the stars").

The earliest tarot cards of The Star pictured six stars grouped around a central seventh star. Some sources believe this was a replica of the six stars which comprise the Big Dipper and revolve around the central North Star.

The Star is Aquarius (January 20–February 18). January (*Januarius* in Latin) is named after the Roman God, *Janus*.

Janus was the two-faced god who ruled doors and gateways, the Roman word for opening or gate being *janua*. Janus was known both as the God of Time and Destiny and also as the God of Beginnings and Endings. He was able to see behind into the past and ahead into the future. Without realizing it, we still celebrate Janus in our holiday of New Year's. On New Year's Eve we commemorate the past and endings by reviewing the preceding year and by singing *Auld Lang Syne* at the passage of midnight. And on January 1st we look forward to the future and beginnings by making a New Year's Resolution for the coming year.

Word Archetype: The Fool

The origin of the word Fool is Old French *fol* and Latin *follis* meaning "bellows, to blow, bag." Word archetypes are: foolish, foot, foible, fun, fable, folly, follow, food, foist, and folk.

Some authorities believe the origination of the Fool and the Fool's Day, now known as April Fool's Day, began when Pope Gregory XIII, in 1582, changed the calendar and moved the New Year from March 25th to January 1st. Those people who remained resistant and who couldn't, or wouldn't, make the proper adjustment on their calendar were called fools, or April's fools. Other scholars say the Fool's Day began when the Green Man of Fertility was celebrated following the week-long celebration of Easter at the Vernal Equinox. *Bacchanalia*, celebrated once every three years in the Spring by the Greeks in honor of *Bacchus*, the God of wine and joy, was a wild and primitive Greek orgy connected to the Green Man. We still employ wine at Easter in Holy Communion when we drink the blood of Christ. The change of the calendar may be why in France April's Fools Day is celebrated with *Poisson d'avril*, which means "the fish of April." The fish is, of course, connected to February/March by the sign of Pisces. It is the custom in

France today for confectioners to sell chocolate fish, or "April Fish" on April 1st and for friends to send postcards to one another with fish on them. Also, Bacchus was connected to the sacred fish, *Bakkhos*, a red sea-mullet associated with the ancient Dionysian, Bacchian, and Eleusinian mysteries.

The Fool is known by a variety of generic names and celebrations in all cultures. He is the Fool, the Court Jester, Le Mat, El Loco, the Mad One, the Juggler, the Jokester, and the Trickster. In Northern Europe and England he was called the Green Man, Jack in the Green, Green George, and the Wylde Man. Robert Eisler, in his book, *Man into Wolf*, offers numerous well-referenced quotes and documented records of people having spotted and known about the actual existence of *Wylde Men* still living in Europe as late as the 16th century. They were apparently a race of people, sometimes said to be dark and hairy, who lived in the woods and hills and wore garments of grass, leaves, and grape ivy, thus their nickname of the Green Man connected to the grapes of wine.

Of all the tarot archetypes, the Fool is the most universally well-known. The Fool is the only Major Arcanum that still remains in a deck of playing cards, as the Joker. In many tarot decks, he is pictured with a wolf or a dog snapping at his heels, which may be the symbol of February snapping at the heels of January, because the wolf is associated with February (The Hanged Man) and January is associated with a man (Aquarius-Janus). The wolf is known in relation to the Fool as "El Loco."

XVIII—THE MOON
XII—THE HANGED MAN

Astrological Sign: Moon—Pisces
Astrological Planet: The Hanged Man—Neptune

Astrological Form of the Moon: I believe.
Astrological Motion of the Hanged Man: I seek myself and I don't seek myself.

Runestones: Moon—*Isa*, the rune that impedes, a standstill, said to be born of ice; the Goddess Isis.
Hanged Man—*Perth*, the rune of mystery, initiation, becoming whole, forces beyond our control.

Colors: VIOLET-RED; magenta, mauve, deep rose, wine

Chakra: Sixth chakra—the Brow Chakra. *Intuition.* Light, color, seeing, thought, information, meditation (inner and outer), visualization, imagination, spiritual perception, dreams, fantasies, spaciness, fear of faith (doubt). The chakra of *purpose* and *patience.*

Stones: Rubies, garnets, sugalite, rubellite (violet-red tourmaline), and violet-red chalcedonies.

Notes: Moon—B
Hanged Man—G#

Qaballah: Moon: Simple Letter—Sleep
Path—*Qoph*, The Corporal Intelligence
Meaning—Back of Head, Ear
Hanged Man: Maternal Letter—Water
Path—*Mem*, The Stable Intelligence
Meaning—Water

Plant Essences: The Moon—Sandalwood, Marjoram, Melissa or Lemon Balm
The Hanged Man—Mugwort, Spikenard or Valerian, Myrrh

Psychic Energy: Clairvoyance—means "clear seeing." The ability to "see" without the limitations of the physical eyes or timespace. Also Oneiromancy, the ability to see through dreams.

Huna: The High Self. That part of us which is our spirit, grace, our connection to God, and our soul's mate. In Huna the three selves are called the *Unihipili, Uhane*, and *Aumakua*. Native Americans called the three selves the *Hare* (timid subconscious), the *Coyote* (sly conscious), and the *Raven* (soaring superconscious). To the Greeks they were *Aphrodite* (feminine subconscious); *Hermes* (reasoning conscious); and the *Hermaphrodite* (whole superconscious).

Word Archetype: The Moon

The origin of the word Moon in Sanskrit is *masa*, meaning "moon" or "month." In Old High Greek it is *mēnē* or *mēn*, in Old English *mona*, and in Latin *mensis*. Word archetypes are: Mona Lisa, mouth, money, menstruation, menopause, maniac, mania, monster, monk, man, men, woman, women, moor, moose, moot, morning, mourning, morose, mane, manicure, manna, menat (amulet), maiden, many, moron, moan, merry, marry, and all derivatives of the name Mary, Mara, Marie, et. al.

In French and Latin, the word for Moon is *luna*, meaning "to shine." Derivatives are lunatic, loony, lunar, lunch, lung, lumination, and Lemniscate (a symbol in the shape of an eight sometimes pictured on the cards of the Magician, Strength, and two of discs).

Word Archetype: The Hanged Man

The word hang derives from the Gothic *hanhan*, Middle English *hon*, and the Old English *hangian*. It is probable that hang originally derived from *An*, the first name we officially know of for God, recorded by the Sumerians more than 6,000 years ago. Word archetypes of hang are: hank (coil or loop), hone, honey, honor, hook, hoop, hope, hole, whole, halo,[16] hallow, anger, angle, angel, ankh, hangover, and hand.

The month of the Hanged Man is February (February 18–March 19), originally derived from *Fenris*, the cosmic wolf of the Norse. *Febris* is the Roman feast of purification and is taken from the Latin, *februare*, meaning "to make pure."

The Hanged Man is associated with the "savior-god-man" in most religions. Jesus was hung from a cross, and Odin, the Viking god, hanged himself from a giant Ash tree named Yggdrasil for nine days until he discovered the secret of the sacred runes. Some claim Merlin was hanged on the branches of a tree when he jumped off a cliff, but most medieval scholars discount this and say that Merlin took to the woods toward the end of his life and went back to living the life of the hermit he so cherished. Even as late as the 20th century saviors have been hanged. Joseph Smith, founder of the Church of Latter Day Saints (the Mormons), was lynched by a crowd in Illinois. But not all saviors are hanged, although some do suffer equally odious executions or tortures. Osiris was nailed alive inside a coffin. Prometheus was chained to the side of a mountain for several hundred years until Hercules rescued him (*Her*cules really was a *hero*); and Baal of the Mountains ate mud and died. On the whole, however, it seems that most saviors opt to depart when the

[16] *Ha* from "han" and *lo* from "lune."

general populace gets a little irritable, not by dying, but rather by simply splitting to another scene. In his latter years Buddha traveled and taught. The Aztec God, Quetzalcoatl, got on a boat and paddled away to parts unknown, professedly to also teach. King Arthur sailed off over the horizon to Avalon; and ancient Sumerian texts say that Thoth, that very magical and very wondrous Egyptian wizard of yore, took to his feathered heels and winged it to the desert.

The Hanged Man and February are associated with the wolf and the dog.[17] One of the oldest legends existing combines the dog and a first Hanged savior, a woman. *Icarius canis* or Procyon (little dog), now a bright star in *Canis Minor,* once was Maera, the faithful dog of Icarius during the reign of King Pandion in Athens. The God Bacchus taught Icarius the art of winemaking, and one day Icarius gave the wine to some shepherds which intoxicated them. Terrified by their condition they believed themselves poisoned and murdered Icarius and buried his body beneath a tree on Mount Hymetus. His dog, Maera, went to Icarius' daughter, Erigone, and by tugging at her robe led her to the grave. Overwhelmed by grief, Erigone hanged herself from the tree which overshadowed her father's grave, and faithful Maera's body was later also found lying lifeless beside the grave.

Sirius, the star most revered by the Egyptians, makes its ascendancy in August and reaches its culmination (descent) on February 11th. Sirius, located in the constellation of *Canis Major,* was, and still is, called the Dog Star and was allied with all canines and lupines. In Egypt, *Anupis* was the jackel-headed God known as Anupis of the Hill, Guardian and Protector of Souls. In Germanic lore, he was *Fenrir,* the giant wolf-son of Loki, and in Scandinavia he was *Fenris,* the Cosmic Wolf. Among the Anglo-Saxons (Angles and Saxons), February was *Wulfmonath* (Wolf Month). *Lupercus* (lupine),

[17]That the Hanged Man is related to both the savior-god and the dog is archetypal in that dog is god spelled backward.

sometimes called *Faunis*, was the Roman God of Fertility, Courtship, and Mating, who like *Anupis,* was also associated with hills and woods. The Romans celebrated his day on February 15th which may be the origin of our Valentine's Day (the culmination of Sirius) because of his association to lovemaking and mating. Sirius was also called the Bow Star (bow-wow and the bow and arrow of Cupid).

NOTES

Chapter 6 LAYOUTS

The Hermit

How many Zen Buddhists does it take to screw in a light bulb?

Two. One to do it and one not to do it.

A layout is the way the cards are "laid out" in a particular pattern or arrangement so that each position in the pattern has a specific meaning. There are popular layouts that are typically associated with tarot, such as the Celtic Cross and the Astrological Spread, and many others found in books and along with tarot decks. When working with the cards regularly, a taroist usually ends up becoming familiar with at least several different spreads because there are certain layouts that are more suited for specific questions than others.

Like the tarot, a layout is symbolic. The definition of a symbol is: "something that stands for or suggests something by reason of its relationship, association, convention, or accidental resemblance to something else." C. G. Jung often possessed a startlingly clear way of defining concepts, and of the symbol, in comparison to the allegory, he wrote: "An allegory is a paraphrase of a conscious content, whereas *a symbol is the best possible expression for an unconscious content whose nature can only be guessed, because it is still unknown*."[1] Even though such things as cards, layouts, astrology, visions, and dreams are symbols, this does not mean that they do not have manifest merit on their own; because,

[1]C. G. Jung, *The Archetypes & the Collective Unconscious*, p. 6 (Italics mine).

if looked at from a greater perspective, everything that we are able to perceive is a symbol. As Oswald Wirth pointed out in *The Tarot of the Magicians*, "Everything is a symbol, for everything proceeds from a generating idea which is related to transcendent conception."[2]

The conscientious reader may notice that the definition of a symbol is practically synonymous to that of an archetype and a correspondence. An archetype, too, is an unconscious content whose nature can only be guessed, and if we recall from Chapter One, it is also a representation of something else. The dictionary says: "An archetype is a prototype, or a copy of the original."

Seen in the context of archetypes being copies of the original, and since the universe is an eternal-infinity of limitless form and motion, it is not amiss to say that people are archetypes as well, supposedly made in the image of God. But if everything is created from the original Archetype of God, or from the thought of God, than it is also valid that not only people, but *everything* is made in the image of God, for the holy books—*The Bible, The Koran, The Bhagavad-Gita*—say that God created the light, the heavens and the earth, creatures, the stars, and the firmament. And in the respect that everything is an image, an archetype of the original, everything is not only a symbol, but a symbol in the image of God—whose nature can only be guessed because it is still unknown.

Many people see a cow not so much as a living, breathing, feeling creature, but as a symbol of their milk and cheese, or hamburgers and steaks. Some people may not appreciate a fine gem as a rare composition of precious minerals that is millions of years old, but as a symbol of their personal power, social status, and adornment. And an insect may not be seen as a lifeform with its own legitimate claim to life, but instead as a symbol of fear or annoyance. But if these creatures and objects are a symbol of food, power, or

[2]Oswald Wirth, *The Tarot of the Magicians* (York Beach, ME: Samuel Weiser, 1985), p. 145.

fear, equally it may be said that for the cow and insect it is people who are perhaps the symbol of power or fear. It certainly seems fair that to the world of bacteria, fungi, germs, viruses, and cells that people may be symbols, and even symbols used for the vast microscopic world's personal gain, even perhaps as we use the earth and animals for ours. Bacteria and viruses could perceive people as simply domiciles in which to set up housekeeping and to live out their visceral lives to their own personal satisfaction and growth. And that they are quite successful at using us, even far more so than we at using them, has an interesting truth to it, for they were here billions of years before we were, and there's no reason to believe they won't be here billions of years after we're long gone and fodder for fungi, pushing up the daisies.

It is doubtful that anything is a symbol in the respect that a symbol is lifeless and unconscious in its own realm, just as it is equally doubtful that any archetype is lifeless. We tend to attribute life only to those "forms" we readily recognize as being most like our own, but "form" is merely a slower vibration of "motion," and in science and mysticism form, motion, and vibration are the same thing. Talking about form and motion is much like talking about space and time, which science and mysticism also realize are the same thing. Kurt Gödel, hailed as the greatest logician of the 20th century, and who has been compared with his friends Albert Einstein and Franz Kafka, said that the passage of time and space doesn't even really exist, that timespace, too, is a symbol of the human mind, arising from confusing "the *given* with the *real*." In his book, *Infinity and the Mind*, Rudy Rucker quotes Gödel: "Passage of time arises because we think of occupying different realities. In fact, we occupy only different givens. There is only one reality."[3]

What it seems to boil down to is that everything is something scientists fuzzily and somewhat haplessly refer to as *energy*, or vibration. In tarot, whether this energy takes

---

[3]Rudy Rucker, *Infinity and the Mind* (New York: Bantam Books, 1983), p. 183.

the form of a card or the motion of a layout, how we go about observing and interpreting the energy which we call the symbols of the tarot, or the energy of anything, is always a collectively-personal affair which, as Jung said, "takes its colour from the individual consciousness in which it happens to appear."[4] We can assume without too much subversion of convention that what Jung perhaps really meant when he said a symbol is an unconscious content whose nature can only be guessed because it is still unknown, is: A symbol is an unconscious content (to *us*) whose nature can only be guessed (by *us*), because it is still unknown (to *us*).

When doing tarot and attributing certain meanings to cards and to specific positions in a layout, we are employing what we call symbols in order to tap the personal and collective unconscious. Because the tarot is cosmogonal symbols, if we study it and work with it long enough, we begin to see that the cards may be read successfully (or unsuccessfully) by someone not because the cards or reader themselves are necessarily more magical, psychic, bewitched, prophetic (or perhaps dismally unprophetic) than anything else, but because, like symbols and archetypes, the cards reflect the qualities of the present energy and thus embrace whatever may be that person's personal reality. And since there really is no timespace—only the present—the past and future may also be understood. As goes the moment, so fall the cards. Which is true of everything in life, and what anyone sees and makes of a layout of cards is the same as what they see in cows, gems, insects, other people, and in all of life. In this respect, so appropriate to divination, Jung adds: "Our task is not, therefore, to deny the archetype, but to dissolve the projections, in order to restore the contents to the individual who has involuntarily lost them by projecting them outside himself."[5] In other words, the answer is not outside the problem, but the answer *is* the problem, or the answer is always staring us in the face if we can but see it.

---

[4]C. G. Jung. *The Archetypes & the Collective Unconscious.*, p. 5.
[5]Ibid., p. 84.

When doing layouts, if you want to capture the most of whatever your reality is, there are probably a few exoterical rules of traditional thumb that are helpful to follow:

1. Concentrate and meditate on your question while shuffling the cards. It is important to be at ease, not in a rush, and to not be interrupted. You may ask the same question over and over again until the cows come home, but if while you're shuffling the cards and asking the question, you are feeling or thinking about something else, that something else which you are feeling is what the cards will respond to and reflect. The principle of love in the Universe determines that like-attracts-like. Energy, or vibration, seeks its own, and the layout is a reflection of the person's subconscious emotions and feelings. This does not mean the layout does not work. Quite the contrary, it demonstrates that it does because subconscious fears and desires are followed by conscious and unconscious thought which are followed by astral and physical manifestation.

2. When preparing to do a layout, all 78 cards may be shuffled together as one, or they can be separated into two or three parts and each part shuffled separately. For instance, you may only want to use one court card for a significator and take the remainder of the court cards out of the deck for the reading. Or, for the *Half Moon* spread, you may prefer to use only the Major Arcana for the first nine cards and only the Minor Arcana for the second nine cards, in which case you would first shuffle and lay out the Major Arcana for the first nine, then shuffle and lay out the Minor Arcana for the second nine. It's a matter of whatever you prefer to do—to employ all of the deck together as one, or divided into two or three parts.

3. Shuffle the cards by shuffling them from one hand into the other hand, not by flipping them on top of one another like when playing cards. Shuffling them the latter way scatters energy instead of enveloping or sharing it.

4. Most taroists believe it is not a good idea to turn over any card until *all* the cards have been laid out (face down), and not to turn over a card until you are *finished* shuffling. If you turn over cards and look at them before you've completely finished shuffling, you start thinking about the cards you're looking at instead of continuing to meditate and concentrate on your question, and thus you may influence the remainder of the shuffle with conscious speculation.

THE CELTIC CROSS

The Celtic Cross Spread is commonly thought to be the oldest known layout. It has withstood the test of time and space because like many other ternary symbols, its form and motion are transpersonal. There are many variations to the Celtic Cross, but regardless of locution, a good Celtic Cross spread will always maintain within its form and motion the ability to transcend the barriers of individual consciousness through a collective and recognizable harmony of symmetry.

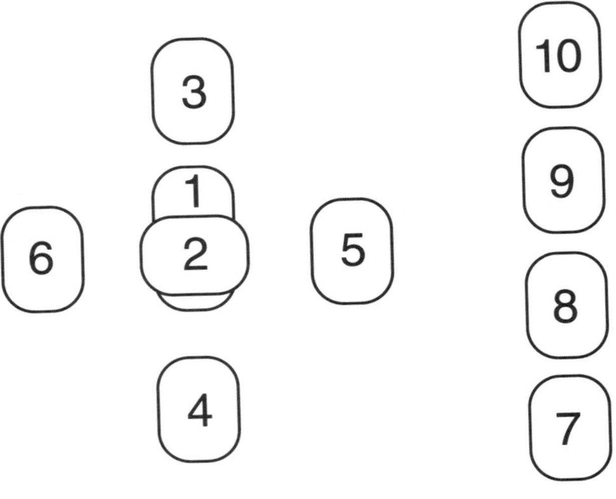

As you lay out the cards repeat this triumvirate:

1. Finds you.
2. Crosses you.
3. Crowns you.
4. Beneath you.
5. Behind you.
6. Before you.
7. For your house and home.
8. For your hopes and fears.
9. For what you don't expect.
10. For what is sure to be.[6]

1. *Finds you.* This is you, or the client, whoever the reading is for. The basis of the question. The significator.

2. *Crosses you.* A difficulty hindering the situation, or the extended lightbeam by which you may see yourself clear of the situation. Also this is the final outcome of the cross, sometimes only later understood with "hindsight."

3. *Crowns you.* This is the wholer energy, or High Self, coming in. The energy playing out into the rest of the spread. Go back to this card for the overall vibration in the reading.

4. *Beneath you.* This is what is, or will, take place on the physical plane; actual manifestation on the physical plane.

5. *Behind you.* The past, usually the recent past. This is also the subconscious, because the subconscious is memory and the past.

6. *Before you.* This is the future, usually the near future. This is also the conscious, because the conscious mind doesn't live in the present but dreams of the future.

7. *For your house and home.* What is, or soon will be, taking place in your immediate surroundings, family environment, and around those most close to you. Indicates a place of residence, either real and/or spiritual.

---

[6]I have been unable to locate the source of the charm spoken in this spread. If anyone knows its origin, I would appreciate hearing from you so credit can be given in the next edition.

8. *For your hopes and fears.* Your secret wishes and desires, doubts, and fears that are affecting the present situation.

9. *For what you don't expect.* The unexpected stroke of fortune, good or bad. What you do not expect.

10. *For what is sure to be.* This is the inevitable, what is going to happen, no matter what.

THREE-CARD SPREAD

This Three-Card Spread is used for answering a quick question when you don't have a lot of time or you just want a quick answer. It can symbolize any issue or question, and it is an easy layout but a good one for getting down to brass tacks. For instance, if you have been asked to do something and are not sure if you want to or not, card #1 indicates the *yes* reason you should or why you want to; card #2 shows the reason you shouldn't (or the *no* reasons); and card #3 shows your indecision and the pros and cons of both, the *maybe* of the issue. The suggestions offered here are the positions for various relationships, but you can make up your own relationships among the three cards, depending on the question. If you're trying to decide between getting a job or going back to school, you could make card #1 work; card #2 school; and card #3 both or neither, card #3 perhaps signifying you might go to school part-time and work part-time, or perhaps do neither and consider a completely different avenue.

1	2	3
Subconscious	Conscious	Superconscious
Past	Present	Future
The other person	Yourself	A third party
Yes	No	Maybe
Body	Mind	Spirit
What I do to others	What others do to me	Synthesis of both
How George perceives me	How I perceive George	The relationship
George's perspective	My perspective	The situation

THE HALF MOON SPREAD

The Half Moon Spread, taken from Marthy Jones' *It's in the Cards.*[7] It is a reading to be done when you do not have a specific question. It is a short-term reading to be considered on a short-term basis. I find it most often gives a two to four week forecast.

Shuffle cards. Lay nine cards face down in a half-moon. Shuffle again. Lay nine more cards face down on top of first nine cards. Read in pairs, going from left to right.

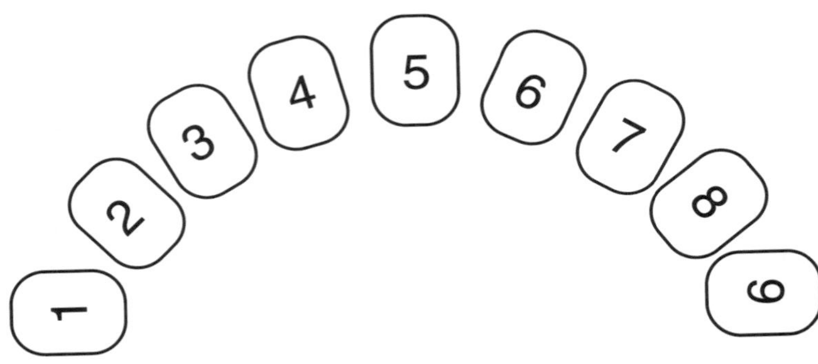

1. Someone you will meet;
2. Someone you will love;
3. Someone who tires or wearies you;
4. Something which brings peace or comfort;
5. Something hanging over your head;
6. Something which helps you;
7. Something which surprises or astonishes you;
8. Something longed for;
9. Something pleasant that will take place.

[7]Marthy Jones, *It's in the Cards* (York Beach, ME: Samuel Weiser, 1986), pp. 27–28.

NOTES

NOTES

WHY DIVINATION WORKS

The Hanged Man
If there is a God, give me a sign! . . . See, I told you that the knulpt smflrt glpptner. . .

—Steve Martin

The renowned physicist, F. David Peat, once wrote: "Everything causes everything else."[1]

C. G. Jung said: "The entire universe is contained within the smallest of particles, which then corresponds to the whole."[2] Said the writer-philosopher, André Gide: "Unhappiness comes from looking about and subordinating to oneself what one sees."[3] And Gautama (the Buddha) when asked, "What is Nirvana?" answered: "Nirvana is the consequence of understanding that all things are equal."

Because of the latest research being undertaken in many modern sciences, it is now being physically demonstrated that what these and other astute thinkers have been saying all along is true—everything in the universe is intimately connected with everything else. The most commonly discussed science where this is currently being confirmed is Quantum Physics.

The Electron Paramagnetic Resonance Effect (EPR Effect), a mechanics of physics, was mathematically theorized

[1]F. David Peat, *Synchronicity: The Bridge Between Matter and Mind* (New York: Bantam Books, 1987), p. 47.
[2]C. G. Jung, *Psyche & Symbol* (Garden City: Doubleday/Anchor, 1958), p. 250.
[3]André Gide, *The Fruits of the Earth* (Mount Vernon, NY: The Peter Pauper Press, 1969), p. 14.

by physicist John Stewart Bell in 1964 and later proven by physicist John Clauser in a laboratory experiment in which sub-atomic photons were exposed to the same polarization and then fired in opposite directions. Clauser, assisted by Stuart Freedman, discovered that after two polarized photons were separated, they still responded to the same stimulus. In other words, when one was stimulated, the other, although a distance away, also responded. Once exposed, the two related photons could no longer be considered separate objects, but in some way continued to remain mysteriously linked. Some physicists theorize that after sharing a common polarization, no matter how far apart two particles may eventually become from one another, or how much time passes, they will continue to share the same polarization and a commonality with one another, even perhaps for eternity and throughout infinity.

Eternity and infinity is a very long time in an awful lot of space for two things to share experiences. But, apparently, this is exactly what particles do. For as incredible as it may sound, we all have particles inside us right now from the original "Big Bang" and from every single person and living creature who has ever lived. Physicist Louise B. Young, in her book, *The Unchanged Universe,* talks about this timelessness and spacelessness of particles:

"*It is generally believed that all the protons which exist today—at least one in every atom in the universe—were created in the first one hundred millionth of a second after the Cosmic Birth.* Recently scientists have been watching with sophisticated instruments for signs that the proton may, in fact, occasionally disintegrate spontaneously, and they have reached the conclusion that if the proton decays at all its average life-time must be at least 100,000,000,000,000,000,000,000,000,000,000 years. . . . This extraordinary tenacious unit of matter serves as the nucleus of the hydrogen atom, the simplest and most abundant atom in the cosmos."[4]

---

[4]Louise B. Young. *The Unchanged Universe* (New York: Simon & Schuster 1986), p. 39. (Italics mine).

Physicist Jean Charon, in his book, *The Unknown Spirit: the Unity of Matter and Spirit in Space and Time*, also talks about the timelessness (eternity) and spacelessness (infinity) of particles. He says: "There are more electrons in a cubic centimetre of the air of our planet than there are stars in the cosmos. . . . As we know, Julius Caesar was murdered in 44 B.C. As anybody does at his last breath, he expelled approximately one litre of air from his lungs into the atmosphere. Now, here is the question: at each inhalation, and in whatever place on the planet, are we not breathing in some of the electrons that constituted the air molecules from Caesar's dying breath? We can say that this last litre of air from Caesar has been uniformly diluted on the planet during the course of time, and that this has happened throughout the atmospheric layers reaching 100 km high all around the planet. A simple calculation will provide the answer. 'Yes, we currently breathe in about 100 Caesarian electrons at each inhalation.' "[5]

It is likely no one will ever be able to prove empirically that particles are infinite and eternal, but the time and space physicists have discovered that particles do encompass is so phenomenal that there are not many of us who are likely to quibble the point. The scientific postulate that certain particles never decay and that every single living creature manifestly shares particles with every other living creature, and since it is particles which comprise all matter and space, goes a long way toward verifying what mystics have been telling us all along—everything is connected, and whatever happens to any one of us eventually happens to us all.

Physics isn't by any means the only science which has deduced that life may be intimately connected infinitely and eternally, even in such manifest ways as we've never dreamed of, because modern researchers of all types—computer programmers, mathematicians, astronomers, astrophysicists, neurologists—are delving into their own special fields and coming up with similar prototypes of the universe.

---

[5]Jean Charon, *The Unknown Spirit: The Unity of Matter and Spirit in Space and Time* (London: Coventure, Ltd., 1983), p. 100.

The Holographic Paradigm of modern light technology demonstrates the same principle of the unity of life. Now that science is capable of producing a hologram on the physical level, we are able to actually visually see how all parts are connected, or contained within a whole, quite literally. A laser beam is concentrated, focused light in the electromagnetic spectrum, which makes it like other light except it enables us to see things that our physical eyes don't register in ordinary diffused light. A hologram is produced by splitting a laser beam so that the laser reflects back on itself. The result is a three-dimensional image that in all ways, except for its lack of material barrier, looks and acts exactly like three-dimensional reality. Many of us saw our first hologram in the movie *Star Wars* when R2D2 projected the holographic image of Princess Lea to Obewankanobee. The really interesting thing about a hologram is that all of its parts are contained as smaller wholes within its single larger whole. If a hologram of an apple is cut into 16 different pieces, each of the 16 pieces contains an image of the *entire* apple. Scientists don't know why or how this is so, but from holographics (whole sight) and holophonics (whole sound), has arisen the Holographic Paradigm, which is the theory that the entire universe is a giant Super Hologram and that *all* things in it are but smaller wholes which are complete images contained within the larger whole. The holographic phenomenon has confirmed to some people that life is not limited to only that narrow band of the physical which the five human senses register but may experience itself limitlessly and boundlessly. If it is recalled what was discussed in Chapter 1, this is what Hermes proposed over 3000 years ago and what is referred to as the Hermetic Law of Correspondence: As above, so below. And as below, so above. As given in the Latin translation of the text of the Emerald Tablets of Hermes Trismegistus, the Hermetic Law of Correspondence precisely reads: "Quod est inferius est sicut quod est superius et quod est superius est sicut quod est inferius ad perpetranda miracula rei unius." ("What is inferior is as what is superior and what is superior is as what is inferior in order to perpetuate the miracle of the unified god.")[6] For those readers wishing more information on the Holographic Paradigm, Michael Talbot explains it beautifully in his book *The Holographic Universe.*

C. G. Jung, Marie von Franz, F. David Peat, and many other scholars have also described the same principle of universal unity using Jung's theory of synchronicity. The definition of a synchronicity is: "an occurrence in time or space in which two or more apparently unrelated events or objects have the same or similar meaning." More simply, Jung said a synchronicity is a "meaningful coincidence."[7]

Briefly recapitulated, here are a few synchronicities that have occurred to me in my life. They are not particularly outstanding examples, and most readers can come up with similar "coincidences" of their own.

1. My dog, my cat, and my friend's dog were all born on December 24th. All were purchased before their birthdates were known, and I didn't even notice the synchronicity for several years. As a slight additional synchronicitous note, my son, two of my friends, one of his friends, and myself were also born on the 24th of a month. More of our pets and acquaintances may have also been born on the 24th of a month, but we haven't checked.

2. In 1961, my family and I moved from Illinois to England. On my first day of school in England, I discovered one of my new classmates was a boy who had been my next-door neighbor in Arkansas three years earlier.

3. As an adult, at the same time I was living on *Horseshoe* Lane in Indiana, my sister was living on *Palomino* Drive in Florida. She married a man in Florida who was from Indiana, and I married a man in Indiana whose parents lived in Florida.

---

[6]Mouni Sadhu, *The Tarot* (N. Hollywood, CA: Wilshire Book Company, 1968), p. 44.

[7]C.G. Jung, *Synchronicity: An Acausal Connecting Principle* (Princeton, NJ: Princeton University Press, 1973), pp. 21–25.

Whether in actual fact coincidences ever really occur, or whether all of life is so planned that everything only appears to be unrelated when in actuality everything is very related, is now being seriously debated among some of the world's top scholars of synchronicity. Many researchers believe that there is an underlying universal common symmetry beneath all things, that everything is synchronicitous, and it is only the few rare times we are able to briefly capture a glimpse of a larger pattern at work that we incorrectly call it a coincidence.

And all this is the reason divination works. Because even though we are not normally able to perceive it is so, apparently, everything works. If you are able to see a piece of a hologram you've got a pretty good idea of the entire hologram. If you are able to glimpse a synchronicity, you may be able to see the part it takes in the larger pattern. Or in other words, *all things are in all things.*

I've often said that a good enough diviner can read anything—cards, rune stones, a crystal ball, tea leaves, even the cracks in a wall. Because the world is a likeness of itself—or because God created in Its own Image—as quantum physics, the Holographic Paradigm, synchronicity, and many other models may suggest—what is around us at any given moment is what we are most like, but we only recognize that piece of the likeness that we are able to perceive. We are only aware of whatever dimension, plane, event, situation, or part of life we are perceiving, and the reason we are perceiving it in the first place is because it *is* that part we are *most* like. When we lay out tarot cards, we are attempting to look at a part of life that we would not normally recognize. And whether we are successful at this or not, either way we will see our own reflection in the cards, just as surely as if they are a brightly polished mirror reflecting back to us our own self-same image.

If this seems simplistic, perhaps it is, because, in the end, it is possible that the universe itself is simple. It is usually only people who tend to complicate matters. Theology and mythology claim our entire problem to begin with is because of the original Fall from Grace. The Fall from Grace occurred when Adam and Eve (or their cultural counterparts in other religions) were expelled (or chose to leave, depending on which version of the story you are reading) from the Garden of Eden and became separated from God. The story of Adam and Eve may be literally true, or it may be a mythological allegory, but either way, it is supposedly when mankind first began to believe itself separated from God. And since God is one and the All, it is also when we began to see ourselves separated and divided from everything else as well. Apparently humanity hasn't changed all that much since Adam and Eve originally did their thing because we still see ourselves as individuals, separated from God, and from other people, and from other creatures. Curiously, we generally see ourselves as better than all the above. Which, according to the Sufis, is what caused the Fall, or separation, and still continues to cause it. That we cannot see the Whole as One and believe ourselves to be separate bodies and minds seems to come about because each of us is limited to what it is we are each personally aware of. Or as Jung once wrote, "One sees what one sees best oneself."[8] All conflict is the failure to perceive other realities.

In theory, divination can work for anyone. And in theory, anything can be read, even a goldfish bowl. However, the ability to divine anything accurately depends on how well the reader is able to see beyond him- or herself. If people are blinded by their own projections, if they are subconsciously fixed in their personal beliefs so that they are unable to get beyond their own individual fears and desires (their own personal angles on the Angel), they will not be able to see anything but their own subconscious in a reading, no matter for whom they are doing the reading. Since, in reality, the universe is one single undivided whole, the

[8]C. G. Jung, *Psychological Types* (Princeton, NJ: Princeton University Press, 1974), p. 9.

more people feel separated from anything in it, the less they will be able to see anything but their own personal beliefs in other people and in virtually everything that exists. Because everyone sees their own likeness, or angle, best, or because like-attracts-like, it often happens that people seek answers from other people who have the same problems, ideas, and situations in life as they themselves have. For this reason, psychiatrists, counselors, and taroists often appear to know the answer to certain problems, but the advice or reading offered will be as limited, or as unlimited, as the readers and querents themselves are.

Successful divination is not haphazard, nor is it chance. It is a coded reflection of the universe acting in ourselves and in everything that exists. The cards do not *make* happen what we see in them, they merely reflect what is already here. They reflect that part of the Whole that we are able to recognize. Regardless of whether we do tarot for fun, profit, a sense of power, growth, or spiritual seeking—it does work. And like everything else in life—our jobs, relationships, goals, cars, and coffeepots—it works in exact proportion to what we give to it and to what we are able to receive from it. It is perhaps as C. G. Jung once wrote: "The spirit and meaning of Christ are present and perceptible to us even without the aid of miracles. Miracles only appeal to the understanding of those who cannot perceive the meaning. They are mere substitutes for the not understood reality of the Spirit."[9]

---

[9]C. G. Jung, *Psychology & Religion—West & East*, ¶ 554.

TAROT BIBLIOGRAPHY

Tarot books and decks may be purchased from most major bookstores, from their publishers, or direct from Samuel Weiser, Box 612, York Beach, ME 03910–0612.

Arrien, Angeles. *The Tarot Handbook: Practical Applications of Ancient Visual Symbols.* Sonoma, CA. Arcus Publishing Company, 1987.

Buryn, Ed. *The William Blake Tarot of the Creative Imagination Book and Deck.* London: HarperCollins Publishers, 1995.

Butler, Bill. *Dictionary of the Tarot.* New York: Schocken Books, 1977.

Cowie, Norma. *Exploring the Patterns of the Tarot.* White Rock, British Columbia: NC Publishing, 1987.

———. *Tarot for Successful Living.* White Rock, British Columbia: NC Publishing, 1983. (Write NC Publishing, P. O. Box 75051, White Rock, B.C. V4A 9M4 Canada.)

Crowley, Aleister. *The Book of Thoth.* York Beach, ME: Samuel Weiser, 1974.

Crowley, Aleister and Frieda Harris. *Thoth Tarot Deck.* York Beach, ME: Samuel Weiser and Stamford, CT: U. S. Games, 1977.

Eakins, Joyce, *Tarot of the Spirit Tarot Deck.* Stamford, CT: U.S. Games Systems, 1992.

Eakins, Joyce and Pamela Eakins. *Tarot of the Spirit Set.* York Beach, ME: Samuel Weiser, 1994.

Eakins, Pamela. *Tarot of the Spirit.* York Beach, ME: Samuel Weiser, 1992.

Fairfield, Gail. *Choice-Centered Tarot.* Smithville, IN: Ramp Creek Publishing, 1981.

Fairfield, Gail and Patti Provo. *Inspiration Tarot.* York Beach, ME: Samuel Weiser, 1991.

Greer, Mary K. *The Essence of Magic: Tarot, Ritual and Aromatherapy.* N. Hollywood, CA: Newcastle Publishing Co., 1993.

———. *Magical Women of the Golden Dawn.* Rochester, VT: Park Street Press, 1995.

———. *Tarot Constellations: Patterns of Personal Destiny.* N. Hollywood, CA: Newcastle Publishing Co., 1987.

———. *Tarot for Your Self: A Workbook for Personal Transformation.* N. Hollywood, CA: Newcastle Publishing Co., 1984.

———. *Tarot Mirrors: Reflections of Personal Meaning.* N. Hollywood, CA: Newcastle Publishing Co., 1988.

Greer, Mary K. and Rachel Pollack, eds. *New Thoughts on Tarot.* N. Hollywood, CA: Newcastle Publishing Co., 1989.

Jones, Marthy. *It's in the Cards.* York Beach, ME: Samuel Weiser, 1986.

Kaplan, Stuart R. *The Encyclopedia of Tarot, Volumes I, II & III.* Stamford, CT: U. S. Games Systems, 1978, 1985, 1991.

Noble, Vicki. *Motherpeace: A Way to the Goddess Through Myth, Art & Tarot.* San Francisco: HarperCollins, San Francisco, 1983.

_______. *Shakti Woman: Feeling our Fate, Healing our World.* San Francisco, California: HarperSanFrancisco, 1991.

Noble, Vicki and Jonathan Tenney. *The Motherpeace Tarot Playbook.* Oakland, CA: Wingbow Press, 1986.

Noble, Vicki and Karen Vogel. *Mini Motherpeace Round Tarot Deck.* Stamford, CT: U. S. Games Systems, 1992.

_______. *Motherpeace Round Tarot Deck.* Stamford, CT: U.S. Games Systems, 1983.

Pollack, Rachel. *The Haindl Tarot, Volume 1.* North Hollywood, CA: Newcastle Publishing Co., 1990.

_______. *The Haindl Tarot, Volume 2.* North Hollywood, CA: Newcastle Publishing Co., 1990.

_______. *The New Tarot.* New York: Overlook, 1990.

_______. *Tarot: The Open Labyrinth.* London: Aquarian Press, 1986.

_______. *Salvador Dali's Tarot.* Salem, NH: Salem House, 1985.

_______. *Seventy-Eight Degrees of Wisdom.* London: Aquarian Press, 1980.

_______. *Seventy-Eight Degrees of Wisdom, Part 2.* London: Aquarian Press, 1983.

_______. *The Shining Woman Tarot Deck.* London: Aquarian Press, 1993.

_______. *Teach Yourself Fortune Telling.* New York: Henry Holt, 1986.

Pollack, Rachel and Caitlin Matthews. *Tarot Tales.* London: Century Hutchinson, 1989.

Riley, Jana. *The Tarot Book.* York Beach, ME: Samuel Weiser, 1992.

Sadhu, Mouni. *The Tarot.* N. Hollywood, CA: Wilshire Book Company, 1968.

Sharman-Burke, Juliet. *The Complete Book of Tarot.* London: Pan Books, 1985; New York: St. Martin's Press, 1986.

Sharman-Burke, Juliet, and Liz Greene. *The Mythic Tarot.* New York: Simon & Schuster, 1986; and London: Rider/Random House, 1986.

_______. *The Mythic Tarot Deck.* Illustrated by Tricia Newell. New York: Simon & Schuster, 1986.

Stewart, R. J. *The Complete Merlin Tarot.* London: Aquarian Press, 1992.

Stewart. R. J., and Miranda Gray. *The Merlin Tarot Deck.* London: Aquarian Press, 1992.

Stewart, R. J., and Stuart Littlejohn. *The Dreampower Tarot Book and Deck.* London: Aquarian Press, 1994. For further information, write to BCM 3721, London WC1N 3XX, United Kingdom.

Waite, Arthur Edward. *The Pictorial Key to the Tarot.* York Beach, ME: Samuel Weiser, 1973; and Stamford, CT: U. S. Games Systems, 1977.

———. *The Rider-Waite Tarot Deck.* Painted by Pamela Colman Smith. Stamford, CT: U. S. Games Systems, 1977.

Walker, Barbara G. *The Barbara Walker Tarot Deck.* Stamford, CT: U.S. Games Systems, 1986.

———. *The Secrets of the Tarot: Origins, History, & Symbolism.* San Francisco: HarperSanFrancisco, 1984.

———. *The Woman's Dictionary of Symbols & Sacred Objects.* San Francisco: HarperSanFrancisco, 1988.

———. *The Woman's Encyclopedia of Myths & Secrets.* San Francisco: HarperSanFrancisco, 1983.

———. *Women's Rituals: A Sourcebook.* San Francisco: HarperSanFrancisco, 1990.

Wang, Robert. *Introduction to The Golden Dawn Tarot.* York Beach, ME: Samuel Weiser, 1978.

———. *The Qabalistic Tarot: A Textbook of Mystical Philosophy.* York Beach, ME: Samuel Weiser, 1987.

Wanless, James. *The Nature of Success Wild Cards.* Carmel, CA: Merrill-West Publishing, Inc.

———. *New Age Tarot: Guide to the Thoth Deck.* Carmel, CA: Merrill-West Publishing, 1988.

———. *Star Tree: Homestudy Certification Course.* (Write Merrill-West Publishing for information: Box 1227, Carmel, CA 93921).

———. *The Voyager Tarot Deck.* Carmel, CA: Merrill-West Publishing, 1985.

———. *Voyager Tarot: Way of the Great Oracle.* Carmel, CA: Merrill-West Publishing, 1989.

Wanless, James and Angeles Arrien. *Wheel of Tarot: A New Revolution.* Carmel, CA: Merrill-West Publishing, 1992.

Wirth, Oswald. *The Tarot of the Magicians.* York Beach, ME: Samuel Weiser, 1986.

———. *The Wirth Tarot Deck.* Stamford, CT: U. S. Games Systems, 1976.

GENERAL BIBLIOGRAPHY

A Course in Miracles. Glen Ellen, CA: Foundation for Inner Peace, 1985.

Baigent, Michael, Richard Leigh and Henry Lincoln. *Holy Blood, Holy Grail.* New York: Dell, 1983.

________. *The Messianic Legacy*. New York: Dell, 1986.

Brau, Jean-Louis, Helen Weaver and Allan Edmands. *Larousse Encyclopedia of Astrology*. New York: McGraw-Hill, 1977.

Blum, Ralph. *The Book of Runes*. New York: St. Martin, 1982.

Bonewitz, Ra. *The Cosmic Crystal Spiral.* Shaftesbury, England: Element, 1986.

Capra, Fritjof. *The Tao of Physics*. New York: Bantam Books, 1984.

Charon, Jean. *The Unknown Spirit: The Unity of Matter and Spirit in Space and Time*. London: Coventure, Ltd., 1983.

Cipriani, Curzio, and Alessandro Borellia. *Simon & Schuster's Guide to Gems and Precious Stones*. Edited by Kennie Lyman. New York: Simon & Schuster, 1986.

Cirlot, J. E. *A Dictionary of Symbols*. London: Routledge & Kegan Paul Ltd., 1971.

Cole, K. C. *Sympathetic Vibrations: Reflections on Physics as a Way of Life*. New York: William Morrow, 1985.

Collier's Encyclopedia. New York: MacMillan Educational Company, 1991.

Cooper, J. C. *An Illustrated Encyclopedia of Traditional Symbols*. London and New York: Thames Hudson, 1990.

Cotterell, Arthur. *The MacMillan Illustrated Encyclopedia of Myths & Legends*. New York: MacMillan 1989.

Couzens, Reginald C. *The Stories of the Months and Days*. Detroit, MI: Omnigraphics, 1990.

Dossey, Donald E. *Holiday, Folklore, Phobias and Fun*. Los Angeles, CA: Outcomes Unlimited Press, Inc., 1992.

Eisler, Robert. *Man Into Wolf: An Anthropological Interpretation of Sadism, Masochism, and Lycanthropy*. London: Routledge & Kegan Paul, Ltd., 1951.

Evans-Wentz, W. Y. *The Fairy Faith in Celtic Countries*. New York: University Books, 1966.

Gardner, John W., and Francesca Gardner Reese. *Quotations of Wit and Wisdom*. New York: Norton & Co., 1975.

Gide, André. *The Fruits of the Earth*. Mt. Vernon, NY: The Peter Pauper Press, 1969.

Hall, Manly P. *The Secret Teachings of All Ages*. Los Angeles, CA: The Philosophical Research Society, 1977.

The Holy Bible, King James Version. Cleveland: World Publishing Company.

Howie, M. O. *The Cults of the Dog*. Saffron Walden, England: C. W. Daniel, Ltd., 1972.

Jung, C. G. *Collected Works of C. G. Jung, No. 9, Pt. 1. The Archetypes & the Collective Unconscious*. G. Adler, et al, eds. R. F. Hull, trans. Bollingen Series, No. 20. Princeton, NJ: Princeton University Press, 1968.

_______. *Collected Works of C. G. Jung, No. 6. Psychological Types*. G. Adler, ed. R. F. Hull, & H. G. Baynes, trans. Bollingen Series No. 20. Princeton, NJ: Princeton University Press, 1971.

_______. *Collected Works of C. G. Jung, No. 12. Psychology and Alchemy*. G. Adler, et al, eds. R. F. Hull, trans. Bollingen Series No. 20. Princeton, NJ: Princeton University Press, 1968.

_______. *Collected Works of C. G. Jung, No. 11. Psychology & Religion—West & East*. G. Adler, ed. R. F. Hull, trans. Bollingen Series No. 20. Princeton, NJ: Princeton University Press, 1969.

Jung, C. G. *Memories, Dreams, Reflections*. New York: Vintage Books, 1965.

Jung, C. G. *Psyche & Symbol: A Selection from the Writings of C. G. Jung*. Violet de Laszlo, ed. Garden City: Doubleday Anchor Books, 1958.

Jung, C. G. *Synchronicity: An Acausal Connecting Principle*. G. Adler, ed. R. F. Hull, trans. Bollingen Series No. 20. Princeton, NJ: Princeton University Press, 1973.

Keirsey, David and Marilyn Bates. *Please Understand Me: Character & Temperament Types*. Del Mar, CA: Prometheus Nemesis, 1978.

Long, Max Freedom. *Growing into Light*. Marina del Rey, CA: DeVorss, 1955.

_______. *Recovering the Ancient Magic*. Cape Girardeau, MO: Huna Press, 1978.

_______. *The Secret Science Behind Miracles*. Marina del Rey, CA: DeVorss, 1988.

Mella, Dorothee L. *Stone Power*. New York: Warner Books, 1986.

Men, Hunbatz. *Secrets of Mayan Science—Religion*. Santa Fe, NM: Bear & Company, 1990.

Metcalf, Fred, editor. *The Penguin Dictionary of Modern Humorous Quotations*. London & New York: Penguin, 1987.

Myers, Isabel Briggs and Peter B. *Gifts Differing*. Palo Alto, CA: Consulting Psychologists Press, 1980.

Ouspensky, P. D. *Tertium Organum*. New York: Vintage Books, 1982.

Page, R. I. *Reading the Past Runes*. Berkeley, CA: University of California Press, 1987.

Peat, F. David. *Synchronicity: The Bridge between Matter and Mind.* New York: Bantam Books, 1987.

Prophet, Elizabeth Clare. *Forbidden Mysteries of Enoch.* Livingston, MT: Summit University Press, 1983.

Pyles, Thomas. *The Origins and Developments of the English Language.* New York: Harcourt Brace Jovanovich, 1971.

Robins, Don. *The Secret Language of Stone.* London: Rider & Co., 1988.

Robinson, James M. editor. *Nag Hammadi Library.* Translated by members of The Coptic Gnostic Library Project of the Institute for Antiquity and Christianity. San Francisco: HarperSanFrancisco, 1981.

Rucker, Rudy. *Infinity and the Mind.* New York: Bantam Books, 1983.

Shipley, Joseph T. *Dictionary of Word Origins.* New York: Philosophical Library, 1945.

Sitchin, Zecharia. *The Earth Chronicles* (4 book series). New York: Avon Books, 1976–1990.

Skeat, Walter W. *A Concise Etymological Dictionary of the English Language.* New York: Perigee/Putnam, 1963.

Talbot, Michael. *The Holographic Universe.* New York: HarperCollins, 1991.

Temple, Robert K. G. *The Sirius Mystery.* Rochester, VT: Destiny, 1987.

Thompson, Keith. *Angels and Aliens: UFO's and the Mythic Imagination.* New York: Addison-Wesley, 1991.

Valle, Jacques. *Passport to Magonia.* Chicago, IL: Contemporary Books, 1993.

Von Franz, Marie-Louise. *On Divination and Synchronicity.* Toronto, Canada: Inner City Books, 1980.

Webster's Encyclopedic Unabridged Dictionary of the English Language. New York: Portland House, 1989.

Webster's Ninth New Collegiate Dictionary. Springfield, MA: Merriam-Webster, 1985.

West, John Anthony. *Serpent in the Sky: The High Wisdom of Ancient Egypt.* New York: Julian Press, 1987.

Wilhelm, Richard, translator, and C. G. Jung. *The Secret of the Golden Flower: A Chinese Book of Life.* Orlando, FL: Harcourt Brace Jovanovich, 1962.

Young, Louise B. *The Unchanged Universe.* New York: Simon & Schuster, 1986.

INDEX

D

E

F

G

N

O

P

Q

R

U

V

W

Y

Z

Photo by Wayne Kochenderfer

Jana Riley has been studying esoteric subjects since 1974. She is a graduate of Indiana University, with a B.S. in Business and Management. Since 1976, she has owned and operated a small advertising firm, while teaching tarot classes and workshops, lecturing locally, and working with charts and tarot cards for many clients. Ms. Riley lives in Indiana and is currently working on her next book.